IRVING WALLACE

A WRITER'S PROFILE

Profiles in Popular Culture
No. 1

General Editors

RAY B. BROWNE

SAM L. GROGG, Jr.

JOHN LEVERENCE

IRVING WALLACE
A WRITER'S PROFILE

BY

John Leverence

With an introduction by JEROME WEIDMAN, an interview by SAM L. GROGG, Jr., and an afterword by RAY B. BROWNE

The Popular Press 1974
Bowling Green, Ohio 43403

Cover design by John Leverence.

For

Margaret

Acknowledgments

Without the cooperation of Irving Wallace this book could have never been written. Mr. Wallace provided extensive research materials to The Center For The Study of Popular Culture, these forming the basis for this study. He supplemented them with hundreds of photographs, reams of manuscripts, letters and other records of his long and prolific career. He and Mrs. Wallace meticulously examined the manuscript and galley stages of the book for factual errors, and Mr. Wallace spent weeks fleshing out the interview sections.

Special thanks also go to Jerome Weidman, who took time out from his own writing to provide the profile's introduction.

Paul Gitlin and Richard Snyder saw the book to market. Michael Korda kindly consented to allow the use of his editorial letters. Jim Harner provided invaluable assistance with bibliographic research. Pat Browne, Dorothy Betts and Nora Sheldon worked long and hard to put the book into print. Lois Howe, who did most of the offset composition, deserves special recognition for her faith as well as her typing.

Sam Grogg spent the better part of five months writing, proofing, indexing, and generally contributing to the positive atmosphere that finally produced this book. Ray Browne, publisher of the Popular Press and Director of The Center, gave the initial backing for the project, and followed it through with his personal guidance and professional attention.

John Leverence
Bowling Green 1974

Contents

Jerome Weidman and Irving Wallace on the Champs Elysees, Paris, 1953.

Introduction

by Jerome Weidman

It was the year Jerry Wald and Norman Krasna owned R.K.O.
Or thought they did. And why shouldn't they? Howard Hughes
had bought the studio between blondes. Between brunettes he
stopped in to take a look at his purchase. While he looked, an
industry held its breath. What would Mr. Hughes say?

"Paint it," Mr. Hughes said.

It was not enough. Even though he used the best paint money
could buy, the overhead kept piling up.

"What should I do?" Mr. Hughes asked.

Of nobody in particular.

"Make pictures," nobody in particular replied.

That's where the advice stopped. It did not specify what kind
of pictures. Just pictures. To eat up the overhead. And the two
boys in the Hollywood of that time who were noted for their
capacity to eat up overhead were Jerry Wald and Norman Krasna.

They no longer are. Wald is dead. For practical eating-up-
overhead purposes, Krasna might just as well be. He lives in
Switzerland.

In those days they lived in Beverly Hills. A place where Mr.
Hughes recruited much of his personnel, male as well as female.
He recruited Wald and Krasna, turned over to them the R.K.O.
studio, and ordered them by contract to make fifty movies in five
years.

People who are good at eating up overhead are good at simple
arithmetic. Fifty movies? Five years? That's ten movies a year.
And wait—in those days somebody always remembered—that's a
lot of stories.

If you're in the business of eating up overhead, to whom do

you turn for stories? Not to Chauncey DePew. Or George Jessel.
These boys dealt in a different kind of story. Wald and Krasna
turned to people who set stories down on paper.

Mr. Hughes, who owned many things, owned TWA. So at
the taxpayer's expense Wald and Krasna started flying to Beverly
Hills from all over the world tax deductible people who earned
their bread by writing stories.

The author of these notes was summoned in the final phase
of this international in-gathering. My name in the phone book is
listed under "W." The only writer tapped after me was Israel
Zangwill. He did not show up. Mr. Zangwill had died in London
shortly before the typewriter was invented.

When I arrived at the R.K.O. studio Mr. Wald was in conference. Mr. Krasna had not yet come in. Mr. Hughes never came in.
I was assigned an office and told to wait.

It is an activity I have never found irksome. I have no trouble
getting through waiting time. My fingernails grow rapidly, and I
always carry a neat little pocket manicure kit.

Three days later my fingernails were down to the quick. I
was prepared to continue down to my knuckles. Wald and Krasna
paid handsomely for waiting. More handsomely, I learned later,
than they paid for writing. But my nail file broke.

I was pretty sure there were places in southern California
where I could purchase a substitute. But I did not know my way
around, and I had learned at my mother's knee one of life's basic
rules: never ask directions from a stranger. Even if he doesn't
know how to get where you want to go, he will tell you. I was
considering various ways to solve my problem when there was a
knock on the door.

"Come in," I called.

What came in was a pipe, projecting from a face that had
clearly been borrowed from the Admiration cigar ads.

"Are you all right?"

The words emerged around the pipe stem in small clouds of
concern.

"I think so," I said. "Why do you ask?"

"I've got the office next door. For three days I've been

listening to you file your nails, and then a few minutes ago the sound stopped."

I held up the broken nail file.

"Let's go out and buy you a new one," the pipe said.

We did. It proved to be one of the most sensible shopping trips of my life. Out of it came not only the best ten-cent nail file I have ever owned, and still do. Out of that shopping trip came an enduring and cherished friendship. The face into which the pipe had been, and still is, stuck belonged to Irving Wallace.

In those days Irving was a highly successful member of a somewhat lustreless group that hovered uncomfortably in a rather low position in the Hollywood pecking order: the "seven-fifty-a-week" writer. That, by the way, is seven *hundred* and fifty. And not seven hundred and fifty zlotas. In those days all figures in Hollywood that did not belong to Jane Russell were quoted in dollars.

For his seven hundred and fifty dollars a week Irving wrote what were then known as "tit-and-sanders." *Beau Geste* is to this example of the cinema art as the ceiling of the Sistine Chapel is to house painting.

Irving worked steadily. However, he was not happy. He did not want to write tit-and-sanders for a lousy seven hundred and fifty dollars a week. He wanted to "write."

"Write what?" I said.

Two months later Irving showed me. I received at my home in Connecticut an advance copy of a book soon to be published by Alfred A. Knopf. On the title page it said *The Square Pegs* by Irving Wallace.

What I said was, "Oy!"

I had liked this guy. His generosity, his kindness, his lovely wife, their well-stocked bar and groaning board had got me through Wald and Krasna. Now he turned out to be just another writer. I have spent much of my life with writers. Very few of them are generous. None is kind. Not many have lovely wives. Only some are generous with their whiskey. And when their boards groan it is usually because the boards, like the guests, have heard that one before. Many times.

"What am I going to do with this thing?" I said.

"Read it," my wife said.

I did, the next day, on the plane to California. TWA, of course. Wald was not yet dead. Krasna had not yet moved to Switzerland. Howard Hughes was still trying desperately to burn up overhead. They were down to the "W's" again.

When I checked in at R.K.O. Wald was in conference. Krasna had not yet come in. Mr. Hughes never came in. I was assigned to an office and told to wait. I got out my nail file and went to work. Thirty seconds later there was a tap on my door.

"Come in," I called.

The pipe came in first, of course. It was followed by the face. Under it there was a plate with a dozen Brownies.

"I knew you were coming," Irving said, "so Sylvia baked a cake."

We munched them while I told him what I thought about *The Square Pegs*. Nobody has ever told me things like that about my own work, but no matter. I went on for a while. When I paused to pick up another Brownie, Irving said, "You mean you like the book?"

"I like it very much. This book shows you have the makings of a novelist. I'm not saying you are Tolstoi. Maybe you are. How does anybody know until they write a novel? Do you want to write one?"

"Yes," Irving said.

Wald and Krasna never succeeded in making fifty pictures for Howard Hughes. But when it came to decorating the offices of their writers they set a mark for other studios to shoot at. It took me only twenty minutes to locate, in an ormulu and onyx escritoire, a copy of the Los Angeles telephone book. The Wald-Krasna interior designer had slip-covered it in mutation mink. I pushed the telephone book across the desk toward Irving.

"Take a look at that," I said.

"Why?" Irving said.

"It contains a list of all the people in this area who want to write novels," I said.

"You mean—?" Irving said.

"Don't start sentences with *you mean*," I said. "The composers of tit-and-sanders do that. Not novelists."

"You mean—?" Irving said again.

Even in those days one of his most charming traits was the capacity to help a floundering friend out of a confused conversational eddy.

"I certainly do," I said. "There are no ground rules for writing novels. You don't have to pass any examinations. Judging by much of what gets published, not even talent or intelligence are necessary. There is only one prerequisite. You have to want to do it."

"You also have to have material," Irving said.

"The only people who do not have material for writing novels are dead people. Anybody still walking around has material. You have more than most. *The Square Pegs* consists of twenty-four meticulously researched and admirably presented biographies of two dozen fascinating people. You have set down their stories in nonfiction form. If you want badly enough to write novels you won't even have to think about material until you get around to writing your twenty-fifth."

Irving went to work on relighting his pipe. In those days he owned one of those lighters that are equipped with a direction button. When the smoker pressed it, the flame shot down into the pipe bowl instead of up toward a cigarette end. Irving always had trouble with his flame direction. I did not know then that the difficulty was self-imposed. The small fumbling performance was a cover for thought. It gave Irving time to assemble his words for his next remark.

"I've been writing non-fiction since I was in college," he said when he had the pipe going again. "I know how to do it. I've also written and published short stories. But I've never written any long fiction. I don't know if I can do it."

"How do you know if you can or can't until you try?" I said.

My talents as a homespun philosopher tended to reach their apogee in Beverly Hills.

"Of course," Irving said, "I've written original stories for the screen. I suppose that could be called long fiction."

I thought it could.

Irving was having trouble again with the direction of his lighter flame. "What are you doing tonight?" he said finally.

"I don't know," I said. "I don't have any plans."

"I do," Irving said.

What I did that night was spend the hours between 8:00 P.M. and 3:00 A.M. in my hotel room with Irving and a stenographer. We took turns dictating. The next morning, at 10:00 A.M., we delivered to Irving's agent four copies of an original story set in Jerusalem immediately following the Crucifixion. The script bore the title: *The Holy Grail*.

At 3:00 P.M. I was filing my fingernails in my office at R.K.O. and helping Irving finish the Brownies that Sylvia had baked for us that morning. The phone rang. I picked it up.

"For you," I said to Irving. "Your agent."

When he hung up Irving said, "For us."

Universal-International had bought *The Holy Grail* for $10,000.

"This beats movie jobs," Irving said.

"It certainly does," I said.

"Want to try more of the same?" he asked.

We tried more of the same.

What Irving and I got for the next five tit-and-sanders on which we collaborated can be stated with accuracy in round figures. More accurately, in one round figure: zero.

Strolling down the Champs Elysees on the day we received word from Irving's agent in Hollywood that our fifth tit-and-sander had struck out, I showed him a royalty statement on my most recent novel that I had received in the morning mail from my agent in New York. Irving studied the statement for a few moments, then went to work on his lighter. He finally got the flame headed in the right direction.

"Is that all you make out of a novel?" he said.

"It's as much as Emily Brontë got out of *Wuthering Heights*," I said.

Irving said nothing. He said nothing for almost a year. Then, one day in my New York apartment, I received a phone call from

Irving in California.

"Well," he said, "I've done it."

"Done what?" I said.

"Written a novel, *The Sins of Philip Fleming*," Irving said.

The words of the cheer leader rose to my lips. They did not cross this barrier into the phone. The tone of Irving's voice had come back to me.

"You don't sound very enthusiastic about it," I said.

"Neither is Alfred A. Knopf," Irving said.

"Oh," I said.

A useful, all-purpose syllable.

"He says it will ruin my reputation," Irving said.

"With whom?" I said.

Irving laughed.

"I never thought of that," he said.

Neither had I, but I had assumed the mantle of the seasoned veteran counseling the rookie. I had to press on.

"There are other publishers," I said.

"That's the trouble," Irving said.

"How do you mean?" I said.

"Another publisher wants to do it," Irving said.

The lack of jubilation in his voice was puzzling.

"You don't sound as though you're going to let him," I said.

"How can I?" Irving said. "Nobody ever heard of him."

"He's heard of you," I said.

"I'm not an imprint on the spine of a book," Irving said. "If I let him publish my book, this publisher *will* be."

Pause. Across the width of a continent I could hear the work on the lighter getting under way.

Finally: "What do you think?"

"I think you need some advice," I said.

"I'll take anything," Irving said.

"You've been wanting to become a novelist for a long time," I said. "The day you get a manuscript published you become a novelist. Here's your chance to become a novelist."

"But *The Square Pegs* was published by Alfred A. Knopf," Irving said. "That's class. This publisher who wants to publish my novel, he's not known at all."

"If you want to go to sea," I said, "obviously it's more pleasant to go in a yacht than in a rowboat. But it's the sea that's important, not the vessel. It's better to go in a rowboat than not to go at all."

"I never thought of that," Irving said.

Neither had I.

"Think about it now," I said.

"You really feel I should let this little-known publisher bring out my novel?" Irving said.

"Publishing your novel could make him into a well-known publisher," I said. "If he's got even a little bit of luck."

As it turned out, he had a lot.

A Writer's Profile

> If successful novelists had a formula,
> they would not have failures, and I
> know of no novelist who has not
> had a failure at one time or another.
> —Irving Wallace, *The Sunday
> Gentleman*

What does Irving Wallace know of failure? What does any novelist who has sold ninety-two million books and is one of the five most widely read writers of his time know but success? He is the one who made a quarter of a million dollars in thirteen months from *The Chapman Report*. He is the one who sold *The Prize* to the movies for another two hundred and fifty thousand dollars. And certainly he is the one whose Midas Touch has brought him six figures on a single paperback reprint sale.

This is what he says: "Money is equated with not being honest. But the real villain is being hungry. Because you'll write anything—and I've been on that side of the street."

Neither part of the story tells the whole tale. The success and the money mean nothing without the poverty and desperation of the thirty years that preceded his first success, *The Chapman Report* of 1960. And the long decades of frustration need their complement in the years after *Chapman*. Otherwise, like a caricature, the lines of any Wallace profile are diminished or intensified through pure editorial bias.

This profile of Irving Wallace, based on private letters, journals, unpublished manuscripts, personal recollections, and other sources never before available to a researcher, is an attempt to make more whole and more objectively visible this man and his extraordinary career. It is neither definitive nor is it blessed with the perspective of time. Rather, it is a look at people, events and ideas that have defined his character and his work. Its purpose is not to be prescriptive of attitudes about Wallace, but to be descriptive of the facts of his life and the fiction of his novels.

And so the profile must extend as far forward as the books he has not written but wants to write, and go back into the past, even to January of 1916, to the sixth month of Bessie Wallace's first pregnancy.

She fell off a chair and for almost three days there was no life felt inside her. The doctor told her the pregnancy had ended. But on the third day Bessie knew he was wrong. On Purim Sunday, March 19, 1916, she gave birth to a 7½ pound son who was named Irving.

The child was named after his maternal grandfather, a bookkeeper and Talmudic scholar of Narevka, Russia.

Bessie had emigrated to the United States in 1907. She was seventeen years old when she accompanied her brother Bernard and her sister Gertrude on a journey from Narevka to the port of Bremen. "I'll never forget Bremen," she told her children years later. "There, for the first time in my life, I saw electric lights. It was the most modern city in the world, and after it, even the cities in America were disappointments. The museum there was wonderful. There were mummies, thousands of years old, made to breathe by machinery. I was never so frightened."

A fourteen day crossing in third class was followed by a train ride to Chicago; Bessie Liss was there reunited with her older sister, Yetta. At first they shared a four room apartment. Then, after Bessie found a job as one of four hundred women in the Cable Corset Company, where she was paid $6 a week, she took a private room (with board) for $5 a month. Later, as an early union member and Socialist, she went on strike with others against the girdle manufacturers.

Bessie was as romantic in her youth as in her later years. Raised on Tolstoi's *Anna Karenina,* she always wanted to marry for love. In fact, she would say that one reason she left Russia was

Bessie and Alex Wallace at their wedding, August 17, 1913.

Bessie Wallace and son.

He was four months old.

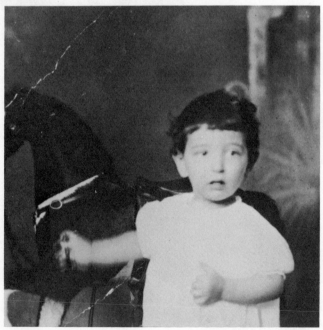

Age one.   Chicago, 1917.

because she did not want to be married off by her family through a *shadchen*—a matchmaker.

Alex Wallace, Wallechinsky before Ellis Island, had arrived in America at the age of fourteen. He was from the Russian town of Vasilishki. In 1912 he lived with relatives in Chicago and worked as a counterman in a dry goods store. One of Alex's stepsisters was marrying a man who had come from Narevka. Naturally, Alex was at the wedding, and there he met Bessie. Although he was not able to walk her home, since he was already committed to escorting a female cousin, Alex was determined to see Bessie again. After Alex got Bessie's half-brother, Sam, a job in the store where he was working, he then asked Sam to reciprocate the favor with tickets to a Jewish play being performed in Chicago. Alex invited Bessie to the play, appeared carrying a box of candy, and began a year and a half courtship that evolved into marriage on August 17, 1913. Bessie was twenty-three and Alex was twenty-one.

Fifty years later, in 1963, Bessie Wallace remembered the circumstances which led to the family's migration from Chicago to Kenosha, Wisconsin: "Dad was working as a salesman in Chicago. We had a nice six-room apartment for which we paid $23 a month. Alex told traveling salesmen friends if they ever heard of a really good job, to let him know. One advised him to take a job in a small town. One day a salesman was in Kenosha, Wisconsin, and the owner of the North Side Bargain Store asked if he knew of an experienced clerk. The salesman mentioned Alex, who went on to Kenosha for three months alone before determining we could live there and sending for me and for Irving, who was by then one year old."

Kenosha was an attractive little city (pop. 50,000) located on Lake Michigan about fifty miles north of Chicago. Bessie and Alex made this place their home from 1917 until early 1936. Mrs. Marcella Rodgers, a neighbor and friend, can still go back in memory to the North Side Bargain Store where "two little boys played hide and seek under the bargain tables. Your mother," she wrote one of the little boys in 1970, "would say, 'now don't bother the ladies. They want to buy something.' But one day the Bargain Store burned to the ground, and it has never been replaced. The

I. W. age eleven, a Kenosha cub scout.
With sister Ester and Mother.

I. W. in 1923, Kenosha. Seven years old.

old neighborhood has changed many times, but the Bargain Store was to the North Side wives the same as the corner pub or saloon was to the tired working men. It was taken for granted that no matter what you needed, you would find it there. And many a gossipy conversation was held while looking for a purchase."

The fire that took the North Side Bargain Store brought together Alex and his younger brother, Abe. They built another store at 4426 Sheridan Road—Wallace Brothers General Merchandise. Business flourished, and the Wallaces felt the promise of Golden America. They were happy to have the work and became prosperous because of it. "*Arbeit macht die Leben suesser*" (Work makes one's life sweeter) was a favorite phrase of Bessie Wallace. Alex, being less garrulous, kept a glass paperholder on his desk that said it for him: "The world owes no man a living." These were immigrants who believed in the work ethic and, at least for the time being, were well-sustained in their faith.

In 1929 the store was visited by two men who believed in another sort of ethic. They had guns and threatened to use them if Alex did not clean out the cash drawer. He had little choice, especially with his thirteen-year-old son looking up the barrel of a pistol. Afterwards the *Wisconsin News* of Milwaukee reported the hold-up of Alex Wallace and his son "Norman."

The Wallaces were orthodox Jews, belonged to the Kenosha synagogue, and sent their children to Hebrew school every day. Years later, when asked why he had not written a distinctly Jewish novel, Irving Wallace replied that it was probably because of Kenosha. "I was raised in the Midwest, in an atmosphere devoid of anti-Semitism. My friends in Kenosha were Jewish as well as Italian and Polish Catholics and Swedes, and I never heard the word 'kike' until I was nineteen and going to college in Berkeley. Ben Hecht, who was raised in Racine, eleven miles from me, once wrote he had never known anti-Semitism until he grew up and moved to Chicago. No one believed him, but I did."

The Wallaces gave their two children (a daughter, Esther, had been born in 1923) a respect for the two concepts basic to the Jewish personal ideal: *Landan* (learning) and *Chassid* (piety). The children were urged to read the best of European and American

KENOSHA EVENING NEWS
EDITORIAL DEPARTMENT
ERNEST F. MARLATT, EDITOR
KENOSHA, WISCONSIN

February 19, 1931

Mr. Irving Wallace
4042 Sheridan Road
Kenosha, Wisconsin

Dear Sir:

 I am returning to you the story
"Courage Makes the Man" which you submitted
to us for publication. We feel that this is
not the field for your articles but that
they should be submitted to a magazine and
not to a newspaper.

 It is true that we carry a serial
story but we do not plan to publish short
stories which are clearly in the province of
a magazine.

 Thanking you for submitting it to
us, I am

Respectfully,

Ernest F. Marlatt

EFM:ED Ernest F. Marlatt

Rejection letter — "Courage Makes the Man."

literature—especially Tolstoi and Balzac, Stendhal and Lewis. But Irving was also a son of America, and in the 1920's and 30's that meant a passion for sports. He supplemented the family reading with *The All-America Sport Magazine, Sports Aces,* and *Dime Sports.* Then he read *A Young Man of Manhattan* by Katherine Brush, a novel about a sports writer's glamorous life. And at Hurd's Drug Store he picked up a copy of *The Writer's Yearbook* and learned that stories did not just appear in magazines, but they were written for and sold to magazines.

He decided to become a sports writer.

In the October-November, 1932 issue of *Quill and Scroll,* the official publication of the International Honorary Society for High School Journalists, sixteen-year-old Irving Wallace recounted his sportswriter's beginnings: "Even when my mother cut my hair by placing a dish on my head I can remember I wanted to be a writer. In junior high school my classmates used to poke fun at me by saying, 'You've written half of the paper, Irv.' No egotism, because my material wasn't good, I'll admit. But I sure turned out plenty of pages of short stories and news articles."

Many of these sports articles appeared in his regular "Sport News" column of the *Kenews,* Central High School's newspaper. In 1931 he wrote a two-part article on women in sports: "Athletic Girls, You Can Have Them." This was followed by an article titled "Male Athletes: The Big Oxes!" "I was talking to a bright young lady the other day; she said that article I had written about athletic gals had her approval, but that she believed the fellows weren't anything to brag about themselves." After a strained parody of a "dumb athlete's" lack of poise and articulation, the article concluded that "When bigger and better bores are made, most of our high school and collegiate athletes will make them" (*Kenews,* September 18, 1931).

Wallace also did straight reporting on athletic events or school activities. These included the familiar topics of class enrollment, dance announcements, school elections, and faculty news. He and his Jay Gatsby alter-ego collaborated on the book reviews:

"The other day I was sitting on my veranda overlooking the lake, I felt at ease with the world. I had just finished a hard game

NEWS FLASHES . . . Irving Wallace

WASHINGTON STUDENTS ENTERTAINED BY HIGH CLASS PERFORMERS !

You don't have to go to Broadway to see high class entertainment that was proven when the trio from Hollywood, California appeared here.

The male member of the trio entertained with what we would call a squeeze box or in other words a concertina.....One of the female members of the company played a violin and the other member of the fair sex sang and gave some very good readings.

Miss Wallendorf, dramatic coach of the school, was interviewed on what she thought of the program.

"As far as I am concerned," said Miss Wallendorf, "That was the best program of that type ever shown in this school, that is, since I have been here". And may I add, when Miss Wallendorf sex a program is good, you can bet your boots its a humdigger.

ROOM 22 Holds a Mock Election.

The students of the 9 A home room 22 held an election on November 4, and here are the results:

GOVERNOR: LaFollette 25
          Hammersley 3
SEC OF STATE: Dammann— 18
          Frogsten— 7
ASSEMBLY 1st District & 2nd
Cooper 25   Piper   25
Kiernan 0   Birchard   0
COUNTY CLERK: Russell 18
          Niederprim 10
SHERIFF: Robinson — 18
          Willems — 10
DISTRICT ATTORNEY: Barnett — 16
          Dittmann 12
CORONER: Schmitz — 21
          Kimball — 6
COUNTY TREASURER : Lauer - 14
          Bendegom - 13

The 9 A Oral English classes are going to have a "Thrift Speaking Contest", the best speakers will give their speechs to the home room groups on Mondays.

ASSEMBLY PROGRAMS.

Harken, the Washington Winner will classify all programs given in assembly. The programs will be rated mainly on the interest they create and not on the acting. This will prevent any hard feelings.

Here is our system of rating:
(4 stars)...Very good
(3 stars)...Good
(2 stars)...A little better than fair.
(1 star)....Fair
(0 stars)...Good(to induce sleep)

(1 star)... A short play was given in dedication of Columbus day, by the students of the first hour 9 A Oral English class. It was concerned with a group of students trying to find material for a topic on the discovery of America.

(2) stars)...A play was given by the Washington troop of girl scouts. The scene was in the cour of good health. Girls guilty of various bad health rules were convicted and started on the road to good health. Very funny in parts

(3 stars)... This is the kind of assembly program that we call good it contained:

Introduction of Washington's new school song, "A Toast to Washington by Marie Leonelli.

An ensemble of Kenosha Junior High school's star music talent.

Three talks on school were given, the one given by John Zibbenski was especially good.

A pantomite "School Days" was given

All in all, this was an interesting program.

Sandy dropped a nickel
Into a ten foot creek
Sandy was a Scotchman
The funeral is next week.

I. W.'s "News Flashes" in the Washington Junior High *Winner.*
November, 1930.

of ping-pong, and that feeling of well being, which comes on all of us, was upon me. When up from the great stone gate that leads to my small estate I heard the chug-chug of the editor's Ford. 'Curses,' I muttered in my quiet bass. 'Here comes that girl to disturb my peace.'

"And sure enough, in a few minutes, the editor herself broke into view and was upon me. 'Aha,' she chuckled. 'Here you are, Irving. I knew I would find you. You must review the latest novel for the *Kenews*. No one else but you can do it.'

"Moved by her faint praise, I permitted myself to be forced into breaking my peaceful afternoon by reading the book for her. With my accustomed speed I set to work, carefully skipping all allusions and descriptions. I completed the book in time to dress for dinner, for I read swiftly, and arrived in time for a most pleasing meal with my next door neighbor.

"The book, by the way, is pretty good" (*Kenews*, February 11, 1931).

In the 1934 *Buds*, Central High's *Quill and Scroll* yearbook, Irving objectified his alter-ego when he wrote about heroes:

"My best heroes are in fiction. They have lived, unstained by reality. The thing that makes bloated mortal heroes go 'poof' in the eyes of worshippers is the very fact that they are mortal. . . . Ah! how I pray for the sacrifice of d'Artagnan, for the skill of Frank Merriwell, for the ingenuity of Jeeves, for the color of Robin Hood."

The fantasy life of the budding journalist was more than a light homage to fictional heroes and alter-egos. In a general way it reflected the depression years with their popular models of heroism—the Anthony Adverse or Frank Merriwell types who overcame terrible misfortunes to Triumph In The End. But the fantasies of the 1930's were detached from the self and projected onto fictional heroes. The fantasies of Irving Wallace were directed right back to himself—or at least to one part of him. He certainly thought popular heroes were "the nuts," but he didn't have the time, the money, or the complaisance to follow their shell game. Knowing the hand is quicker than the eye, he trusted himself. During the next thirty years, the lean and desperate ones, there

EDITORIAL ROOMS
THE SATURDAY EVENING POST
The Curtis Publishing Company
George Horace Lorimer Editor
PHILADELPHIA

August 11, 1921.

Dear Mr. Wallace:

Your article, "The Horse Laugh", which you have been kind enough to submit for our consideration, has been read with interest. We have not found, however, that it quite meets the special requirements of The Saturday Evening Post and the manuscript is returned herewith.

Thank you for letting us see it.

Yours very truly,

The Editors

Rejection slip from *The Saturday Evening Post*.

was less doubt about *whether* he would Triumph In The End than impatient chagrin about just *when* it would happen. It should be noted well that by the time he entered junior high school he knew exactly what he wanted, and then he persisted until he got it. Years later he summed it up with this revealing self-characterization:

"Have an ideal, but not an idol. If you have an idol, that makes you second-rate.

"There are certain men who are satisfied to be sycophants, dwell in reflected glory, sharing illumination from a bright name. But not he. From youth he would not subserve himself in this way. He wanted to give the light, not bask in it. He wanted, in a sense, to be the ulcer giver, not getter."

And remember this. Alex Wallace had made a prosperous living, but by the time Irving was a teen-ager the depression had reduced Golden America into a Pyrite Wasteland. Nathanael West, another writer who knew the depression well, once wanted to write a story about a character who was trying to get one foot on the Ladder of Success and they were always moving the ladder on him, but they couldn't touch the dream. For Irving Wallace, the dream was to write. If Hard Times threatened the dream, then the only thing to do was write and sell, write and sell, over and over again until the selling did not make any difference and there was only the writing. Beyond the security of money was the real pay off—to write it so well that anyone reading it would know it exactly as it was imagined or felt or experienced.

But what makes the jump across the synapse from imagination to articulation is never just right, so you do it over again, always certain that the pursuit can never be won. And when you think you have finally won then there should be a cerebral click and a recorded message telling you how badly you have lost. It is the bitter recognition of every writer that whatever is done is finally less than what it was supposed to be. But there is something sweet in there along with the bitterness. If there is no final Triumph In The End, there are small skirmishes that can be won. A good scene, a comic twist, a proper jab of irony—these are the small pleasures that Bessie Wallace would say make *das Leben*

THE HORSE LAUGH

The $182.04 stride..... Top Flight won $219,000 in 7 races in
1931
1,203 strides in 28,875 feet

Average plater does 52 feet per second
Stake horse does 54 feet per second

27 ft per stride

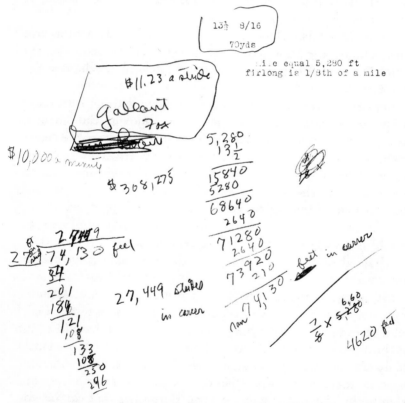

I. W.'s original notes for "The Horse Laugh," his first article sold to a magazine. He kept no carbon and the original was lost at the publisher's. This and two other pages of figures are all that remain.

suesser.

After the store folded Alex Wallace had low-income jobs working for other people, struggling along with most of America in the early years of the depression. Irving went to work in 1929 when he was thirteen as a sports stringer for the *Wisconsin News*. He was paid a few cents per printed inch. He moonlighted by selling several filler items (odd-lot pieces used to complete newspaper columns) to *The Sporting News*.

The next year he wrote nonfiction articles for magazines and sent them to the markets listed in his *Writer's Yearbook*. His first submitted article, "Visiting Buffalo Bill's Grave on Pike's Peak," was a six page recollection of a family trip to Colorado. It was rejected by *St. Nicholas Magazine*.

"What is this thing called Romance?"—his next attempt—was promptly rejected by the Kenosha *Evening News*, and on February 19, 1931, they sent back the five hundred word essay "Courage Makes The Man."

But the winter of 1931 was not without its small successes. The January issue of the *Washington Winner*, Irving's junior high school paper, featured "The Great Basketball Mystery," a short story remarkable for its inclusion within two pages of the mysterious "Operative Z-13," a kidnapped Albert Einstein, and a basketball game between the 9-A boys and the Washington School faculty. The boys won the game.

That January Irving graduated from junior high as class president and news editor of the *Winner*. He transferred to Kenosha's Central High School and completed the first half of the tenth grade in early June. A month later he had a remarkable idea:

"It occurred to me, one day, in the sluggish era of Herbert Hoover, that it might be possible to write a very interesting article on the fact that race horses, working no more than two to three minutes a week, earned considerably more than their human colleagues, the sweating golfers, pugilists, hockey players. On this somewhat fantastic premise, based on an imaginary interview with a famous thoroughbred, I wrote 'The Horse Laugh.' It was rejected by Horace Lorimer of *The Saturday Evening Post* who, unable to resist budding genius, advised me to peddle it to a more

"We Make No Promises
We Cannot Fulfill"

THE NORTH TOWN
STATE BANK BLDG.
North Town Bank Bldg.

Circulation Manager
FRANK DIDGE
Phone Sheldrake 4700

EXECUTIVE
CHARLES L. HALL
JOHN P. HANLEY

EDITORIAL
RAY JURGEN, Editor
LESLIE KERR
R. SCHOTTENFELS

"THE PHOENIX PRESS"

THE PHOENIX PUBLISHING CO.
2337 DEVON AVENUE
CHICAGO. ILL.

HORSE~JOCKEY

August 18, 1931

Mr. Irving Wallace
6023-19th Ave.,
Kenosha, Wis.

Dear Mr. Wallace:

We are receiving quite a bit of suitable material
for Horse & Jockey Magazine, and we have not been paying
more thank $5.00 for regular size short story articles
and perhpas as high as $10.00 for two page feature articles.

We are inclosing check for your story and ask
that you send your picture so that we can run it along
with the story similar to the style being used by Liberty.

We are sending sample copy of Magazine under
separate cover.

Yours truly,

Chas L Hall
President

PHOENIX PUBLISHING CO.

CLH/rf

Expert opinions on racing and other lines in the field of sports expressed in the columns of the Horse and Jockey magazine are offered as a matter of news gathered and written by those best qualified to do so. Subscription Rates $1.50 a year. Foreign Countries $2.00 a year.

Letter from Charles L. Hall announcing I. W.'s sale of "The Horse Laugh" — first magazine article sale.

Racing Oddities

by IRVING WALLACE

YOU may be the best handicapper in your city, or a heavy bettor, or the average turf follower who can purchase no more than a two-dollar pasteboard — but whoever you are—have you ever put on your thinking cap and thought to yourself just what makes horse racing the vivid, fresh, interesting sport it is today?

Naturally, any sport which presents such a wide field for betting will always be one of the leading sports of the world. But pause for a moment to think just what makes competition of any type interesting. It is the love of the unusual.

And on the turf the unusual is always hovering around. I believe every turf follower should at least have in mind a few of the things that has made racing the sport of kings—and the people.

The shortest priced winner in the history of racing was Man O' War, the sage of American turf. In 1920 this great horse won the Lawrence Realization against Damask at the record odds of 1 to 100.

And while we are on the subject of odds it might be well to mention the record longshot. Here is the story: Mrs. Answorth, wife of a Liverpool, England, physician, decided to bet two shillings (50c) on a horse named Coole to win a hurdle race at Haydack Park, England. The odds on Coole were 3400 to 1. Well, Coole bounded across the finish line ahead of the pack and won. Mrs. Answorth collected $1,705 for her 50c wager. Whew!

Previous to the event I mentioned above the longshot record was held by Robledo who won at Shanghai, China, in 1929 and paid off at 3037 to 1.

In our fiction of today we usually find a stereotyped plot which tells us that the villain's horse is disqualified and we are overjoyed to find out that our hero's colt wins because of the disqualification. In real life that plot is really enacted, but we do have costly disqualifications. For an instance:

FRED ARCHER HOLDS WINNING RECORD FOR JOCKEYS. HE WON 2,775 RACES BETWEEN 1810 AND 1876

EARLE SANDE IN THREE YEARS WON ONLY 956 RACES

September 13, 1930, was a dreary day for the owners of Arc Light. In the 3-mile Grand National Steeplechase held at Belmont, N. Y., for a prize of $28,350, Arc Light came galloping in first. But Tourist II was the horse that collected. Arc Light was disqualified and placed last for bothering Tourist II. This was the most expensive disqualification in the history of the turf.

Back in the 70's a horse named Little Reb won four races in less than 24 hours. He won the last race at New Orleans, one afternoon, and swept the next day's card of three races. Ah, for the good old days!

Will Shakespeare once said, "Oh consistency, thou art a jewel!" And for the bettors there is nothing like a consistent race horse. Kingston was one of that type. Kingston was never out of the money in 74 starts. . . . Another racer, Clifford, was out of the money only twice in 64 starts. His last race was at the age of seven when he finished third to Ben Brush and Hastings.

TOP FLIGHT WAS WORTH A $182 A STRIDE IN 1931

Many historical and hysterical moments can be recorded under the heading of "Dead Heats."

In Newmarket, England, at the Houghton meeting on October 22, 1885, four horses in a field of five ran a dead heat. They were Gamester, The Unexpected, Over Reach, and Lady Golightly, for a $50 sweepstake.

In the month of October, 1903, Lock Lochie, High Flier and Barindi ran a dead heat at Moorfield in Australia. A runoff was held and all three of the horses ran a dead heat again. So the owners finally divided the purse.

The Northern Jockey Club Course in Australia, in 1896, was the scene of another of these hair-raising dead heats.

Yellow Plush, Tom, and Syndicate dead heated in their regular race. A runoff was ordered and Tom and Yellow Plush again finishing in a dead heat. Again the horses held a runoff which Tom won by a mere nose.

. . . According to Robert Ripley, Top Flight was the possessor of a $182.00 stride in the year of 1931. The filly won $219,000 in seven races. It took 1,203 strides in 28,875 feet. Which means $182 per stride.

Working on the same basis we find that Sun Beau won $110,925 as a six-year-old in 1931. The Beau took 5,280 strides. And so, for every stride taken by Sun Beau we find he gets $21.00.

Show me, if you can, any other living thing that can collect $182 for every stride it takes at the ripe old age of two. Show me, if possible, any six-year-old living being that collects $21 per stride.

The oldest winning horse in the history of the game was John Burwell, who at the [*Continued on next page*]

Irving Wallace's first published article.

specialized market. I promptly mailed it to the *Horse and Jockey* magazine of Chicago. I received in return five dollars and a request for my picture."

The picture was of a fifteen-year-old with a pimple on his nose. It was never published and neither was "The Horse Laugh." The five dollars paid for the essay was held against Irving's account at *Horse and Jockey*. A little over a year later, on October 17, 1932, *Horse and Jockey* accepted his article, "Racing Oddities II." They did not pay him for it but counted the previous five dollar payment for "The Horse Laugh" as payment for "Racing Oddities II." In effect, Irving lost his first five dollars when he made his second five dollars.

But that is getting ahead of the story. On July 2, 1932, Irving wrote the first "Racing Oddities"—"Racing Oddities II" being the second. *Horse and Jockey* bought it on July 21, 1932, for five dollars and published it in the August 1932 issue, pages fifteen and sixteen. Then and there he became a professional, published magazine writer. It was a mildly auspicious beginning to the twenty years in which he would write over a thousand articles, half of them finding their way into print.

His last two and a half years of high school were busy ones. In September, 1931, Irving was the sports, front page, and editorial chief of the *Kenews*. On December 4 he began writing the "Sportorials" column. Beginning in early 1932 he wrote a column for the *Kenosha Bulletin*, a local weekly. On March 31 he participated in the State Debate Championship at Madison, Wisconsin. Central High won seven debates and the winners' trophy.

But debating did not always go well. On February 24, 1933, the Kenosha team lost a debate to Oconomowoc High School. The judge's comments on Irving Wallace were less than flattering:

"Utterance cluttered and a bit hard to understand at times. Pained facial expression, nasal stenosis. Seemed to be working very hard with his lips but not succeeding very well in articulation. Talked to opponents too much . . . Phrasing not so good . . . Frequently pulls words apart which belong together. Unfortunate use of word 'intangible' . . . Overdid action—especially the gesture thrusting out the little finger of his left hand."

He's Best Student Feature Writer

The outstanding newspaper feature writer among 20,000 High school students in the United States is Irving Wallace, (above) Kenosha High school mid-year graduate. He was awarded first place in a contest conducted by Quill and Scroll, national High school journalism society. The Kenosha student also ranked high in the ratings of the National Forensic League for debaters, and has been active in many affairs in the High school.

Irving Wallace debating. 1931

That August, after the "Racing Oddities" article was published, Irving sent *Quill and Scroll* his professional advice for writing and selling sport stories:

"I have learned from what little experience I have had that the only way to become a writer is to write! Write for the wastebasket, for magazines, for the school paper or annual—but write, revise, correct and write more. You will be happy next year if you start now."

And write he did. Soon after school began in the fall of 1932, he signed up for *Quill and Scroll*'s international editorial contest. The contestants crowded into room 306 on Tuesday, October 18. At three o'clock sharp Miss Charlotte A. Moody, Central's journalism teacher, signaled them to begin. At four-thirty she collected the papers. She took them home that evening and read them. The following afternoon the best editorial, "A Change for a Change," supporting Franklin D. Roosevelt's election over President Hoover, was in the mail to *Quill and Scroll*. The results of the contest were announced in November. Among eight hundred entries, Irving Wallace's "A Change for a Change" placed second.

Throughout the next two years Irving continued to debate and write. In October, 1933, the Kenosha debators won ten out of twelve league debates in Wisconsin, finished second in the regionals in Wheaton, Illinois. The Medill School of Journalism at Northwestern University named him the country's number one high school feature writer in a competition of three thousand students. With Lowell Richardson, a Central student, he won Medill's Grand Gold Cup for high school news writing and his second national writing award in two years.

On August 13, 1933, he tried a baseball short story, "Sacrifice-Hit." He sold it to *The Challenge* of Nashville, Tennessee, for twelve dollars. ("There's more to baseball than heavy hitting, as little Willie Hansen learned.") "Sacrifice-Hit" was the first short story sale. *The Challenge* published it May 6, 1934, pages one and four.

Somewhere between his extra-curricular and publishing activities Irving spent time in class. Graduating on February 2, 1934,

Illustrator: McCullough Partee

The second baseman, way off his sack, couldn't get Willie.

I. W's first

published short

story, sold for

$12 in 1934 to

The Challenge.

SACRIFICE HIT

THERE'S MORE TO BASEBALL THAN HEAVY HITTING
AS LITTLE WILLIE HANSEN LEARNED

Irving Wallace

THE minor league baseball team, the Bears, was in spring training. The manager was doing his best to whip a pennant team in shape, because if he didn't he wouldn't be manager very long. The team was just a team—what they needed was a good hitter or two; there were prospects among the rookies—

But wait. I won't rush ahead of my story. Speaking of the rookies trying to make good on the Bears, there was one little, scrawny fellow. Good-looking? Yes. Clean-cut, better yet. His name was Hansen, Willie Hansen. No one knew much about him; looked as if he had been found in a seed catalogue. For a week no one paid any attention to him. Finally one day the manager saw him hanging around and called him over.

"Well? What are you supposed to be doing here?"

"I play ball," mumbled Willie.

"Does anyone else think so?"

"Not sure."

"Well, what's your name?"

"People call me Hansen," said Willie.

"Well, then I guess that is your name," said the manager.

"I guess so," admitted Willie.

"What do you do?" asked the manager.

"I play the infield," answered Willie.

(Continued on page four)

Irving Wallace, fourth from left, as Miss Fly in high school play, "The Web."

A high school sports writer on his day off.

with an 81.94 cumulative grade average, his best subjects were public speaking (96), journalism (93), and modern history (89). He managed an 82 average in English. His worst subject was second year German (72). *Macht Arbeit die Leben suesser?*

The 1934 *Spy,* Central's yearbook, summarized his three years of senior high:

"Irving Wallace, 'Iggle': Washington Junior, Editor-in-Chief of *Kenews,* Pres. of Forum Club, Pres. of Journalism Club, Pres. of Quill and Scroll, Chief of Prep Club, National Forensic League, Pres. of Junior Class, Tennis Club, Pep Club, Little Theatre, Debate Team."

In January of 1973 Wallace addressed his daughter's high school graduation in South Woodstock, Vermont, and recollected his own:

"All I remember of it was that I was bored mindless. I was impatient for the ceremony to be ended so that I could split, get away, be on my own after twelve relentless years of schooling. It was only after I got out of school that my real learning began."

It began with a $1.30 ad in the April, 1934 issue of *Writer's Digest:*

"ADVENTURE HO!— Motoring through North and South America? Want to accompany you in search of material. I'm good companion; author of one hundred stories. Write your plans. Irving Wallace, 6103 - 18th Avenue, Kenosha, Wisconsin."

Some of the responses were more curious than practical. One gentleman invited him to take a *bobsled* trip to Alaska in search of gold. Another proposed a trek across the United States—to be accomplished by walking backwards.

Then a letter arrived from a Mr. W. W. Williams, a Honduran government official:

"Sir, I am from Central America, and there are few who know Honduras as well or better than I. I have lived here a long time, and made a special study of the country. It is the least known of all the Republics, has no history written, no railroad or dirt road from the Atlantic to the capitol. You travel by mule trains where you cannot walk.

"Then there is the *La Fuentede Sangre* (The Fountain of

5,000 Miles of Adventure Ahead of Them

These three Wisconsin youths are planning a 5,000 mile adventure into Central and South America. They will leave Kenosha Sept. 9 for Mexico City to begin a search for the Fountain of Blood in Honduras and the missing Fawcett expedition in Brazil. Left to right are Irving Wallace, 18, and Vladimir Horidovetz, 18, both of Kenosha, and Paul Behm, 23, leader of the expedition whose home is at Cedarburg.

"The Wisconsin Collegiate Expedition." L-R: I. W., Paul Behm, Wally Horidovetz.

Blood), that strangest of all phenomena.

"It is a cave from whence is said to flow a red liquid. It is south of the jungle village of La Virtud, far in the interior, so that no one has ever been there to make a real scientific analysis. But the red liquid is exactly like blood, since dogs, birds, and insects eat it with relish. This is a sacred Fountain of mystery and myth—"

That settled it. Somehow he would find The Fountain of Blood.

Irving recruited his school mate, Wally Horidovetz, and Paul Behm, a twenty-three-year-old world traveler and University of Wisconsin student. He gathered letters of introduction from Secretary of State Hull, Governor Schmedermann of Wisconsin, Dr. Glenn Franks, the President of the University of Wisconsin. He even went so far as to obtain a character reference from the local sheriff "to prove I had never robbed banks."

They called themselves "The Wisconsin Collegiate Expedition."

My Adventure Trail is the unpublished, full-length book that recounted the trip. It began as a handwritten diary, was expanded into a book after Irving returned from the trip, and was later rewritten completely when he decided to convert it from a romantic to a more honest and realistic book. The first version gave this motive for the trip:

"That would be romance, and how! While others wrote of China, of Africa, of Tahiti, of Easter Island, I had to confine my articles to the Wisconsin Woods, Lake Michigan, Sand Dunes. Writing of those places didn't constitute my idea of being a full-fledged travel writer. In my travels, I had always dreamed that someday I might don a spotless white duck suit, a white tropical helmet, and smoke a carved antique pipe. When I traveled, I dreamed that pretty young girls would nudge each other, and whisper—'There he is. Wallace, the great adventure writer.'"

The rewrite was considerably altered:

"My motive for traveling was a simple motive. I was damn sick and tired of roosting in one place; I yearned to Do Things. But mostly, I suspect, I yearned to make money. I wanted to see

September 9 - Sunday - 1934 - Leaving!

It is ten o'clock in the morning. — Yesterday was a most eventful day. Puca had a stagg farewell. We all rode around and talked until 1:30. I then said goodbye to Milt and Scheer, and it was plenty difficult. Said goodbye to Dot Johnson (she cried) when I kissed her farewell.

— Left Reno at 12:30. Left folks at the state line. Both Ma & Pa cried terribly.

: We are now in Bloomington, Illinois, our first stop overnight, 200 miles from Reno. We are seated in the YMCA, writing at 10 in the evening. We ate on the running board of the car — salome sandwiches Hardy had.

Our car, Petasuo, went well, except for part of the top tearing off.

There is not much more to record. The ride was enjoyable; and people stare at our painted car and attire wherever we go. I am enjoying this very much.

NOTE!

Presents: $3.00 & candy from Aunt Rose & Abe
Fudge from Hilda Roberts
Cigarette package from Jerry Vanderwoll

Also had goodbye calls from Harriet Schlager, Mr. Silverberg, Miss Wilkinson, Ruth Sepp, Frannie Achen, Dot Johnson.

(Expenses: .00)

1934 Central and South American trip journal, page one.

Passport for 1934 trip.

unusual sights, photograph them, be impressed by them—and then make money writing about them." These were the strains of alter-ego fantasy and practical professionalism we have witnessed earlier. They were not incompatible, but each a necessity in the pursuit of that complex synthesis of ambition and fantasy that has been referred to as the dream. Perhaps with this more mature recognition of what he wanted and what he thought he could discard, we might properly refer to the dream as The Dream.

The fantasy of the tropical garb and carved pipe could not be sustained or gained without the financial base provided by the practical businessman. But the practical necessities of making a living were, for Irving Wallace, meaningless without the romantic fancy. Wallace had to be the patron and at the same time be the recipient of that patronage. Of course, his art, being absolutely dependent on his business acumen, could easily be ruined by it. He called it "going soft." It was something he had to be careful about —not then, but later.

Only when there was enough money that he never had to worry about money could the business man be retired and reincarnated as an agent or an accountant. Then the creative personality could be allowed the full force of his energy. To be poor was to be divided; to be financially secure was to be whole again. The Dream.

The search for The Fountain of Blood was begun on Sunday, September 9, 1934. "Left Keno at 12:30," he wrote in his daily journal. "Left folks at the state line. Both Ma and Pa cried terribly. Our car, Petasus, went well, except for part of the top tearing off."

Nine days later they arrived at the Roosevelt Hotel in New Orleans. "We found his room to be no. 38 on floor 12 and were admitted by his henchmen. Huey Long, decked in white pajamas, greeted us, shook hands—and seated on the bed with him, we fired questions—he is the master showman."

September 21-Friday:

"Went over to Mexico at night.

"A new world!

"Foreign speech, attractive natives, odd food—God! how can

Irving Wallace on the way up

Mt. Ixtaccihuatl.

At the summit.

I describe it. Went to a 10¢ a dance joint, 'The Pullman,' where
we danced with professional harlots!' "

September 26—Wednesday:

"At 7 this morning we set out to climb 6,000 foot Saddle
Mountain.

"We hiked 10 miles to the mountain. There we started up a
stoney trail, into brushes, into a million cactus plants, into slabs
of stone. We climbed until 1:30—and just at the summit I told
the others to go on—I could never reach the top. (Neither did
they.)

"So alone, I started down, lost my way, bumped on a rock
and passed out, lost my $23 camera. I thought I was going to die.
The sun blinded me, the cactus cut, my fingers bled, my legs
buckled—I couldn't stand, kept falling—stumbling—rolling.

"I got to a road, I don't know how. Then I just lay down
and slept. I was happy I wasn't going to die.

"I'm sick of mountain climbing."*

On October 3 the Kenosha *Evening News* printed a modified
version of the climb. In it he did not mention his inability to complete the chore, but he did manage a fictional twist: "We emerged
from the clouds onto the peak, onto the summit! Alas, alack! We

---

*This experience emerged twenty-four years later in Wallace's first pub-
lished novel, *The Sins of Philip Fleming*:

"Once, in his youth, in the year between high school and the university,
he had spent the summer with several young friends in Colombia, and one
Sunday they had undertaken to scale an eight-thousand-foot mountain. At a
distance, and from the maps, it had appeared a routine task. But on the
overgrown trail hemmed in by trees and sharp bramble, stifled by exhaustion
and heat, he had found the task too formidable. He had decided to forego
the summit, and return to the patio of his cool pension, and so had separated
from the others to return to the village alone. Halfway down, soaked in
perspiration, his defeated legs stiff as stilts, he had collapsed. Rising at dusk,
he had lost the path through this jungle of hostile green, but knew that
safety was in continuous descent. He had gone on and on, downward, sight-
less and uncontrolled, bumping into trees and tearing his skin on pointed
thorns, and nowhere, it seemed, was there a way out. It was a small hell of
blind man's bluff, until, with night, he reached the foot of the mountain, and
saw automobile lights flashing on a nearby highway, and stumbled to safety"
(published New York: Frederick Fell, 1959, p. 106).

Irving Wallace, Fred Sabatini, Wally Horidovetz, Paul Behm.

Irving Wallace before the plane that took the expedition to Chaletange, Salvador.

had climbed the wrong peak—for there, hundreds of feet away, waved a flag on a neighboring top." [The Mexican flag was permanently implanted on Saddle Mountain.] This was untrue.

Mountain climbing seemed to be a favorite topic for Wallace's use of what Norman Mailer has called "factoids"—facts that are not facts until they appear in print. There is no mention in the diary of adverse weather during the November 2 climb of Mount Ixtaccihautl, a sixteen thousand foot peak outside Mexico City. The photographs taken that day provide further evidence of a clear day. *My Adventure Trail* states that the day of the climb was marked by clear skies. The night before the final ascent to the top "A million stars were blinking above" and the next morning "the sun rose over the hills." But for the readers of the Kenosha *Evening News* our correspondent added a violent storm that merited the headline: "Kenosha Boys . . . Battle Blizzard to Reach Summit of Ixtaccihautl."

Descending the mountain, at least for the Kenoshans who read the *Evening News*, was a "breathtaking march." In *My Adventure Trail* we are told it was a "terrible strain." The folks back home read that the last thousand feet were accomplished by sliding—in the casual manner of the experts. The journal entry reads, "I almost killed myself." Years later, in *The Sunday Gentleman,* Wallace partially explained these creative embellishments on the facts by quoting the words of the sign that hung in most Hearst newsrooms: "Make 'em say, 'gee whiz!' "

October 9—Tuesday.

[While in Mexico the boys met another traveler, Fred Sabatini.]

"Eating at Madrid Cafe, Fred got a date with the well-figured waitress. He simply said to her, 'You have nice eyes. Are you married?', etc.

"I must say one thing. I like Fred's philosophy. As he said to the woman, 'I've seen the world and life. I've lived enough of life, and now I don't care what happens to me. I get what I want, do what I want—enjoy life.'

"I wish I could be more like Fred. I am a better writer than he, but oh! he has that heavenly carefreeness about him—which

Before The Fountain of Blood, Honduras jungles. Irving Wallace at far right with neck scarf.

Irving Wallace, Wally Horidovetz, and Paul Behm at The Fountain of Blood. The bottles hold samples from the Fountain.

is something I must attempt to attain. He is frank and devil-may-care. If he likes a girl—well, he simply tells her. I shall strive for that."

The Wisconsin Collegiate Expedition paused in Mexico City long enough to scale Mount Ixtaccihuatl on a clear day during a blizzard, and then they were off to Honduras to find The Fountain of Blood.

On Saturday, December 8, they flew to Chaletango, Salvador. An all-day hike through a pestilential jungle brought them to the village of Hombre de Jesus in Honduras.

"We could find no native to show us their sacred worshipping place. Finally, a tall, skinny peon named Martinez came up and said he could lead us directly to the Fountain, 30 kilometers away through the jungles."

Martinez was given three dollars for guiding them to the Fountain. After three months and five thousand miles it seemed a fair price.

"We left at about 20 to 9:00 A.M. on foot with practically no luggage. A gang of six other natives joined us and we trudged on, jumping fences, hiking over trails. At first it was easy, but then it became very stiff and Martinez set a stiffer pace.

"Down the last mountain, through a valley of eight-foot grass. We cut away with our machetes. I was so tired I just let the weeds and bugs hit my face and arms. I didn't give a damn.

"Up a last mountain and down to a canyon, wherein a river flowed. Up around jagged rocks inch by inch and down to the extreme end of the canyon.

"The natives shouted. I ran along the pebbles and about 12 feet up I saw a huge cave—my Star, The Fountain of Blood! It was exactly 12:30 noon.

"It was rather mystic . . . the red fluid was so mysterious. We went some fifteen yards deep into the black of the cave, but hundreds of bats started flapping and we retreated . . . the stink was overwhelming.

"We took some 40 shots, and eight bottles of the fluid, and retreated.

"Yes, we are the first white men ever to lay eyes on the

After The Fountain of Blood discovery the expedition was received by President Andres Menendez of Salvador.

L-R: Paul Behm, President Menendez, Irving Wallace, Colonel Manuel, Wally Horidovetz.

"The 4th seat from me is a beautiful woman — about 25, painted lips, gorgeous Mexican complexion. Big shoulders & breasts, & beautiful narrow hips. She sits by window & stares at me by the hour. She leans over & looks at me & under different conditions it would be easier to understand. She knows her stuff & I believe, contain a delightful story — for she is "attractive" &

I. Wallace

From a pocket notebook Irving Wallace kept on the Central-South American trip, this written on a train outside Vera Cruz.

Fountain.   A Mr. Squires from England got three-fourths of the way . . . but he didn't reach it. He sent his native guide ahead to get the fluid, but the bottle broke before he got home. We have seen it first, obtained the first photos, and first bottles of the fluid."*

By December 14 the boys were in San Salvador to be received by General Andres Menendez, President of Salvador. From there they traveled to Panama, Colombia, Cuba, and were back in the United States by January 4.

Only one article, "The Mighty Mount Ixtaccihuatl," was sold during the trip. It netted $16.60. The $25.00 the *Evening News* advanced Irving for his dispatches had been spent prior to the journey on a portable typewriter. On January 1, 1935, three days before arriving in Miami, he had two dollars left for spending money on the three-day bus ride to Kenosha. "Oh well," he wrote in his final journal entry. "It has been a great trip, a really great trip—and has molded me no little."

Back to Kenosha meant back to work. In 1935 he wrote sixty-six magazine articles and *My Adventure Trail*. Forty-three articles sold, netting him $378.44. The book, rejected by two publishers, was shelved.

In March he went to work for the *Southport Bugle*, a paper begun by a group of Kenosha labor leaders. Irving did most of the writing—three hundred and eighty-six typeset inches in the paper's four-issue existence. The Wallace touch can be seen in the issue numbers: "First Volume, Second Spasm" (the second issue) was followed by "First Volume, Third Brainstorm" and "First

---

*Natives of Salvador thought the red fluid was the blood of Christ; Honduran mythology proposed it was the blood of a mighty giant buried under the cave. The bottles were sent to the University of Wisconsin where a chemical analysis was performed. The results: "It is a colloidal suspension of mineral matter in water. The odor is due to the products formed in the decay, putrefaction and fermentation of the dead bats, bat dung and other organic matter. Not only does this material produce the foul odor, but it also helps, no doubt, in keeping the colloidal material in suspension.

"Material in colloidal suspension very generally has distinctive colors. In this particular case, the color was golden brown by transmitted light and had the appearance of red blood when examined in reflected light."

Washing in a Honduras stream.

Irving Wallace in Mexico posing with an ancient Toltec serpent. His caption: "Beauty and the Beast."

Volume, Fourth Convulsion."

He even managed to include editorial comment in the price listing: "10¢ in Southport [an earlier name for Kenosha], 2 rubles in Soviet Russia;" "Still a dime here but free in Finland. They paid their debt;" and on the last issue, "Still a dime here but free just the same. We're having a lot of fun."

Fun or not, the *Bugle* folded on March 27, 1935. It was Irving's last job as an editorial staffer on a newspaper, and he would not do political reporting for the press again until 1972.

In July, 1935, Williams Institute of Berkeley, California, offered him a scholarship. He had previously turned down several offers, among them were scholarships from the University of Wisconsin, Ripon, and Northwestern. But Williams was different. Important authors were on its visiting faculty: Rupert Hughes, Edwin Markham, Lincoln Steffens, William Saroyan, and Count Korzybski, the general semanticist. This was a place where The Dream could be pursued. Or so it seemed.

With thirty-five dollars from his parents he chipped in with four other men to share the use of a car across country to Berkeley. There, he lived in a slant-roofed attic with a family near the college, paying fifteen dollars a month room and board.

After two terms he knew he had made a mistake. The Williams faculty emphasized the basics of writing for magazines. What good could that do someone who had published almost a hundred magazine pieces? In December, 1935, he left Berkeley and traveled south to Hollywood.

Wallace's feelings about missing college are ambivalent. He could have gone to any number of first-rate colleges, and so there was never a sense that he had been rejected by higher education. He clearly rejected it because it stood in the way of his work. But still, there is a sense of something lost in this 1959 sketch of a fictional character—a sense that the author might share:

"He had never been to college or university and it gnawed at him. No amount of forced reading—far beyond what any college required—could ever fill this void.

"The mere fact of knowledge did not make up for the sheepskin, the piece of paper that indicated a certain leisure and status

WILLIAMS INSTITUTE
ARLINGTON AVENUE
BERKELEY, CALIFORNIA

May 3, 1935

Irving Wallace,
6103 18th Avenue,
Kenosha, Wisconsin

Dear Mr. Wallace:

We are pleased to hear you are going
to be with us this next fall. Enclosed is a form,
which you might fill out and return for our records.

Before you enroll, we should tell you
that our college does not give a degree, as we
planned to do when the School of Authorship circular
was printed. We found that our writers are far more
interested in winning an E. C. (editor's check) than
an A. B., and there is considerable red tape to
get state recognition of a degree-granting college.

The Fall term begins August 26th.

Hoping to see you then, I am

Very truly,

James Duncan
Director

Luggage   . . . $12
Travel   . . . $12
Travel Exp. . . . $ 5.50   (room, food, incidentals)
Tuition   . . . $50.00
Berkeley
Room and B . . . $48.00   (8 weeks at $6 per week)
                              $ 24 = 4 weeks
To Chicago, etc. $ 3.00 $106.50
                    $130.50

To Berkeley = $1.00
Trunk = .75
                $1.75
Clothes Bch = $5
                $6.75

$113.25

From Williams Institute, Berkeley.

I. W.'s budget for his trip from Kenosha to Williams
College, Berkeley, 1935.

Williams College, Berkeley.

EPISODE IN THE NIGHT

by . Irving Wallace .

I was walking down Main Street. Rather inspirational. White, crisp snow on the ground. It made queer crunching noises as I walked over it. The wind whipping up from Lake Michigan was clean and hard. I enjoyed it.

At the corner I paused to light a cigarette. Someone tapped me on the left shoulder. I wheeled about. It was a girl. She was rather short, shapely, and looked chic in a fine winter coat and stubby overshoes.

"What about a cigarette, buddy?" she asked.

"Sure," I said, pulling one out of the package. "Sure, have a cigarette."

She placed the cigarette between parted red lips. Well-curved, full lips. I lit a match. It went out in the wind. I cupped my hands, lit another, and she sucked hard until her tobacco was aglow.

"Thanks," she said.

I noticed she had nice round eyes. Brown eyes. And her hair was brunette. It peeked out from under her hat.

"A bit brisk out, isn't it?" I said.

"Yes. I'm not used to this kind of weather. I mean

First page of a 1935 short story written at Williams.

class.

"Because his background was first generation, and erratic, and poor, he now made a fetish of collecting honors. He heard about a public relations firm that got you honors—and so on his wall, laminated in magnificent frames, were awards from B'nai Brith, Optimist Club, YMCA, Sane Nuclear Policy Association—most impressive—knighthood from everyone—but the final approval continued to elude him—even this high-powered firm could not get him an honorary degree from a respectable university.

"After a few drinks, when angrier than usual, he would bespeak his rationale: the professional scholars who remained on campus as adults, teaching, researching, were 'frightened of life and the outside world' . . . they with their Princeton Clubs and Williams Clubs and their alumni magazines and fraternity reunions and special snobberies—they were the immature retarded juveniles. He despised them and wished more than anything he were in their boots."

But in 1935 Wallace was uncomfortable and unhappy in college. His father was the same in Kenosha. In late January of 1936 Alex Wallace left Kenosha to join his son in California. They took a room together at the Re-Tan Hotel, 1732 Whitney Avenue, Hollywood.

Writing for magazines had been Wallace's primary source of income since he was fifteen, but the three to four hundred dollars a year that subsidized him as a teen-ager living at home was no longer sufficient. He wrote furiously. On January 28 *The Modern Psychologist* accepted a short essay for publication but would not pay for it. In February he sold fillers to a drug store flyer—payment of one dollar. In March he sold a baseball story to *All-American Sports* for five dollars; the following month the same magazine bought a nonfiction article on the origin of slang expressions for another five dollars, and on April 17 they paid him fifteen dollars for a short story about an unfortunate baseball catcher whose face was paralyzed—"Mann in the Iron Mask."

On August 10 he sold a story concerning hockey violence to *All-American Sports* for seven dollars. The money came just in time to buy his parents a twenty-third anniversary gift. Bessie

Mann in the Iron Mask

By IRVING WALLACE

YOU can't tell me nothing about cool, calm people. Oh, I know Helen Wills Moody is supposed to be the "Little Poker Face," and I know they say Joe Louis has ice tea in his veins. Yeah, and I know all about Buster Keaton's great stone profile. Toss all those frozen faces together and they add up to the sphinx. But, shucks, alongside of Hunky Mann the sphinx is a laughing hyena.

You can believe me, because I've seen Hunky through hell and hurri-cane—in other words, through one baseball campaign in the Allied League, and I only seen him twitch a facial muscle once. Honest to gosh, just once.

I tell you, I seen Hunky Mann spit out two teeth when a fast ball caressed his lips, and I seen him going after a foul ball and bounce off the backstop, and that mummy mug of his never changed.

But once it was different, and I'm aiming to tell you about it.

Wallace and Esther had moved to Los Angeles that March, when Alex found a drugstore job.

The failures of the winter, spring and summer were almost enough to convince Irving that he would starve, lose his confidence, or both. Then Breeze Brandon came along.

Breeze was a scientific boxer who appeared in "Powder Puff Puncher," a story sold to *Thrilling Sports* on the first day of September, 1936. Breeze netted his creator the incredible sum of seventy-five dollars—more than twice what had been earned the previous nine months. His crises of cash and confidence would recur again and again in the next few years, but with "Powder Puff Puncher" precious time had been bought, and he could continue writing.

The magazine work was done for three reasons: 1) to earn money; 2) to have a job where he could write every day; 3) to gain more experience with his craft. As in any profession, an apprenticeship had to be served. In 1944 he wrote a memoir of his magazine days titled *With Their Pants Down* (unpublished). This is what he said about magazine writing:

"Any responsible reporter, determined to hold onto his integrity as he would a winning sweepstakes ticket, soon finds he is censored by what his medium will or will not accept. If he is working for a big magazine he soon finds that magazine a straitjacket. He realizes the magazine is using his earthy epics only as filler material, mere bait, to lure the people into the advertisements. He finds that what he can write and cannot write is governed largely by these advertisements. And, when he approaches magazines that do not carry advertisements, he learns they have political axes to grind. So the writer throws in the towel. He accepts his membership in the Great Brotherhood of Trained Seals."

When the Great Brotherhood closed its doors at midnight on Saturdays, Irving turned to his own writing.

"It was because I believed in the responsibility of the writer to his art as much as I believed that he had other responsibilities beyond writing, it was because of this ambivalent feeling toward my work, that I determined that six days a week were enough to

I

THIS IS WHERE I CAME IN

It is, perhaps, significant that the first interview I ever had was with a horse.

It occured to me, one day, in the sluggish era of Herbert Hoover, that it might be possible to write a very interesting article on the fact that race horses, working no more, than two or three minutes a week, earned considerably more than their human colleagues, the sweating golfers, pugilists, hockey players. On this somewhat fantastic premise, based on an imaginary interview with a famous thoroughbred, I wrote "The Horse Laugh." It was rejected by Horace Lorimer of the Saturday Evening Post who, unable to resist budding genius, advised me to peddle it to a more specialized market. I promptly mailed it to the Horse and Jockey Magazine of Chicago. I received, in return, five dollars and a request for my picture.

It was my beginning. My first sale.

I was thirteen years old at the time.

Since that exalting morning, and in the fifteen rather hectic, ulcerating years that followed, I have interviewed

Page one of manuscript *With Their Pants Down.*

A Complete
Boxing
Novelette

"Breeze! Go in and fight your

POWDER

CHAPTER I

New Champ

THE lightning uppercut caught "Breeze" Brandon square on the jaw. It lifted him off his feet, and sent him spinning, falling.

Suddenly, though it seemed hours later, Brandon emerged from the pit of darkness. The bright Kleig lights above made him blink his eyes. The

The Tide of Ringside Hate is Turned When a

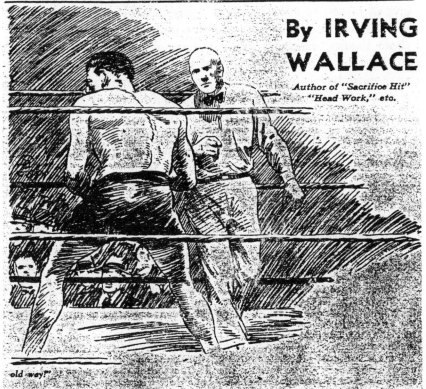

By IRVING WALLACE

Author of "Sacrifice Hit"
"Head Work," etc.

"old way!"

PUFF PUNCHER

cheers and tumult from eighty thousand throats beat against his eardrums.

As his head cleared, he barely made out the grey form of the referee over him. He watched the referee's arm rise and fall. He heard the count:

"—five—six—seven—"

Instinctively Brandon's muscles reacted. They strove to lift his trembling, lean body from the canvas. He knew the old champion, John L. Pearson, was waiting like a tiger in the neutral corner, ready to pounce on him. He knew Limpy, his manager, was sweating blood. In a split second, as he struggled to a knee, he knew he had to rise and win.

He had battled five years for this chance. Had boxed in Navy matches, amateur tourneys, prelim club bouts; had scientifically jabbed his way to the top. He had finally obtained a match with old Pearson, the killer, and ten-year champ of champs.

All through the battle, amid the hoots of the mob, Brandon had boxed the

Scientific Boxer Becomes a Two-fisted Slugger!

give of myself to avoid a debtor's prison. The seventh day of the week, I felt, belonged to me. And so almost every Sunday, during those twenty magazine years, I devoted to factual articles and stories that were more honest, if less commercial, because they were entirely my own. . . . I hoped they would appear in print, and that I would be paid for them, but if they were not accepted and published, it did not matter."

In 1936 Wallace spent his Sundays writing plays. He submitted his first three-act drama to Edward Clark, proprietor of The Clark Academy Theatre. It was a modest little theatre, as exemplified by Clark's playbills which requested that the patrons use the "rest rooms and auto service" at the Texaco station three doors west.

Two weeks later, on December 2, Clark accepted for production. *And Then Goodnight,* a play written by Wallace in six days and revised in four more days.

Early in 1937 the Ben Bard Playhouse, another little theatre in Hollywood, accepted his second play, "Because of Sex." "Death Incorporated," a one-act drama, was staged at Los Angeles City College. His last produced play was *Ego-Maniac,* a comedy in three acts that Edward Clark presented nightly from December 27 to January 27, 1939-1940. On January 12, 1937, Row, Peterson & Company of Evanston, Illinois, paid Wallace thirty-five dollars to include a one-act play titled "Murder by Morning" in their *Fourth Yearbook of Short Plays: 1938.* This was his first work between book covers.

In the November, 1937 issue of *Writer's Digest* Wallace described the Hollywood market for original plays, and hinted at his ambition to break into screen writing:

"Hollywood is regarded solely as a terminal where blondes with hard eyes and soft heads promenade with pet poodles, and where good authors write bad stuff for magnificent salaries.

"Did you know Hollywood is the best market in the world for the amateur play?

"If you have a dramatic opus, and would like the movie moguls to take a peek at it, shoot it to Hollywood.

"The major studios send story scouts to look over new local

THE FOURTH
Yearbook of Short Plays

Twenty-five
New Non-Royalty Plays Designed
for Study and Production

Selected and Edited by
LEE OWEN SNOOK
DIRECTOR, DIVISION OF DRAMA
ROW, PETERSON & COMPANY

Decorations by
JOSEPH M. O'MALLEY

ROW, PETERSON & COMPANY
EVANSTON, ILLINOIS
NEW YORK   SAN FRANCISCO

Anthology in which Irving Wallace's only published play appeared.

Murder by Morning

IRVING WALLACE

The author speaks: "I was born in Chicago. Raised in Kenosha, Wisconsin. After being raised, I joined an expedition into Honduras jungles. Acquired publicity and bedbugs. On the way home, interviewed Huey Long, Sloppy Joe, Kathleen Norris, and Dizzy Dean.

"I was educated at Kenosha Central High School, Williams School of Authorship (Berkeley, California), Los Angeles College, and countless public libraries. Made my stage debut at the age of six in 'The Spirit of America.' I was the Spirit. I forgot my only line, and was on the wrong side of the curtain when it fell. After various similar experiences, I gave up the stage and turned to the ink-pot.

"My initial magazine piece was accepted on my fifteenth birthday. Since then I have sold two hundred stories and worked on five newspapers. At present I am batting out a syndicated movie column.

"Influenced by Hollywood, I took up playwriting last year, and was prostrated for a week when my first three full-length dramas were purchased by producers.

"I enjoy satirizing pomposity and Americana. I enjoy ridiculing intolerance and war. . . . I've never written a back-stage, musical comedy, never named a butler Meadows or Jarvis, never expected my first play to be grabbed by the Theatre Guild—which all makes me feel I'm entitled to the Pulitzer Prize."

CHARACTERS

HERMAN WINKLE, *a writer of detective stories*
SHEILA O'CONNER, *his secretary*
ANITA ANDERSEN, *his temporary heart-interest*
VAN PATTEN, *Anita's volunteer protector*
MR. MAGNON, *the big bold publisher*

SCENE: *The workroom of Herman Winkle, writer of mystery thrillers*

TIME: *The present; evening*

Yearbook purchasers may procure this play, in pamphlet form, at 50 cents per copy.

The curtain rises on the workroom of HERMAN WINKLE, *renowned father of a hundred bouncing murder novels. There are a number of usual things in his room: a conventional Persian carpet on which stands a desk and typewriter, a sofa, an easy chair, and a sundry assortment of lamps. There are also a number of unusual objects in this room: a variety of bleached skulls. On the wall hang large portraits of Edgar Allen Poe and Conan Doyle, and an autographed, enlarged photo of Al Capone. Sandwiched between these pictures is an old-fashioned rusty revolver mounted on a board with a large sign underneath reading: "This gun killed Jesse James."*

All about the room are strewn various gaudy-covered magazines. On an end-table stands a decanter half filled with wine, and beside it is an oriental pipe, one of those snaky affairs that make you think of harems and hula. This, then, is the abode of a modern author of modern detective tales.

After the curtain rises, we find our hero, HERMAN WINKLE, *with his back to the audience. When he finally turns, we note that he is talking to himself. Furthermore, we notice that he is loading a gun. Carefully he injects six bullets into the cylinder. Taking our attention away from the weapon, we get a better look at* WINKLE. *He is of medium height, and attired in a lavish dressing gown. He possesses an intelligent face on which every emotion is written plainly throughout the drama. Moreover, he is the proud owner of a fearless moustache.*

After several seconds, he completes the business of loading his gun. He goes over to his desk and rings a bell. Then, hurriedly, and not unlike Jack the Ripper, he slinks to the left and crouches tensely beside the sofa. He is juggling his re-

plays. I've been in the theater at the opening of my own shows, and seen the scouts, some of whom I know personally.

". . . if you've got something, anything on the theatrical ball, you'll land, be produced. You will receive no initial pay—except experience, publicity, criticism, and the chance of a Broadway or screen sale."

Wallace's first original story for the screen was a mystery tale featuring a detective who faintly resembled Robert Ripley, the renowned cartoonist and oddity hunter. It was handled by the William Morris Agency in 1936. No buyers were found.

Although he wanted to get into the movies (for the money), the chances of having a story bought were so remote that he couldn't afford the time to speculate in films. Throughout 1937, except on Sundays, he stayed with magazine writing. In 1969 he wrote a friend:

"Once, in 1937, there wasn't a dime. My father could get no job, I could sell no story—I was about to give up writing and take a job—meanwhile I borrowed money from a close friend to buy bread, eggs, milk, what we lived on for weeks—then suddenly my father got a job and I broke through with sales to *Coronet* and *Ken* magazine (a political mag put out by *Esquire*)."

Less than four months after his twenty-first birthday, Wallace made his first sale to *Coronet*. "He played Jonah" earned seventy-five dollars.

Ken paid the same amount on August 8, 1938, for "The Vatican Fights Back," a nonfiction article on the Pope's problems with Mussolini and Hitler which typified the style of magazine articles sold to a popular market in 1938:

"The smallest independent state in the world, no larger than a golf course, and with a total population of 1,003 is today fighting a two-fisted fight against the twin menaces of dictatorship and intolerance."

Wallace became adept at the hard-driving reportorial style demanded by the mass magazines. Implicit in some criticism of his later novels is the charge that he never overcame the habits of his apprenticeship, that his novels are full of unnecessary and distracting facts. Wallace admits that he loves facts, especially

March 15th to April 10th, 1937 (Nightly excepting Sundays) at 8:30 p.m.

THE EDWARD CLARK ACADEMY PLAYERS

Present

"And Then Goodnight"

A New Three Act Comedy Drama

By

IRVING WALLACE

ALSO

"A One Horse Town"

A One Act Comedy

By

EDWARD CLARK

Both Plays Directed by Mr. Clark

NEXT ATTRACTION

"The Piker," by Leon Gordon - April 26th to May 22nd

To My Patrons:

You are respectfully requested to consider that these players are students of this Academy (Unless otherwise indicated), some of whom have but recently taken up the work.

They may, in your judgment, here and there be cast in roles as yet not quite within their reach, but that is no fault of theirs since it is my policy and system of training, to throw them overboard, so to speak, to sink or swim.

Acting can be learned only by acting—by practical experience, rather than by theory—for "that which is to be learned, must first be experienced."

Hence, this little theatre of mine is run along stock company lines, giving the students an opportunity to play all manner of parts, alternating roles, for a total of 240 performances during a year's term.

Here, there are no classes, no exercises, no hired teachers, no enrollment time limit, no faculty—in other words, "all there is, I am." And with a lifetime of stage and screen behind me, as author, actor, producer, and director, I think I may modestly assume that I have a goodly amount of theatrical knowledge to impart to the embryonic stars of the future.

Open house prevails here at all times, and anyone is welcome to attend and witness any and all rehearsals, for in the magician's vernacular, "I have no rabbits up my sleeve, and no moustache to deceive you."

I thank you,

EDWARD CLARK.

Ad for Irving Wallace's play, "And Then Goodnight."

when he can use odd information to undercut our accepted and comfortable opinions.

In a 1961 press release he observed that his "attitude toward book subjects is fairly reflected by a young newspaperwoman I created as a fictional character in *The Prize*. Here's what I wrote:

" 'Her delight was not in learning of Julius Caesar's campaigns, but in learning that he wore a crown of laurel to hide his increasing baldness. She was not interested in the fact that Francis Scott Key had composed *The Star Spangled Banner,* but in the fact that he had no ear for music. And one day was made when she learned that Daniel Webster had been sued for not paying his butcher's bill.' "

Michael Korda, Wallace's editor at Simon & Schuster, would also like to see less factual information. Wallace wrote him in 1963:

"You don't like it when I digress and hold up the story; you don't like it when I weave in factual material which you feel does not serve forward motion. From an absolute pure story telling standpoint you are right. On the other hand, this kind of periphery thing, this love of occasional facts and factual wonderland detours, is part of the fabric of my writing and personality. It is not a showing off of cheap capsule knowledge, but rather my genuine interest and the interest of my characters in little related off-shoots in their dialogue. This is the way I am."

He retained the technique in his novels not only because of what he considered the intrinsic interest of oddities and because "that's the way he is," but because he learned in magazine writing that facts could render more complex, and perhaps more true, the lives and settings of his fiction. His fact-in-fiction mode is a journalistic technique which, for better or for worse depending on the point of view, he is consciously applying to his fiction. It is more to him than verbal litter on a fictional landscape.

Remember that the necessity of making a living and the pursuit of The Dream were driving on the same track. He wrote six days a week for a living, one day a week for himself, but writing was a common activity in both parts of the working week. The goals of financial security and skill in his craft might have been

CORONET
M A G A Z I N E
919 NORTH MICHIGAN AVENUE
CHICAGO

July 8, 1938

Mr. Irving Wallace
6527 Leland Way
Hollywood, California

Dear Mr. Wallace:

Enclosed is check for $75.00 in payment for
North American magazine rights on your manuscript, HE PLAYED JONAH, including pocket-
size digest rights for which you will receive
full compensation, if and when sold.

Cordially,

Helene Richards,
Secretary to Mr. Gingrich

HR-ef

Enc. check $75.00

Letter of acceptance for Irving Wallace's first sale to *Coronet*.

miles apart, but they came together in the writing. Wallace was a Janus-faced writer: one face looked back at the creditors, and the other looked forward to The Dream.

Inevitably the two strains of writing became inbred. Wallace's novels, the children of these strange bedfellows, should be considered in the context of his writing background—a combination of magazine journalism and, later, film writing.

Early in 1939 he tried to capitalize on the public's fascination for movies and stars with *The Reel Hollywood*, a little magazine he and his friend Jim Scheer produced. Their notion was to publish a weekly magazine about celebrity happenings, give it away in drug stores or hand it out door-to-door, and make money from the sale of advertising. *The Reel Hollywood* lasted one issue —that of September 7, 1939. It not only lost money, but it made Wallace wonder if there was a living in writing about Celebrity Hollywood.

A month later he got his answer when he sold his first article, "The Dietrich Lure," to *Modern Screen*. That sale to the leading Hollywood-Interest magazine led to many more sales. Furthermore, it put his name before the film publicity people and other studio personnel—a must for breaking into studio work. But most important it brought him in touch with Dell Publications, which owned *Modern Screen*, and which employed Sylvia Kahn as its Western Editor. As he later recollected:

"The editor of the magazine in New York was Pearl Finley, and one of her young assistants—an editorial whiz—was Sylvia Kahn, although I did not know this. My correspondence was with Pearl. Well, Sylvia Kahn, as I would learn later, was enchanted by my letters as well as by my writing. Early in 1940, Pearl Finley came out to Los Angeles to install her assistant, Sylvia Kahn, as the new West Coast editor of Dell Publications. Upon their arrival, Pearl phoned me at my parents' house. She was told she could reach me at a pool hall off Hollywood Boulevard, where I frequently played snooker for an hour or two in late afternoons. I was a pool fiend in those days.

"Pearl reached me there, invited me to join her and her assistant, and several other guests, that evening at the Hollywood

THE REEL HOLLYWOOD

Vol. I   No. 1
September 7, 1939

Editors:
IRVING WALLACE
JAMES F. SCHEER

THE LITTLE FELLER PLAYS DICTATOR

AN EXCLUSIVE ARTICLE ON

CHARLIE CHAPLIN

BY

IRVING WALLACE

A rarity - my friend & I wrote & published this give-away news - we lost money.

One afternoon, last week, a khaki-attired messenger boy pulled his bicycle up before a motion picture studio at 1416 N. La Brea Avenue, and delivered a letter postmarked from Washington, D. C.

The letter was addressed to — "Mr. Charles Spencer Chaplin" —and across the envelope was scrawled the word—"Urgent!"

This missive, an unusual document, was written by a branch of the United States War Department, and it suggested that Charlie Chaplin begin work immediately on his planned picture, "The Dictator."

News of this letter leaked out, appeared in several columns, and readers wondered why the Government should be anxious for Charlie Chaplin to begin his latest epic. The reason, insiders deduct, is this—Chaplin's newest film will be a biting satire on Herr Adolph Hitler; it will make Hitler and his Napoleon complex appear both pathetic and humorous; it will be seen all over the world, by all races, and do more than anything else to puncture the heroics of Fascism.

Recently, at a tennis club in Beverly Hills, I chatted with Chaplin about "The Dictator" and was told that the story concerned a bewildered Jewish tailor, a meek and timid tramp, who resembled the fanatical ruler of a Nazi country, and was hired by the Gestapo as a double, but by accident found himself boosted into power.

The show will be a comedy, and Chaplin will play both the timid tailor and the stern dictator, speaking only in a garbled German—a sort of combined pig Latin and

Oddity Publications, Editorial and Business offices, 6527 Leland Way, Hollywood, Calif., Telephone HI-4783; GL-8139. Distributed free. The Reel Hollywood, published weekly by the La Chall Printing Co., 1616 Cahuenga Blvd., Hollywood, Calif. Copyright 1939. All Rights Reserved.

The Reel Hollywood — first and last issue.

Knickerbocker Hotel for cocktails and a preview of *Dr. Ehrlich's Magic Bullet,* which was to be sneaked a few blocks away. I accepted.

"That evening, wearing my best turtle neck sweater, I went calling upon Pearl Finley. I walked into her hotel suite, and after meeting her, my eyes held on another woman—the very young, absolutely beautiful blonde named Sylvia, whom I was to marry. I never forgot that moment of our first meeting, and years after, with little change, I used it in my novel, *The Prize.* It's in Chapter III. My protagonist, Andrew Craig, a young writer—guess who?—has just been discharged from the Signal Corps at Fort Dix. He is invited to a New Year's Eve Party:

" 'Fortified by two drinks, he arrived in the plush apartment after ten o'clock. The food was, indeed, good, but what was better was Miss Harriet Decker. When Wilson had introduced him to the nearest drunks at hand, Harriet had been stretched supine on the sofa, in stocking feet, her head in someone's lap, as was the fashion for that age that year. She was one of many guests horizontal, but the only guest completely sober. She had acknowledged Craig by shading her eyes, passing her gaze up his lank figure, saying 'Hi, up there.'

"That's the fictionalized version of how in fact I met Sylvia, who was to become my wife about sixteen months later."

Irving Wallace and Sylvia Kahn were married June 3, 1941, in a private ceremony at the Santa Barbara court house. When they returned to Los Angeles from the wedding they were both greeted by summonses. Sylvia was being sued by Errol Flynn for an exposé she had written about him (she won), and Irving was being called up for interrogation by the Army Intelligence.

This is what interested the Army G-2.

By early 1940 Wallace had established a solid reputation with the large national magazines, especially with *Liberty.* They paid him three hundred dollars on February 23, 1940, for an article he ghosted for Los Angeles Mayor Fletcher Bowron. On April 17 they paid him four hundred dollars for ghosting an article for Gracie Allen. Later in June he sold them yet another ghostwritten article, "We'll Give America Wings." It appeared in the September 7,

Sylvia Kahn and Irving Wallace a few months before their marriage.

1940, issue of *Liberty* as the work of Donald Douglas, the aircraft manufacturer. Douglas told *Liberty*'s readers that America could sleep easy despite the Nazi menace; his factories could produce sufficient fighter planes if Hitler pushed the United States into a war with Germany.

It was a timely article and established Wallace as more than a Hollywood reporter. *Liberty* was so impressed with him that they granted him an assignment in the Far East.

When the *M. S. Tatuta Maru* left Los Angeles for San Francisco, Honolulu and Yokohama on July 17, 1940, Irving Wallace, foreign correspondent, was on it.

Mitsuru Toyama, eighty-six year old head of the militant Black Dragon Society, told him the Japanese were ready to establish a "New Order in Asia" which excluded Western influence. Clearly he meant to kick the Westerners out of Asia. He was talking about war.

Then there was Foreign Minister Yosuke Matsuoka who harangued our correspondent with Japan's plans to join Hitler in a world war. Wallace relayed the story to Larry Smith of the International News Service, who broke the story worldwide on October 3, 1941. In 1943 Alice-Leone Moats published *Blind-Date With Mars,* a book about the events leading up to World War II. On pages 54 and 55 she wrote:

"The Foreign Minister himself refused to see me. The official spokesman said His Excellency had made it a policy not to meet any foreign journalists regarding their profession. This policy was due to the fact that Matsuoka had given an interview to a *Liberty* correspondent who had then passed it on to I.N.S. According to the interview, Matsuoka had been extremely outspoken against America. This was just at the wrong moment, when the Prime Minister was following a policy of threatening the United States enough but not too much. Matsuoka announced that he had been misquoted, which may have been true, but in view of his well-known loquacity it is also possible that he was actually as indiscreet as the interview made him sound."

On Christmas day, 1961, Wallace made this notation on the flyleaf of his copy of *Blind-Date With Mars*: "I am the *Liberty*

Irving Wallace with Mitsuru Toyama, leader of the Black Dragon Society. Japan, 1940.

correspondent.   I did interview Foreign Minister Matsuoka in
Tokyo during 1940. He did threaten America with war."

With Their Pants Down recounts another such interview and
its aftermath:

"I went to see Japan's leading Naval strategist, short, wiry
Admiral Nobumasa Suetsgo. Years ago Suetsgo advocated super-
submarines, under-water arsenals capable of cruising around the
world. Years ago, too, he created an international sensation by
demanding that the white race be booted out of Asia. 'We are
ready to defend our island,' he said."

For this and an interview with Admiral Nomura, who wanted
peace and was the Japanese Ambassador to the United States on
"the day that will live in infamy," Wallace was visited at his hotel
by the Tokyo Police. "Be careful, Wallace-San," he was told.
"Our eyes are open."

On August 29 he flew to Shanghai for more interviews.
Although closely watched by The Secret Police of the Japanese
occupation forces, Wallace eluded them to contact Dr. Miner
Searle Bates, an authority on opium traffic. Dr. Bates revealed that
the Japanese army was flooding areas of China with low-priced
opium and heroin. Upon Wallace's return to Tokyo he was again
visited by the police, who wanted to know if he had learned anything interesting about opium. "It was a tough one, but I talked
fast. I explained that my primary interest had been in Japan's
magnificent effort to break the Chinese of their unfortunate opium
habit." The police seemed satisfied and left.

But he did not get off so easily in another interview. If the
Japanese politely implied they would have his neck, Olivia de
Havilland swore she would. It began when he decided to write an
article on "Go," a popular Japanese game. He arranged an interview with one W. A. De Havilland, a "Go" expert living in Tokyo.
Mr. De Havilland said "his wife had left him years before, for a
California gentleman named Mr. Fontaine—and with her she had
taken the two girls, Olivia and Joan." It appeared, further, that
Olivia and Joan were now famous and wealthy movie stars, and
that they refused to help their "threadbare" father. De Havilland
decided to get even with the girls by placing prepaid advertise-

Irving Wallace at the Imperial Hotel, Tokyo.

Below — in Nanking, China.

ments in the Hollywood *Variety* and *Reporter*, two important trade papers. The advertisements stated simply that the father of Olivia de Havilland and Joan Fontaine found it necessary, for support of himself and his Japanese wife, to sell all of Olivia's baby effects, letters, photographs. Wallace persuaded Mr. De Havilland not to send the ads, and got him to agree to a mild article. It appeared in the January, 1941, issue of *Modern Screen.* When Olivia de Havilland saw it she promised Jerry Asher, Warner's publicity contact, that if she ever met up with Wallace she would slap his face, and then some. Asher tried to explain Wallace's intercession with her father, but Olivia did not believe him. For his efforts, Wallace sent Asher a little gift, to which Asher replied: "If you dig up an old Japanese mother for Humphrey Bogart, know I'll love you just the same!"

Liberty's correspondent was in the Far East for three and a half months. After surveying the generally impoverished and demoralized populace during the first month, he concluded that Japan was too weak for war and would remain neutral, or at least keep out of a fight. Most of the later months he spent interviewing Japanese military men and, based on their aggressive jingoism, he reversed his earlier opinion. Ready or not, Japan would go to war because the military wanted it that way. The war that did follow confirmed the latter prediction. Had Wallace not gotten the military side of the situation he would have been left with the inaccurate prediction he published on September 4, 1940, in Morton Thompson's column in the Hollywood *Citizen-News*:

"This is the Japan that bogeymen say might be a threat to the United States. Why, when I get home, if anyone mentions the term Yellow Peril to me, I'll buy them a second-class ticket to Tokyo—which should be cure enough. . . . There is nothing to worry about."

Wallace's more accurate view of the situation appeared in Walter Winchell's column during December, 1940. The Japanese government was furious. Through its English-language propaganda newspaper, *The Times-Advertiser* of Tokyo, it disputed the correspondent's claims about the military's belligerence and announced that both Wallace and Winchell were never to set foot in Japan or

Japanese artist's watercolor of Irving Wallace in 1940.

its possessions again.

Wallace had felt the uneasiness in Japan from the day he arrived in Yokohama and port officials scissored out several pages from his copy of John Gunther's *Inside Asia.* The book having been revised to fit Japan's view of Asia, it was returned to the owner.   When Wallace released Matsuoka's imprudent remarks about Japan's war readiness, the already tense military had to either dismiss Matsuoka as not representative of Japanese thinking, or attempt to discredit Wallace. Reasonably enough, they called Wallace a liar and banned him from the country. Six years later, in 1947, he was further honored by a Facist military junta. General Franco so disliked Wallace's "Will The Spanish Town Live Again?" (*Saturday Evening Post*, July 5, 1947), that he ordered him to never again enter Spain.   Today Wallace is welcome in both countries.

The Far East trip was a journalistic and financial success. *Liberty* bought three articles for $1100, *American Legion* two for $300, *Esquire* one for $100, *Scribner's Commentary* one for $75, *Parade* one for $75, and *Foreign Service* one for $50.

Encouraged by the magazine editors' interest, he decided to write a full-length book on the Japanese situation. Working six days for magazines, he spent his nights and Sundays putting together an outline of *Japan's Mein Kampf.* On Saturday, December 6, 1941, he sent copies of the outline to five publishers. The next day was Pearl Harbor. By Tuesday, December 9, he had received notice from all five publishers of their interest in the book. He worked frantically through December and January to produce a four hundred page manuscript, finishing it on January 29. But *Japan's Mein Kampf* was too historical, too objectively analytical for an America swept by war fever. By June 5 all the publishers had turned it down, and again he was left with a dead manuscript. It would be three years before he would try again, fail again, and twelve years before his first book would finally be accepted for publication.

But first there was the Second World War.

"Caught up in the war fever, I decided not to wait for the draft but to enlist, especially if I could get into a branch of service

Irving Wallace

while in First

Motion Picture

Unit, 1942.

THE ZERO'S HOUR   *by Pvt. Irving Wallace*

When American prisoners in Tokyo, engulfed by silence, tried to learn how the war was progressing, their sullen Nipponese guards told them, "You are losing—you will be conquered—because we have a mystery airplane that is crushing you!"

The mystery plane, tricky and light, but without a Sunday punch, like a Jap boxer, was the wonder plane of the world, the secret darling of the Imperial Japanese Navy—the fabulous Zero!

Today, after countless tangles with the Zero, after endless defeats and growing victories against Japan's "Navy Naught," there are dozens of question marks. Where did it come from? Who thought of it? What is it like?

So, as one who saw the Zero before it had a nickname, and when it was still the Mitsubishi Navy fighter T-00, and as one who heard about it while it was still a maiden, let me file a brief report.

For example, few persons outside Yedo knew how the streamlined, single-seater, low-winged monoplane, sporting the Rising Sun, was born. Actually, it was quite simple—

The Zero was born in the fall of 1931 because a near-sighted little newspaper editor named Taketora Ogata decided to throw a contest. And I can tell the story now because, just before Pearl Harbor, I saw this Ogata, and heard it from his own lips.

Taketora Ogata is Editor-In-Chief of the Tokyo *Asahi*, the daily newspaper which has a fleet of five airplanes at its private hanger. We were discussing air power, and Ogata, a belligerent character, said, "If Japan fights America, we will have the greater air power—because for ten years we have concentrated on air power—ever since 1931, when you in America decided our planes and pilots were a joke."

According to his story, in 1931, the *Asahi*, in an effort to bolster Nipponese aviation prestige, offered a prize of $25,000 to the first pilot able to fly non-stop from Tokyo to America's West Coast. The *Asahi* made the offer feeling certain that one of its own Japanese pilots, in a new Japanese plane, already prepared would succeed in spanning the Pacific.

Everything went wrong. Three Jap-

anese fliers took off. Two cracked up. One was lost. Other little yellow men continued to prepare.

Meantime, Clyde Pangborn, the great American flyer, and his passenger companion and sponsor, Hugh Herndon, Jr., attempting to beat the round-the-world record established by Post and Gatty, landed at Harbarovsk, Siberia, far behind schedule. There they heard of the $25,000 *Asahi* prize and decided to try for it. So, without bothering about passports and such niceties, they flew to Tokyo and set their craft down at the Tachikawa airport. They were immediately arrested. Pangborn had no flight permit. And Herndon, for lack of something else to do, had taken 16 mm. films of the Ominato Naval Base.

Pangborn and Herndon might have been released at once, except that the Japanese wanted to give their own pilots and planes time to grab the *Asahi* award. So the Americans were detained for trial while three more Japanese aviators started across the Pacific—and failed miserably.

At last, after fines had been imposed, Pangborn and Herndon could be held

Page 3

In 1942 Irving Wallace was the editorial assistant for *Contact*, the magazine of the F.M.P.U.   This article appeared in the November 20, 1942 issue.

where I could be more useful carrying a typewriter than carrying a rifle. The Marines wanted combat correspondents. I volunteered. I passed all of the Marine physical except one test—the Marines said I was color blind—and rejected me. Then I heard that the Air Forces had taken over the old Hal Roach film studios, and were converting them into a military base to produce training and orientation motion pictures. I submitted my application to a cavalry officer named Ronald Reagan, and it was processed, and I was accepted."

Wallace was sworn into the army on October 6, 1942, sent to Fort MacArthur for three days of very basic training, and on the tenth of October assigned to the First Motion Picture Unit of the Army Air Forces in Culver City, California.

His superiors were not sure what they should do with him. He had lived in Hollywood, had written about movies and their stars, but he had never written a screenplay or worked in a film studio. He could claim experience in magazine writing and he had a shelf full of unpublished books, but the F.M.P.U. was a film studio where established film writers and directors were continuing their civilian trades in uniform. What could be done with Private Wallace? Major Paul Mantz, Hollywood's hottest stunt pilot, settled that question.

Mantz headed the F.M.P.U. in 1942. He decided he wanted to write a book about flying—for flyers. He could not write, but he heard that one of his men could. Wallace recounted the circumstances:

"I had been on the post only three days, and I had my first assignment. It was the perfect job for me, and I knew that I could do it well. Only two things bothered me. First, I had really wanted to do my share in defeating Hitler and Tojo, yet all I was about to do was fire a paper bullet—which would do little to halt enemy aggression. Second, I was the only person in our Army Air Forces Company who was afraid of airplanes. I had never understood what made an airplane fly, and I still don't. I have, and had, a phobia about heights. This is the man who was assigned to become literary alter ego to the great stunt pilot, Paul Mantz."

The project lasted less than a month; the book never got past research notes. "I don't think it was ever meant to be. I think it was a whim he found acceptable, briefly, and then abandoned for better things. Those who can, do; those who can't, teach (or write). He preferred to go out and do . . . and our collaboration and his book died aborning."

In early 1944 Wallace was transferred to the U. S. Army Signal Corps Photographic Center in Los Angeles. During his three years with the Signal Corps, Wallace worked on over twenty-five orientation films, with topics ranging from "Baseball in Japan" to "Facts About Lend Lease." He worked with directors John Huston and Frank Capra, scriptwriter Carl Foreman, and children's book author Ted Geisel ("Dr. Seuss").

The major project at the Center was the "Why We Fight" series. One film in the series, *Know Your Enemy Japan,* is discussed in detail on pages 288 to 293 of this book.

During the making of the "Why We Fight" series, Wallace and Huston got to know each other socially, and Huston related stories about some of his unusual friends. One was Franz H., a doctor of sorts from Vienna. Dr. Franz did not believe in chance, but insisted that if he knew every meticulous detail about someone's past he could predict that person's future. He even kept a chart on himself. The chart predicted he would commit suicide. It was right.

Another friend of Huston's was Albert Boni, the publisher. Once he was presented with a code that proved Francis Bacon wrote Shakespeare's plays. He applied it. It worked. The code was a sensation until an office boy used it to prove that everything from the Bible to the *Daily Racing Form* had been authored by Bacon.

On November 8, 1945, Wallace was transferred to the Signal Corps on Long Island. In New York he met the Everleigh Sisters, once the proprietors of Chicago's most renowned "Social Club" (read "brothel"). The Everleighs did not admit who they were, only went so far as to say they knew the famous sisters. In 1968 he would pay homage to them in a collection of essays titled *The Sunday Gentleman.*

Another essay in that collection began with an assignment to

Sunday - May 7 - 1944 - New York -
Sgt. Irving Wallace

Dear Sir

Your Letter
addressed to my sister Aida
Lester and to me —
lies on my desk ...
There is Truth in the
Axiom — That asserts —
" A Letter mirrors the

Letter from Minna "Lester," an assumed name the Everleigh sisters used after they retired from the Chicago bordello. On this and the following page, Minna denies she is an Everleigh.

Soul of The Writer' !!!
Your letter portrays culture
courtesy - intellect - literary
and aromatic genius ...
Therefore this candid
heart-prompted response ...
Dear sgt. Wallace —
Aida and Minna Lester's
past is not linked with
The Everleigh Club —

Irving Wallace and Sylvia at a Hollywood premiere, 1944 or 1945. Irving Wallace's caption: "My wife Sylvia, an important editor, got us invited free via her press pass to all premieres and previews."

write about prosthetics. On December 3, 1945, then Sergeant Irving Wallace reported to Lawson General Hospital, Atlanta, for a fourteen day study of amputee rehabilitation. His later essay about the experience, "The Amps," is a cooly understated account of the stygian world of blown-up men.

Lawson General would also serve him well in the writing of *The Prize* (1962). Dr. Max Strattman, a Nobel Prize winner in that novel, is introduced to the reader as he undergoes a physical examination at Lawson.

Late in January, 1946, Irving reported to Fort Dix, New Jersey, for discharge from the army. He almost did not make it. His letter to Sylvia Wallace, written Tuesday night, January 29, 1946, from the Signal Corps post on Long Island:

"I had felt this was a critical day and told everyone so but, of course, there was no way of knowing. I was awfully tired this morning (as I am, more so, now) after days of sleepless nights and ups and downs and waiting. About ten this morning Nathan rushed up to me saying someone had phoned him the final list was out and in the orderly room. We thought it might be a false alarm, but we hurried over. The room was jammed with men getting clearance slips. We asked someone if our names were on the list. He said no, we'd both missed it. We asked him to look for sure. He did. Looked up, said, 'Nathan's not here.' Looked down, looked up, said, 'Hey, Wallace, you're here at the bottom. You and four others were written in.' I had been next in line, would have missed, as Nathan did, if Cahill, our swell first sergeant, hadn't agreed to stay on a few weeks to help the officers with payroll and other details."

On February 3 he was officially discharged as Armed Forces Personnel #19160843, Technician Third Grade, Signal Corps Photographic Center. Decorations: American Service Medal, Good Conduct Medal, World War II Victory Medal. His paper bullets no longer needed by the army, he returned home to fire some at Hollywood.

Trained as a film writer in the army, he had broken through the studio barrier in 1943 with two screenplays: *Jive Junction* (produced); *He's My Uncle* (shelved). On March 10, 1944, Repub-

1945

Irving Wallace's caption: "When all the great Disney artists were drafted into the army, they were funneled into the Signal Corps Photographic Center to produce animated short features. I wrote a short piece for the Center magazine about what earthquakes had done to our enemy Japan in the past — and predicted another one (I meant our bombers) would soon level Tokyo again. A week later an actual earthquake staggered Tokyo. Immediately cartoons of me as Nostradamus by ex-Disney animators filled my room, and this was one of them."

Income Tax for 1945.

any writing, anywhere, no matter when written, on which I must pay tax.

	Total Income	agents deductions
January-February		
March	$ 508.80	45.
May	$ 572.50	60.
July	$ 475.	10.
August	$ 650.	65. + 180. *club*
September	$ 100.	
October	$ 50.	$ 5.
November	$ 900.	$90. 225 *club*
December	$ 200	$ 20
	$ 3,456.30	$700.
	+ 750. Movie	
	+ 100. Contest	
	4306.30	

Irving Wallace's income tax for 1945 showing the financial fluctuation of his magazine income.

lic. Studios had purchased his screen original *Anything For a Laugh*. It was filmed quickly and released September 8, 1944. More important for Wallace, it netted him the tremendous sum of $2,430.

Throughout the army years he had worked nights and weekends on magazine articles. A representative year was 1944, during which he wrote ten articles, as well as the *Anything For a Laugh* original and one full-length book (*With Their Pants Down*). These totalled 158,000 words—about seven hundred manuscript pages. The total earnings for 1944's writing came to $3,687. Deduct the $2,430 for the film story and there is $1,257 left. Since the screen original ran only fifteen pages, the other six hundred and eighty-five pages earned the $1,257. At that rate he would have to write more than two thousand magazine and book pages a year to make a living wage. He wanted to stay in magazine writing because he liked the work and he liked being his own boss, but it was becoming a luxury he could hardly afford.

In 1946 the balance swung in the other direction—away from films and toward magazines. He sold his first story to the *Saturday Evening Post* on January 17, "a red-letter day. While I was in New York with the U. S. Army Signal Corps I had dropped in on Mary Benjamin, the leading autograph dealer of the day. I wanted to buy two autographed letters, one by George Bernard Shaw and one by Emile Zola, as gifts. I became fascinated by Miss Benjamin, and wrote 'The Keeper of the Names' about her."

The day he sold the story he wrote his wife to tell the good news:

"I was snoozing at my best this morning when the phone rang. It was 10:30. I answered. It was Paul Reynolds [literary agent], and his historic words were—'*Saturday Evening Post* bought your story. Price $600.' Thanks, dearest. I love you and wish we could have enjoyed it together.

"It's strange to think of the circumstances behind the sale. Benjamin was first subject I saw here, got only half material I wanted, wrote that outline for Pindyke, who got it rejected by *Colliers* and *Liberty* and returned to me. . . . I abandoned the subject until Christmas when, seeing Benjamin again, getting that

THE SATURDAY
EVENING

POST

FOUNDED BY

Benj. Franklin

BEN HIBBS
EDITOR

THE CURTIS
PUBLISHING COMPANY
PHILADELPHIA 5

February 27, 1946

FEB 28 1946

Dear Mr. Reynolds:

    Irving Wallace's KEEPER OF THE NAMES will appear in the March twenty-third issue of the Post.

Sincerely,

The Editor

Mr. Paul R. Reynolds
JAO

Publication notice from *The Saturday Evening Post* marking I. W.'s first sale to them.

Irving and Sylvia Wallace, 1944.

Irving Wallace with parents, 1945.

Shaw and Zola, I was re-inspired . . . and feeling I should be seen in *Coronet,* wrote it cold only for them . . . until, with your advice, deciding to let Reynolds see it first . . . and bingo, *Post.*

"In 1931 I received my first reject from *Post,* from Horace Lorimer, and in 1946, 15 years later, my first sale. But in those days I thought $600 was enough to retire on for life. It's not bad for a shabby story . . . and frankly, I'm more tickled about *Post* than I would be about *Colliers,* which I think I can crack almost at will if I take on their subjects."

This letter shows great enthusiasm for a post-war continuance of magazine writing, but then it is expressive of an emotional moment. There was much about magazine writing he was less enthusiastic about.

There was the editorial attitude that the magazine article or short story must always be subservient to the advertisements. On August 4, 1942, he received the following letter from Oscar Dystel, editor of *Coronet.* (Dystel had accepted Wallace's article on John Hix, a collector of odd facts, but Dystel needed to straighten him out on a few hard facts of commercial publishing before he would print the article):

"I think I should tell you that we apparently disagree on the basic policy regarding the preparation of articles for *Coronet.*

"You see, Irving, *Coronet* is now in the process of building a million or more circulation. And in this process we cannot afford to take slaps at individuals, or to cast them in any unfavorable light where they will become our enemies rather than our boosters. As a result, we have adopted a policy of trying to stay on the sweetness and light side wherever possible. This may seem spineless to one who has contributed to magazines of established major league standing, but I am sure you will understand our position when I tell you that when we publish an article on a personality such as John Hix, we would ordinarily expect him to promote this piece to the skies. Yet if we do such things which definitely do not please him, and with which he definitely disagrees—the article, while it may be extremely interesting from an editorial point of view, loses its promotion value."

Another form of censorship came from the subject of the

YEAR: 1942

	number written	words	sold
JANUARY	5	13,300	3
FEBRUARY	4	7,400	4
MARCH	4	11,500	4
APRIL	6	14,700	4
MAY	3	6,600	2
JUNE	2	13,000	2
JULY	4	10,500	3
AUGUST	3	7,900	3
SEPTEMBER	6	13,300	5
OCTOBER	1	1,800	1
NOVEMBER	2	6,500	1
DECEMBER	1	3,800	1

SUMMARY: I wrote 41 pieces of work
         of which there were
                 35 articles
                 6 short stories

         I wrote 110,300 words
         I made 33 sales

MAGAZINES: Sold to Liberty-7, Coronet-6, American Legion-3,
           Toronto Star-3, Sir-3, Parade-2, This Week-2,
           Foreign Service-2, American, Male, Skyways,
           Esquire, Facts.

INCOME: I received 34 checks totaling $5,398.00. I averaged
        $158.77 per check. I averaged $103.81 per week.

ADDED FACTS: I enlisted in the Army on October 6, 1942.

Work and sales summary, 1942.

article. In 1946 Wallace interviewed Raymond Chandler, America's foremost hard-boiled detective author. Chandler was acerbically candid in his discussion of other mystery writers. He thought S. S. Van Dine's stories "utterly detestable," Agatha Christie's "phony," and Erle Stanley Gardner's Perry Mason tales simply "stunk."

While the article was being readied for publication, a New York publicist heard about the mystery writer's comments on his colleagues and mentioned them in print. Then Chandler had second thoughts. He told Wallace to delete the candid remarks. Reluctantly, the comments were excised.

And then there were problems with the Hollywood stars and those who were paid to keep them orbiting. In 1943 Wallace sold a sketch of the Andrews sisters to *Coronet* magazine. Lou Levy, the singers' manager, contacted Harris Shevelson, editor of *Coronet,* and threatened to take the magazine to court. Levy objected to Wallace's mention that the Andrews sisters were substantially less than attractive. Levy was finally persuaded that it would be difficult to prove in court that the sisters were beautiful, especially after Wallace had lined up a witness, "a Hollywood beauty expert, who was prepared to state in court that one of the sisters looked like Abe Lincoln."

The studios were another censoring agency:

"One of my earliest experiences with M-G-M censorship came after an interview with the charming Miss Rosalind Russell. During the course of the interview, Miss Russell had a cocktail and several cigarettes. In my story, to punctuate quotes, I quite innocently portrayed Miss Russell sipping her bacardi and smoking as she rambled on.

"When my story reached M-G-M there was a shout heard round the world. Memos papered the publicity offices. I was called in, poor bewildered heathen, and gruffly told that M-G-M stars never, never drink in stories—and they never, never, never, never smoke."

In February, 1941, Wallace wrote a candid overall story about Hollywood. In it he quoted William Morris, the dean of movie agents, as he tried to explain the antics of stars: "They are a pathetic group of poorly educated children, driven by forces in-

Studio Press Correspondent

HOLLYWOOD

IRVING WALLACE

MODERN SCREEN
ST. ANTHONY MESSENGER

JULY
AUG.
SEPT.

Publicity Directors Committee

ASSOCIATION OF MOTION PICTURE PRODUCERS, INC.

Press Pass

TO PUBLICITY DEPARTMENT
TWENTIETH CENTURY-FOX FILM CORPORATION
BEVERLY HILLS, CALIFORNIA

NAME   IRVING WALLACE

REPRESENTING   MODERN SCREEN

VALID UNTIL DECEMBER 31, 1941

STUDIO PUBLICITY MANAGER   HARRY BRAND

No. 202   THIS PASS NOT VALID UNLESS SIGNED BY THE HOLDER ON THE REVERSE SIDE

**LIBERTY MAGAZINE
PRESS CARD NO. 021**

1942

THE PERSON WHOSE SIGNATURE IS WRITTEN
ON THIS CARD IS AN AUTHORIZED PRESS
REPRESENTATIVE OF LIBERTY MAGAZINE

SIGNED   EXECUTIVE EDITOR

Some of Irving Wallace's studio press cards from the 1940's.

comprehensible to them, seeking diversion and security. Why, if you'd never had anything but a wardrobe trunk and a lousy second-rate hotel room to call home, you might spread yourself too."

Robert F. Sherwood, the playwright, said the normal Hollywood starlet "who has been boosted suddenly to a dizzy eminence and is rather puzzled by it all . . . awakens in the night with the realization, 'At this moment I am being subjected to vicarious rape by countless hordes of Jugoslavs, Peruvians, Burmese, Abyssinians, Kurds, Latvians and Ku Klux Klansmen!' Is it a wonder that a girl in that predicament finds it difficult to lead a normal life, that her sense of balance is apt to be a bit erratic?"*

Official Hollywood was not amused. Jock Lawrence, then head of the press section of the Motion Picture Producers Association, curtly informed Wallace that he was no longer on the Will Hays list of accredited studio correspondents.

The magazine writing was fraught with disturbing restrictions, to be sure. But beginning with the *Liberty* assignment to Japan he had developed a sense of self-respect about journalism:

"The stories that I wrote six days a week were stories designed to sell to certain markets, to be published, and to earn me enough money to avoid poverty, bankruptcy, masculine failure, the twentieth-century versions of the seventeenth-century debtor's prison. Nor did I ever feel that this was literary prostitution, any more than magazine writers, newspapermen, television and radio writers and commentators today feel that they are committing prostitution. It was a respectable job to be done, just as magazine writers and journalists today are fulfilling a job in communications. It was an accommodation to a mature necessity of life, a way to survive and seek security for one's self and one's dependents . . . those of us who wrote on order did so because it was man's work, and we tried—as others in this position try today—to earn our daily bread with as much honor, integrity, and individual creativity as possible within the confines of the restrictive commercial world

---

*Twenty-three years later, in the 1974 novel *The Fan Club*, Wallace used Sherwood's observations as an entry in a character's personal journal.

Jacque Kapralik's caricature of Universal's *Meet Me at the Fair*.

of magazines and newspapers."

In a job summary he wrote in 1944, Wallace said that he received his formal education at Central High School, Kenosha Wisconsin, "But my main education has been in magazines." By the end of the 1940's he was ready for post-graduate school—the movies.

The antecedents of Wallace's film career go back to the mid-1930's. In 1936 the William Morris Agency handled *Oddity Hunter*, a seven page original screen story. It did not sell. In 1938 he was unsuccessful with *Mister Myth*, a fifteen page story. *The Cradle Genius*, a forty-four page story about a nine-year-old prodigy who refuted Einstein's theory of relativity was turned down by Producer's Releasing Company and M-G-M in 1939. *Petticoat President* and *Twenty-Six Miles to Glory* were other failures that year. Bette Davis wanted to do *Petticoat President*, but her producer, Hal Wallis, told her she could not because it was a costume picture.

In 1943 he wrote thirteen originals, 86,500 words. All were rejected. Between 1936 and 1950 he wrote a total of fifty-seven unsold originals—approximately a quarter of a million futile words.

His first studio work was *One Man's Justice*, written nights during the spring of 1942. It was never produced, but with it he was in the movies.

Jive Junction was his first produced screenplay. For it he received $369.43 and shared screen credit with Malvin Wald and Walter Doniger. *Daily Variety* (November 12, 1943) said it was "none too happy a chance of story material," which was both benevolent and true. The story concerned a high school boy (played by Dickie Moore), an accomplished musician, who opened a canteen for servicemen (*Jive Junction*), and through an incredible string of events took his school orchestra to the championship of a national music competition. Years later, in *The Sins of Philip Fleming*, Wallace wrote this about the movies and their plots:

"In the studios there was a cliché, as phony as the producers who persistently repeated it, that if you could not tell the story you wanted to tell in one sentence, it was not worth making as a movie. 'Give it to me in one sentence, kid,' they would say. 'If

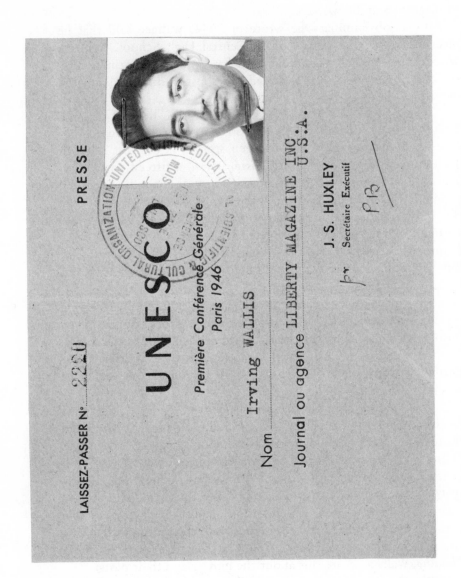

Irving Wallace's *Liberty* press pass for a 1946 UNESCO conference.

Irving Wallace and David Weisbart, the producer of Warner Brothers' *Jump Into Hell*, (Photo: Bert Six)   1954.

you can't you haven't got it yet.' "

On February 5, 1948, David Wallace was born. However beloved of his parents, he *was* another mouth to feed. His parents had just returned from a magazine assignment in Europe. Little money had come of it. To be brief, they were broke. A week before he was mustered out of the army Irving had written Sylvia, "Daddy's coming home." Daddy had come home all right, but the Wallace family's version of the post-war baby boom did not allow him to stay very long. A month after David's birth he went to Washington and New York to research *CID Agent* for producer Buddy Adler. That documentary about the Army Provost Marshal's attempts to uncover black market operations in occupied Europe was never produced, but it earned $2,500 worth of survival money and an opportunity for more studio jobs. Hollywood?

In May he went to work at Warner Brothers on *The West Point Story.* Twenty-seven weeks later, on Christmas Eve, 1948, he picked up his last check from the studio cashier. His income in 1948 was more than he had made from seventeen years of magazine sales—$24,134.63. Hollywood!

Another good year for Wallace's bank account and his confidence was 1950. He knew he could make it in film writing after a brief meeting with William Fadiman, Executive Assistant to Howard Hughes, at that time the owner of RKO-Radio Pictures. Wallace had written a thirteen page original story titled *A Young Wives' Tale* and, with two agents, took it around to the studios. In the foreword Wallace wrote for *Hollywood Now,* William Fadiman's 1972 study of the film industry, he recounted that meeting:

"Somewhat nervously I narrated to Fadiman what he had already read in my thirteen pages. He sat somberly, thoughtfully, through my recital and made notes. When I was out of breath, and finished, he began to pepper me with questions about my characters and plot line and certain possible scenes. The questions were pertinent, and they stimulated me to verbalize many ideas that I had not put on paper.

"At last I was done.

"Suddenly, Fadiman smiled, a warm full smile. 'It's a great

2-9-50   P.1

A YOUNG WIVES' TALE

Throughout America today, in fact throughout the world, there lives a legion of women without their men. These are the war widows. These are the young wives who, in the short years since the rest of the world returned to business and pleasure and normalcy, have had to devise a new way of carrying on alone.

Of the seven million widows in this country today, these young war widows represent a provocative proportion.

Most people have returned to peace. But what has happened to them?

In "The Best Years of Our Lives," we saw what happened to the men who came home to readjust to peace. Here we see what happened to the women whose men did not come home.

This is the story of these young widows, of their turmoil, defeats and victories.

How have they lived? loved? struggled? How have they managed? How have they felt? What are they doing today -- tonight?

A motion picture based on a theme so powerful, dealing with a problem so national, is best told not through the tribulations of one woman, since her story would be too exceptional, but through the realistic adventures of four women, four typical war widows.

They meet, first, in a clapboard Texas town, outside the great airbase where their husbands are preparing to leave for overseas. Their husbands are all air forces officers, members

Page one of Irving Wallace's screen story, *A Young Wives' Tale*.

Magazine ad for *Desert Legion*.

story,' he said. . . . 'As far as I'm concerned we'd like to buy it. There is only one more step. I'll need Howard Hughes' approval.' "

Hughes could not be found. The recluse was so well hidden that before Fadiman could find him Dore Schary at M-G-M bought it. Wallace received $20,000 for the story and his one hundred and eight page screenplay.

From 1943 to 1959 he received screen credit for fourteen films: *Jive Junction* (1943), *That's My Baby* (1944), *The West Point Story* (1950), *Meet Me At The Fair* (1953), *Split Second* (1953), *Desert Legion* (1953), *Gun Fury* (1953), *Bad for Each Other* (1954), *The Gambler From Natchez* (1954), *Jump Into Hell* (1955), *Sincerely Yours* (1955), *The Burning Hills* (1956), *Bombers B-52* (1957), and *The Big Circus* (1959). In addition to these were the unfinished and unproduced screen stories and screenplays, and the several he did not work on long enough to receive screen credit.

"I wrote countless tricked-up idea outlines and present-tense original screen treatments, on speculation, to submit to the film studios. I wrote numerous screenplays, on salary, for every major movie studio. At my lowest point, I wrote ten television scripts for six producers on order.

"I am not complaining about this. It was a plush hell, an infernal region dominated by double-dealing, politics, feuds, pettiness, thievery, cretinism, where the writer suffered indignity, disrespect, disdain, and where he could make more money than he could possibly make in any other salaried medium of writing. There were also, in this region, good people, honest people, highly creative people, and sometimes the product of their collective talents produced a motion picture or television film that equaled or exceeded in artistic value the best current books or plays. But these talented ones, and their best products, were in the minority."

A detailed portrait of his film years is found elsewhere in this book (pp. 274 to 360), but another word is in order. There is no doubt that Wallace learned from film writing, especially how to construct dramatic scenes and write dialogue. And there is no doubt that he lost a lot: subjective writing, descriptive writing, inner monologues, and developing character from story rather than

"THE BALLAD OF OSCAR WILDE"   -1-

FADE IN:

1. EXT. SAN FRANCISCO - PERIOD STREET SCENE (STOCK) - NIGHT 1.

2. EXT. CARLTON HOTEL - FULL SHOT - ENTRANCE - NIGHT   2.

   Several well-dressed couples are entering the hotel.
   PALADIN, in evening dress, walks into view. He is
   carrying a suitcase. He goes into the hotel.

3. INT. CARLTON LOBBY - MEDIUM SHOT - ENTRANCE - NIGHT   3.

   as Paladin comes through. CAMERA PANS him to the hotel
   bulletin board, beneath which a workman is kneeling,
   opening a work kit. Paladin studies the large poster
   on the bulletin board. The lettering reads: "Oscar
   Wilde...England's Foremost Poet, Playwright, Author
   Will Lecture On The Subject: "The American Barbarian"
   ...in San Diego -- Alden's bar: June Sixth at Eight-
   thirty. Platt's Hall June Ninth. Eight-thirty.
   Sponsored jointly by the Civic Cultural Society of
   San Diego and San Francisco." As Paladin watches, the
   workman rises, tacks a strip of paper across the
   poster. We see that the strip reads: "Sold Out."

   CAMERA PULLS BACK as Paladin turns to leave. HEY BOY
   hurries in with a large and formidable bundle of
   newspapers. As he takes suitcase from Paladin --

                    HEY BOY
          You have good vacation?

                    PALADIN
          Too good.
                    (smiling)
          All play and no work makes Paladin
          poor boy.

                    HEY BOY
                    (offering bundle
                    of papers)
          Lots of reading pile up.

                    PALADIN
                    (taking papers)
          Thanks, Hey Boy.

   As Paladin pays him, Hey Boy nods at the poster on the
   bulletin board.

                                    CONTINUED

   Page one from an Irving Wallace script for *Have Gun — Will Travel*.

THOMAS Y. CROWELL COMPANY

PUBLISHERS OF BOOKS

432 FOURTH AVENUE, NEW YORK

May 6, 1938

EDITORIAL DEPARTMENT

TELEPHONE: MURRAY HILL 3-2992
CABLE: "TYCROWELL," NEW YORK

Mr. Irving Wallace
6527 Leland Way
Hollywood, California

Dear Mr. Wallace:

It was very good of you to send us
the manuscript of THE SUNDAY GENTLEMAN: A Life
of Daniel DeFoe, and we have been interested
in reading it. There are several reasons, however, why we are unable to make you a publishing
offer for it. We have an office rule which pre-
vents our giving detailed or specific criticisms
of rejected material--but we did feel that your
book was too short, for one thing. (We have not
overlooked what you said in your letter of April
14 regarding additional material that might be
incorporated into your text). Our readers also
were of the opinion that the book would not have
a sufficiently wide general appeal to make it
a commercially profitable venture for us.

We are holding the manuscript subject
to your instructions. We will return it to you
direct by express collect, or, if you would like
to have us do so, we will forward it without
charge to some other New York publisher.

Very truly yours,

THOMAS Y. CROWELL COMPANY

Elizabeth M. Riley

Rejection letter for *The Sunday Gentleman: A Life of Daniel Defoe.*

tacking characters onto the story. Yet filmwriting was never anything more than an attempt to buy time for the real writing, the
pursuit-of-The-Dream writing. The studios gave him the time and
money to write his first four books and a fierce desire to write a
fifth book—the one that would free him for good. The movies,
like a great deal of the magazine writing, served as both apprenticeship and holding action until everything would come out well in
the end. But how long?

"When I was seventeen, I wrote half a book, *Heroes Of Today,*
recounting the lives of men I admired. . . . It was rejected, never
published. When I was eighteen I wrote half a book, *Sorry, But
You're Wrong,* exploding the fallacies of popular folk beliefs. It
was rejected, never published. When I was nineteen, I wrote my
first complete book, *My Adventure Trail,* an enthusiastic recounting of a journey I had taken into the Honduran jungles. It was rejected, never published. When I was twenty, I wrote another complete book, *The Sunday Gentleman,* a biography of Daniel Defoe.
It was rejected, never published. When I was twenty-two, I wrote
one-third of a book, *Roman Holiday,* a biographical account of the
first twelve Caesars. It was rejected, never published. When I was
twenty-two I compiled and rewrote a book, *Etcetera,* a collection
of some newly written articles together with many I had already
had published in magazines. It was rejected, never published.
When I was twenty-five, I wrote *Japan's Mein Kampf,* a documentary account of the infamous Tanaka Memorial. It was rejected,
never published. When I was twenty-seven, I wrote a full-length
book, *With Their Pants Down,* a candid memoir of celebrities I
had met and interviewed in my writing career. It was rejected,
never published. When I was thirty-four, I wrote two chapters of
a book, *Gabrielle,* a detailed history of the pretty French mur-
deress, Gabrielle Bompard. I was discouraged, never submitted it.
In those years I wrote at least one or two chapters of a half-dozen
novels, but became doubtful about each, and never finished them
or submitted for possible publication what I had finished."

His first novel, *The Sins of Philip Fleming,* concerns a young
man who is trying to build a career in professional writing. At one
point he is discouraged and confused about whether he is ready to

enter a new and important stage in his career and risk the financial and emotional uncertainties that accompany it. To encourage him, a friend tells him an anecdote about Cortez:

" 'Cortez was in Vera Cruz, I think, with his small band of armed hoodlums. He knew that they were badly out-numbered, that the odds were against them, that they'd never be any good as long as their ship was waiting in the harbor to take them home. So Cortez set fire to the ship. . . . And it worked.'

" 'Phil the Fiddler,' said Philip.

" 'Who's that?'

" 'A book Horatio Alger wrote. Same sort of evangelistic tripe.' Philip sat up. 'Look, Nat, sometimes you burn your ship behind you and go straight ahead—and get the shit kicked out of you. They never tell that part of the story.'

" 'It doesn't usually happen.'

" 'The hell it doesn't. Maybe not in books. But for real.' "

Wallace must have experienced the same apprehensions when he became convinced that he had to break away from the studios. His responsibilities were to his family, not only to his Dream. And so he waited. Not until March 30, 1959, the spring evening he sold *The Chapman Report*, would he quit the movies once and for all. That was almost six years from the beginning of his first book, *The Fabulous Originals*.

The Fabulous Originals, a collection of biographies about the real-life counterparts of famous characters in fiction, was begun in August, 1953. By November he had finished the first three chapters and submitted them to the Alfred A. Knopf publishing house in New York. Knopf bought the book on January 13, 1954. Ten months later, writing nights during four separate studio assignments, Wallace finished the manuscript. It was published on October 17, 1955.

The second book, *The Square Pegs,* was begun in April, 1955, and published July 22, 1957; his third book with Knopf, *The Fabulous Showman,* was published November 16, 1959.

Wallace's three books with Knopf were his apprenticeship with published books. He found out quickly that the world of books was a commercial enterprise, that his dream of freedom

The Fabulous Originals

		Real Length	Present Length	Schedule Trim out	Done
I	ANATOMY OF INSPIRATION	30	24½	-5	-5½ ✓
II	BELL	33	30⅓	-3	-2⅓
III	CLAIRMONT	52	44	-10	8
IV	~~TRAIN~~	~~60~~	~~0~~	~~-60~~	~~-60~~ ✓
V	ELLENBOROUGH	75	58	-20	17 ✓
VI	BRODIE	65	56¼	-10	8¾⁺³ ✓
VII	ROGERS	62	55	-10	8 ✓
VIII	SELKIRK	60	55⅓	-10	7⅓ ✓
IX	HARDLY COINCIDENTAL	117	74	-47	-43 ⁺² ✓

175   160 ⁺³ lines

37 to 80
+
540

Work Sheet — *The Fabulous Originals.*

was still a long way off.

The original manuscript of *The Fabulous Originals* ran in excess of 145,000 words. The contract with Knopf called for 80,000 words. His Knopf editor, Philip Vaudrin, urged Wallace to cut 45,000 words from the manuscript. "I know that whatever devices are used the job is going to pain you, but we have to consider our market in terms of the retail price we can expect readers to pay for books of this kind nowadays, and cut we must." There it was again. The commercial practicalities versus The Dream. Wallace was terribly upset, but he did not want to lose his contract. Sensing his author's chagrin, Alfred A. Knopf wrote him on December 1, 1954, sympathizing with his concern about the excisions and scolding him for not being frank about the length of the book when the contract was drawn up. But Wallace's writing charts, records of his day-to-day progress on his books, indicate that in January, 1954, when the book was purchased and the contract was drawn, Wallace had completed fewer than 30,000 words. The book was not planned to run 563 manuscript pages and 150,000 words, but it grew to that size because of the author's fascination with the characters he was writing about. He could not let them be slighted. To do so would betray them and himself. He had waited twenty-five years to do this book, and it seized him without regard for a publisher's contract.

But cuts were demanded and cuts were made. By February 18, 1955, Philip Vaudrin could write that "the manuscript seems to be in very good shape indeed. It is now a very wieldy book, and an even more readable one, I feel, than it was originally. The thinning out has been all to the good."

Years later Wallace recalled what he thought of the thinning out:

"Compromises in the publishing field, minimal though they be, do exist, for reasons of an editor's personal prejudices or a publisher's economic concerns. After spending years preparing and writing my first published book, *The Fabulous Originals,* and receiving an advance of $1,000 and a beribboned contract from Alfred A. Knopf, I was stunned when he forced me to surrender a degree of my creative autonomy before my book went to press, a

The Square Pegs - 1956

Chapter	Subject	Start	Finished	Scheduled to Finish	Pages
2	Harden-Hickey	Jan. 23	Jan. 27	Jan. 27	45
3	Train	Jan. 30	Feb. 1	Feb. 1	50
6	Dexter	Feb. 2	Feb. 15	Feb. 18	62
5	Bacon	Feb. 18	March 20	March 7	83
4	Woodhull	March 21	April 2	March 24	66
7	Norton Symmes Royall	April 3	April 16	March 31 april 7 april 14	81
1	General	April 17	April 20 Fri - 2 o'clock	April 28	31

418 · 335

Work Sheet — *The Square Pegs.*

surrender demanded on economic grounds only. I was stunned because I had regarded Mr. Knopf as entirely a creative publisher with respect for the well-written word. I had not realized that he was of necessity also a tough and shrewd businessman, like most other publishers. Even though my book was not unduly long, Mr. Knopf insisted that he wanted it considerably shorter in order to make its publication cheaper and its profits (the equivalent of 9½% of the retail price was to be mine, I was reminded) greater. It *was* my first about-to-be-published book. Fearful that it might not reach the printer if I defended the Word against the Profit Ledger, I conceded. Of the volume's nine chapters, I was forced to pull out one chapter in its entirety, and cut out two-fifths of another. In short, I needed this publisher more than he needed me, and against my better judgment, I compromised."

Wallace's second editor, Herbert Weinstock, did the editing of *The Square Pegs*. Wallace delivered a 130,000 word manuscript in July of 1956, thirty-four years after he had begun researching it. Of course, he had not worked on it exclusively for all those years, but it had been the autumn of 1932 when he drove from Kenosha down to Zion City, Illinois to see Wilber Glenn Voliva:

"In that year I was an extremely vocal member of the debating society in Kenosha Central High School. Once a month we staged a formal debate on a topic usually more humorous or bizarre than serious. In preparation for one such debate there was a disagreement as to a suitable subject. Suddenly I remembered Voliva, and I put forward his name and his theory. I proposed a debate on the resolution that Voliva was right and Columbus was wrong—in short, that the earth was flat."

He won the debate.

Further research took place "in the libraries of Los Angeles, New York, London, and Paris, reading letters, diaries, and various published material written by those who had known the eccentrics in person or who had previously studied them."

He had done his homework, written long and hard, and was faced with publisher's demands for another substantial excision— this time 30,000 words.

But unlike Vaudrin, Weinstock did not cite sheer length as his

This is the outline of my fourth published book. The original went to New York and is long lost—this is the only existing original carbon copy. Paramount Studios wanted a 40-page profile of Barnum for a movie—and gave me $7,500 to do it. After 4 weeks research, I said I wanted to write a book-length biography. In early October of 1958, I wrote this outline. Based on it, New American Library offered me $4,000 for reprint rights—and I wrote the book following this outline—and on January 19, 1959, Alfred A. Knopf purchased hardcover rights of the completed book for $5,020—beating Little, Brown's bid of $5,000. Based on this outline I began writing the book on October 20, 1958.

Irving Wallace (January 11, 1968)

THE FABULOUS SHOWMAN

Outline for a biography of Phineas T. Barnum

by

Irving Wallace

I.   EXHIBIT ONE: GEN. WASHINGTON'S NURSE

The book opens with a dramatized yet fully factual account of that August morning in 1835 when modern showmanship first came to New York and America. This was the morning young P.T. Barnum put on display Joice Heth, a 161 year old negress who had been George Washington's nurse. It was Barnum's first effort in show business. The chapter relates how Barnum discovered her, authenticated her, sold her.

In his travels with her, I recount Barnum's adventures with Johann Maelzel, who owned the mysterious automaton chess-player that had licked Napoleon and Benjamin Franklin; with Anne Royall, who had interviewed President Adams in the nude; with Signor Vivalla, an incredible Italian juggler.

The day after her death Joice Heth is exposed as a hoax and a fraud - exposed by the very man who had fooled the public with the Moon Hoax of the year before.

II.   EXHIBIT TWO: IVY ISLAND

This chapter tells how Barnum became a showman and paved the way for modern vaudeville, concerts, movies, and television in America. It covers him from his birth to the age of thirty-one . . . the strict Calvanism of his early years . . . his grandfather's marvelous practical jokes, including a memorable one involving Ivy Island (given Barnum as a gift) . . . his meeting with the pioneer showman Hack Bailey and Old Bet the elephant . . . his apprenticeship as a grocery clerk and store owner . . . his courtship of Charity Hallet and elopment with her . . . his fight against blue laws with his own weekly, Herald of Freedom, which lands him in jail . . . his move to New York, after and after the Joice Heth hoax, his adventures with a traveling circus . . . his failures.

III.   EXHIBIT THREE: MERMAID FROM FEEJEE

Through audacity and trickery Barnum, without a penny

Irving Wallace's outline of *The Fabulous Showman*.

Dust jacket – *The Fabulous Showman.*

objection:

"The physical length was not the basis of my suggestion for judicious cutting of all chapters except the last. The basis for that suggestion was a feeling that some of the passages and chapters get to be a little longer than the interest of their material requires."

Both Vaudrin and Weinstock sought to cut their respective books down to contract size, and Wallace could do almost nothing to maintain their original lengths. Throughout the correspondences there is the figure of Alfred A. Knopf himself in the background. He was the one who would make the final decisions on the books—Vaudrin and Weinstock and Wallace followed his lead. Whether Vaudrin spoke of contract and sheer bulk or Weinstock of aesthetics and organization, the fact remained that Alfred Knopf wanted both books cut, and both books were cut.

Wanting to expand his reading audience with a paperback edition of his next book, *The Fabulous Showman,* Wallace contacted Victor Weybright. Weybright's New American Library accepted the book on the condition it did not conflict with a prior Knopf contract. It did not, and Weybright signed for paperback reprint rights to *The Fabulous Showman.*

Knopf wrote Wallace on November 24, 1958, to say he was not upset about the NAL deal since he did not want to advance $4,000 for the Barnum book rights. But when Weybright offered the hardbound rights in auction, Alfred A. Knopf could not buy them for less than $5,000. When *The Fabulous Showman* became the December Literary Guild choice Knopf was further annoyed that he had taken his own author from a paperback reprint house.

Apparently Mrs. Knopf, vice-president of the publishing company, was also annoyed. According to Victor Weybright's letter to Knopf of November 25, Blanche Knopf confronted him with the Wallace matter in an elevator in the Madison Avenue office building that housed both Knopf and NAL. Weybright told Knopf he was very embarrassed by the elevator incident. He went on to assure him that he had never knowingly "raided an author," but had learned not to ask questions when an unhappy author came to him with a good book. He then reminded Knopf that *he* had not sent Willa Cather packing back to Houghton Mifflin when she wanted

Dust jacket – *The Twenty-Seventh Wife.*

Irving Wallace's caption: "After selling *Chapman* to movies we decided to celebrate by having a party for all our best friends. But many of our 'friends' weren't too happy about my good fortune—were jealous, were also resentful that I was leaving movies to be free. Getting these soundings, I chalked up this sign and placed it outside our door for guests to see as they arrived."

to break with them and publish at Knopf.

In the summer of 1958 Wallace had begun writing his first novel, *The Sins of Philip Fleming*. Knopf had turned it down, and Frederick Fell had accepted it. When he rejected *Fleming*, Knopf lost his option on the next novel, *The Chapman Report*. On March 30, 1959, Wallace met Weybright in his suite at the Beverly Hills Hilton and told him he would sell the paperback rights of *The Chapman Report* and *The Twenty-Seventh Wife* for $25,000. Wallace had completed less than two hundred manuscript pages of *Chapman* (it would run 547 pages) and had not yet begun the writing of *The Twenty-Seventh Wife*, a biography of Brigham Young's most rebellious spouse. Weybright agreed. "As Irving told me recently," he wrote in 1967, "despite his large earnings as a journalist and film writer, 'That twenty-five thousand dollars got me out of movies for good.' "

Paul Reynolds, Wallace's literary agent, began looking for a hardcover publisher. Five or six were bidding on it when Alfred Knopf "contacted each one on a personal basis and asked them to withdraw their bids 'on that disgraceful sex book.' All withdrew except Doubleday and Simon and Schuster, and after that I became a Simon and Schuster author."

On October 27, 1959, Simon and Schuster paid a $25,000 advance on *The Chapman Report*. Two months earlier Darryl F. Zanuck Productions had paid $175,000 for the movie rights. Adding these figures to his studio income, Wallace made close to $240,000 in the thirteen months between September 1958 and October 1959.

"Here was the miracle I had dreamed of in my youth. At last, free, independent, confident. I wrote my next book, and my next, and my next, and my next, and each was an international bestseller. By wildest luck and unbelievable good fortune, combined with a love of what I was doing and a love of the stories I had to tell, and the freedom to tell them in my own way, I had won my seven days of Sundays."

The Chapman Report was published on May 23, 1950. The next day Simon and Schuster received a record twelve thousand orders. By early 1961, seventy-five thousand hardback copies had

THE CHAPMAN REPORT

by

Irving Wallace

I.

Once a day, at exactly ten minutes to nine in the
morning, a long, ~~dusty~~ gray sightseeing bus streaked with dust, lumbered up
Sunset Boulevard and entered that suburb of Los Angeles
known as The Briars. The uniformed guide and driver of
the bus adjusted the silver microphone before his lips
and resumed his soporific drone: "Ladies and gentlemen,
we are now passing through The Briars . . ."
          No stir of excitement resulted among the passengers, already
sated by the gaudy homes of motion picture celebrities
in Beverly Hills and Bel-Air, left behind twenty
minutes before. The Briars, they heard, and sensed before
they heard, held no more exotic wonders than the better
sections of the towns they had briefly escaped in Pennsylvania,
Kansas, Georgia, and Idaho. The Briars was, to sight, the
model of perfect normalcy, and therefore, nothing to write home about. Many
of the passengers used this interlude to change their positions,
massage their necks, light cigarettes, or make a remark
to their neighbors, as they waited for the transition to
the more promising Pacific Ocean and its Malibu Colony. But a
few, mostly women with young faces and old hands, continued
to gaze out of their windows, admiring the relaxed, graceful,
rural beauty of the suburb, wondering what the community was

Page one of final manuscript, *The Chapman Report*.

been sold. It was on the bestseller charts for thirty weeks.

New American Library brought out a Signet paperback edition in a first printing of one million copies in the fall of 1960. By early 1961 their inventories were depleted and another one million copies were printed and sold.

Chapman was published in fourteen foreign countries and did well in all but Sweden. As Wallace said in a 1961 press release, "I guess the Swedes are too damn busy indulging in sex to read about it."

It was to have been published during the 1960 Christmas season in Italy until the Vatican asked that it be postponed until Lent. At least until Lent.

The West German Home Ministry threatened to ban it but did not succeed.

Longmans Green bought the English reprint rights for ten thousand dollars. Then, because many of their clients were in the school and religious markets, they bowed under pressure and re-sold to Arthur Barker, Ltd. It was published there in April and immediately became England's number-one bestseller. The London *Times* suggested it be prosecuted as an obscene book. The 1960 *Lady Chatterley's Lover* case, in which Penguin Books successfully defended D. H. Lawrence's novel against the Home Office, was still a matter of chagrin among English conservatives. *Chapman* seemed to be an easier target, but it was never banned.

It was mentioned earlier that Darryl F. Zanuck Productions bought the film rights. This is how the film was sold. On August 18, 1959, Evarts Ziegler, Wallace's Los Angeles agent, sent out seventeen copies of the manuscript to studios and independent producers. There were nine interested bidders. On August 25, at 9:00 a.m., Ziegler sent telegrams to them announcing the terms: $175,000 against five percent of the worldwide gross; $35,000 a year from 1959-1963 inclusive. On August 26 a phone call from Darryl Zanuck in Paris to Buddy Adler of Fox permitted Zanuck's son, Richard, to meet the offer. Minutes later a phone call from Jack Warner on the French Riviera to Steve Trilling of Warner Brothers allowed Trilling to meet the offer. At 6:30 p.m., August 26, Ziegler and Wallace accepted the offer from Zanuck, and the film went to Darryl Zanuck Productions.

The flap about *Chapman*'s overt sexuality was less than justified, especially when that novel is compared with *The Sins of Philip Fleming*. The earlier novel was much more sexually explicit, but no one bothered to attack it. The sexual controversy overlapped into the charges that Wallace had manufactured a bestseller by stringing together frantic sex with a scant story line. But if sex sold *Chapman*, then sex should have sold *Fleming*.

Wallace wrote *Chapman* because he wanted to write about married women and their problems—the sexual problems being minor compared to the insensitivity and stupidity of men. Thematically, *Chapman* is less about sexual matters than about the tensions of suburbia and how they are manifested in a variety of unhappy ways. If *Chapman* was bought and read for its sex, then many readers were disappointed. As Wallace told the Italian press after the novel was temporarily banned in Italy:

"I have not and cannot write obscenely or immorally. I have written of love and sex in candid terms, and I shall again. In *The Chapman Report* I was writing not to stimulate, but to reflect an area of American society with which I am deeply acquainted. Too, I wished to explore certain aspects of female unhappiness and frustration in today's world. I wrote of American women I know— but perhaps I wrote of all women."

In 1966 Bernice Miller, a handwriting analyst in South Africa, a woman who had never met Wallace, wrote this analysis:

"While you are relatively indifferent to individuals in the subjective sense, you are acutely sensitive to outside criticism. You have a great deal of pride. After all, pride is a standard of conduct and involves all the factors that determine how a person lives his life. In short, it is a desire for approval."

Three years later Rosemary Rusinko, an American graphoanalyst, observed the same tendency: "We all accumulate fears as we go through life. A fear of criticism seems to be your chief liability in this respect."

The adverse criticism that greeted *Chapman* deeply disturbed its author. "Well, it's no fun seeing yourself, so often, attacked in print. I don't like it, and I don't like it for my family. At first you want to fight back. My old friend, Jerome Weidman, begged me not to write letters to columnists and reviewers because you can't win. I think that's true—a target can't counterpunch. For a while I desisted—but then it simply got too much for me—and while I was persuaded not to legally sue *Time* magazine or Alfred A. Knopf for circulating factually untrue statements—I did start fighting back with letters. It didn't do much good, although for a while it was good for me inside to let off the steam. But I finally stopped. No more letters, I promise—or very few, at least."

Another source of criticism was the Institute for Sex Research at Indiana University, more commonly known as the Kinsey Institute. Wallace was threatened with a law suit because *his* Dr. Chapman vaguely resembled *their* Dr. Kinsey. Victor Weybright proposed a disclaimer be printed at the beginning of the book. Wallace provided one, which reads in part:

"Among readers of both sexes, there may be a temptation to ascribe to Dr. Chapman and other sexologists in the novel some of the characteristics and methods of real-life sex historians like Drs. Alfred C. Kinsey, G. V. Hamilton, Robert L. Dickinson, Lewis M. Terman, and others. Those who wish to play out the fantasy, and enjoy the fun of it, may do so, but at their own risk, not mine."

In a 1960 press release Wallace said the Sex Institute's concern reflected an astonishing degree of egotism on their part. "They seem to be implying that they invented the scientific study of sex—and that any author who writes about a sex survey is necessarily writing about them. I conceived *The Chapman Report* as a work of pure fiction. I invented every character, the plot and the background. . . . Despite what the Kinsey people have feared, my novel is not an attack on sex surveys in general. It attempts to show both sides. Personally I am in favor of sex surveys and anything similar that promotes wider sex education. I do feel, however, that sex surveys could be vastly improved."

Wallace told Weybright in a letter of November 26, 1959, that he did not think the Sex Research Institute would sue because of the notoriety it would bring. He was right.

Richard D. Zanuck, on the other hand, was privately delighted at the possibility of a law suit. "His only wish was that an injunc-

Dear Friends
Do me the
favor to
get "The Prize"
by Wallace
— book on
the Nobel.
Yrs
U Sinclair

On June 23, 1963, Upton
Sinclair sent this card to
the librarian of the
Monrovia, California, library
reserving a copy of a new
novel. The librarian, Kate
Ainsworth, saved it. Her
husband, author Ed Ainsworth,
mentioned it in an article
in The Saturday Review. This
inspired CBS to show the card
on a program about Upton
Sinclair. Sylvia saw the
show in 1967 and wrote Mrs.
Ainsworth asking if the postcard was for sale. On May 8,
1973, Mrs. Ainsworth sent it
to Sylvia to give me as a
Father's Day gift, writing,
"I loved Uppie Sinclair and
know that you did, too. So,
in love, I send it on to
you."
                    I.W.

tion would come closer to book publication or a suit nearer to the film's release—because it would make book and movie boxoffice smash hits! He said that the day before a sheriff had served him with a suit from Leopold on *Compulsion* and he only regretted it had not occurred when the picture was in release."

On October 29, 1960, Wallace began the formal writing of his next novel, *The Prize*. A detailed account of the research, writing and publishing of that novel is given in Wallace's *The Writing of One Novel* (Simon & Schuster, 1968). A long quotation from *One Novel* is given on pages 400 to 405 of this book.

But another story is how the movie was sold. In May of 1961 Wallace kept a private journal of the movie submission of *The Prize*. He wrote that the selling of *The Prize* took thirteen days, beginning on Sunday, May 14, when Evarts Ziegler sent an advance manuscript copy of the novel to Richard D. Zanuck of 20th Century-Fox. By Wednesday a total of twenty-three advance manuscripts had been sent to producers and agents. On Thursday Wallace and Ziegler received five positive responses. By Saturday Ziegler felt that bidding could begin by Monday or Tuesday. "The fat is in the fire," he said.

By Tuesday Ziegler thought "he could start bidding at once, but preferred to close by the weekend. He said we were working from strength, the sale was in the bag, and it would be a large price. He expects to hear from more studios tomorrow, prefers to have two more signs of interest before sending a wire setting the price, expects to call laggard studios and tell them to get going or they are out."

Ziegler phoned Wallace at noon on Wednesday to tell him M-G-M, Columbia, Warner Brothers, Paramount and several independent producers were interested. "Ziegler says we have a sale. Yesterday he sold a book about three pets for $50,000. 'This one,' he says, 'should bring 90 times as much.' "

That evening Ernest Lehman, the distinguished screenwriter, phoned Wallace to tell him that M-G-M's Pandro Berman wanted to do *The Prize*. Lehman would script it. "Berman told Ernie he wanted to make a big, expensive, dignified, commercial film abroad, and Ernie agreed to write it. Berman is thinking of Greg-

Simon and Schuster's initial ad for *The Prize*.

Assistant director Hank Moonjean leaps in front of an interloping news photographer on the closed set at M-G-M where the nudist colony scene for *The Prize* is being shot.

ory Peck for the lead, and an all-star cast."

Ziegler called Wallace at 11:30 Thursday morning, asked him to come over to the office to be there for any phone calls. No calls. By two o'clock Ziegler had decided to send out contract terms via Red Arrow messengers that afternoon. The deal would close at six o'clock Friday evening. He planned to ask $250,000 cash plus $25,000 for every $500,000 worldwide gross after the film's initial $5,000,000, "the escalator going up to the ceiling of $100,000 additional for me."

Ziegler had planned to leave the office at three, but he decided to wait until four. He had the letters before him, the cash amounts not yet filled in. If there was more studio interest before four he wanted to raise the price above $250,000. No calls.

Friday, May 26. Either the deadline would be met or the book would be withdrawn from sale and marketed again later. Stanley Meyer, an independent, had accepted the deal the night before, but whether he could raise the money was not determined. The book was technically sold, but Wallace wanted Berman to buy it so Ernest Lehman would write it.

At noon he took his wife to Cedars of Lebanon hospital to have a cyst removed in local surgery. While at the hospital, Wallace called Ziegler to find out about the latest developments. He was not there; phone calls were coming in from Paramount and M-G-M. Sylvia came down from surgery and they drove home. Another call to Ziegler. He was still out, but his secretary told Wallace that M-G-M had requested a quick meeting.

At two seventeen Ziegler telephoned to say that M-G-M was about to settle. He would call back.

At three twenty-five Ziegler called. "Three words," he said. "Metro bought it."

The Prize meant more than a big studio sale to its author. "I always loved *The Prize*, since I had a sense of excitement in writing it and since the protagonist was in many ways autobiographical."

Wallace's early mail came from middle-aged readers. By the late 1960's the majority of the fan mail was coming from high school and college students, and young people in their twenties or early thirties. "I couldn't fathom this at first, and finally I came to

I.

It was the first of the letters that Maud Hayden
had taken from the morning's pile on her ~~green~~ desk
blotter. What had attracted her to it, she sheepishly
admitted to herself, was the exotic rows of stamps
across the top of the envelope. They were stamps ~~colored~~
~~in green, red, and indigo,~~ bearing the reproduction of
Gauguin's "The White Horse," ~~and~~ the imprint "Polynésie
Française . . . Poste Aérienne."

From the summit of her mountain of years, Maud ~~knew~~ was painfully aware
that her pleasures had become less and less visible and ~~distinct###~~
distinct with each new autumn. The Great Pleasures remained
definitely clear:
~~clear and defiant;~~ her scholarly accomplishments with Adley
(still respected); her absorption in work (unflagging); her
son, Marc (in his father's footsteps - somewhat); her
recent daughter-in-law, Claire (quiet, lovely, too good to
be true). It was the Smaller Pleasures that were becoming
as elusive and invisible as youth. The brisk early morning
walk in the California sun, especially when Adley/~~was alive~~ was alive,
had been a conscious celebration of each day's birth. Now,
it reminded her only of her arthritis. The ~~scant~~ view, especially
from
~~beyond~~ her upstairs study window, of the soft ribbon of
highway leading from Los Angeles to San Francisco, with
the Santa Barbara beach and whitecaps of the ocean beyond, had always
been esthetically exciting. But now, glancing out of the

Page one of the final manuscript, *The Three Sirens*.

1962   *Irving Wallace*

THE THREE SIRENS

CHAPTER	STARTED	FINISHED	PAGES	BOOK TOTAL	DAYS
I	January 2, 1962	January 6	60	60	5
II	January 8	February 12	158	218	19
III	February 13	March 6	112	330	17
IV	March 7	April 9	140	470	29
V	April 16	May 18	104	574	24
	TOOK OFF TO PROMOTE "THE PRIZE" IN LOS ANGELES AND NEW YORK				
VI	July 9	August 17	97	671	39
VII	August 20	August 30	79	750	11
VIII	August 31	September 7	80	830	7
IX	September 8	September 8	24	854	1
		Finished novel at 4:40 in the afternoon, Saturday.			

Work Sheet — *The Three Sirens.*

understand it. I had been, when I wrote *The Prize*, exactly where the maturing young people are today—suspicious of institutions, of bigness, of authority. In *The Prize* I had taken a sacred international institution, The Nobel Foundation, and I exposed the frailities of the institution, its politics, cynicism, pettiness. In search of truth I had traversed where our young would soon be marching. To have produced a work that would be respected and used by our young—well, that was truly gratifying."

After the June 26, 1961, publication of *The Twenty-Seventh Wife,* the Wallaces left for a European holiday. Six months later *The Three Sirens* was begun.

What *The Chapman Report* owed to sex research was what *The Three Sirens* owed to anthropological forays into the South Seas, notably Margaret Mead's *The Coming of Age in Samoa.* Both novels were loosely based on a scientific activity that numerous people were involved in and some became famous for. No more, no less.

In *The Three Sirens* an American team of anthropologists and laymen descend upon a hidden Polynesian island to study a unique and hitherto undiscovered way of life. In the process they find that their own life styles need careful examination—perhaps more so than the lives of the natives.

Michael Korda, Wallace's editor at Simon and Schuster, liked *Sirens* more than *The Prize.* Wallace disagreed with his editor about his fourth published novel:

"Everyone seems to tell me it is my best novel yet and better than *The Prize*," he wrote Korda. "Good, but I do not believe this. Perhaps they mean the story grows more out of character, and there is less contrivance showing. I don't know. The publishing seasons bring out so many good books, and many are beautiful and important, but they don't read well and fast and excitingly (the reader doesn't 'get lost,' if you know what I mean)—and I'm told this does read well—and so maybe that is its strength. I might add, I rather hope it is a wee more than a good read. Here and there, I have tried to say some things I regard as important—not so much in my dialogue speeches as in my character development—about marriage, the realities of the same, about our standards con-

Edward Alperson (left) and Stanley Meyer (right) paid $300,000 for the film rights to *The Three Sirens*. The film was never made.

cerning appearance, aging, child rearing—about our dreams and their limitations. Much of this may be buried under, lost under, the book's popular façade and under story and explicit this and that—but what matters to me, long after the excitement and attention and after the money is spent is that—I said what I had to say and wanted to say to the best of my ability at a given period in my life. Amen, amen."

A third opinion about the novel came from its readers. Simon and Schuster enclosed Referendum Cards in every tenth copy of *The Three Sirens*. They asked the reader whether the book was enjoyable—why or why not. Some responses:

"Interesting story—well defined characters—well told." (Tom Harmon, radio and television broadcaster.)

"Like *Gone With The Wind*, never a dull page." (Carol Hobart, housewife.)

"Found it slow moving and extremely boring!" (Carol Rosenberg, housewife.)

"How dare you publish such filth? This book has been returned to the place it was bought." (Mrs. J. J. Porter, librarian.)

"I found the book both entertaining and informative." (Leslie J. Luke, registered nurse.)

The film rights were sold to Stanley Meyer and Edward Alperson, two independent producers, for $250,000 cash. They bought it sight unseen on December 3, 1962. The film was never made. On November 12, 1970, Al Hart, the president of the California Bank, foreclosed on the Meyer-Alperson loan and recovered the film rights. He still has them.

If *The Three Sirens* dealt with anthropology, a subject not of general interest to the public, *The Man*, Wallace's next book, would touch two subjects that dominated our concerns from the early years of the 1960's until today—the death, or removal from office by impeachment, of a president, and the plight of Black America.

From the early 1950's Wallace had been eager to write a novel based on the situation of the Negro in contemporary America. He developed two novels and shelved both. He thought they added nothing to what had already been said well by Black authors. On January 30, 1965, radio station KFH/CBS in Wichita, Kansas,

Simon and Schuster's first submitted sketch for the cover of *The Man*. I. W. thought it looked like a man on a flying carpet.

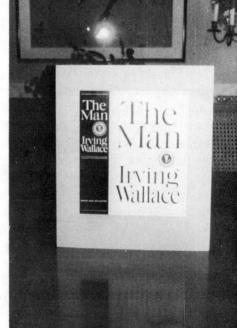

The final cover.

asked Wallace to appear via long-distance telephone to participate in a panel discussion of *The Man*. Because of other commitments he could not appear, but answered their questions in writing. On the conception of *The Man*:

"One night in the early summer of 1963, I suddenly wondered what it would be like if, by accident, a Negro politician were catapulted briefly into the office of the Chief Executive of the land. This gripped me, and the more I thought about it, the more I wished to write about it. And so I began thinking about it, researching it, and suddenly, with considerable dedication, I found myself writing my novel."

The research included a visit to the White House in mid-September of 1963. Pierre Salinger, President Kennedy's news secretary, took him into the Cabinet Room to watch the President swear in new United Nation members. He interviewed Mrs. Lincoln, the President's personal secretary. Preston, President Kennedy's valet, took him on a tour of the private second floor of the White House.

The actual writing of *The Man* began October 31, 1963. Wallace *did not* get the idea of a Presidential death from the November, 1963, assassination. The day President Kennedy was killed, Wallace was in his study completing the first quarter of his 1166 page manuscript of *The Man*. All the scenes of Presidential succession had been written.

The book was completed on March 8, 1964, at 5:16 in the afternoon. But he was not sure that it was right. Wanting to be certain that the Washington presented in the novel was a reasonable facsimile of the real city, he wrote Korda on March 23 asking him if he knew someone "who KNOWS that city a lifetime, the city itself, the branches of government, and can also read my book in thirds and make marginal corrections of any goofs or glaring errors." He was also uncertain about whether he had made any goofs or glaring errors with his Negro characters: "I may try to find one or two Negroes, a man, a woman, to quick read book on same basis."

The time of the novel posed another problem. Although he did not name an exact date for the events of *The Man*, the time is

Evening Clarion

51,722   THURSDAY, APRIL 29, 1965   4d.

FIRST NEGRO PRESIDENT

INSTALLED IN WHITE HOUSE

All World applauds true Democracy

First negro to achieve highest office

SENATOR DOUGLASS DILM... ...OFFICE
NEW PROBLEMS OF FI... ...N TO
LEAD NATION

At 10·35 last night (EDT), ...
American male was sworn ...
of the United States, to succes...
predecessor who died before fu...
full four-year term. In itself, th...
changing of the guard was neith...
nor unusual. It has happened eig...
before in our history. But last nig...
the first time, there was a differe...

Congress an...
voters

A CASSELL bestseller

JUDICIARY COMMITTE...
MEETS TO DE...
CONSTITUT...

THE MAN

a novel by

IRVING WALLACE

Author of THE PRIZE

tremendous in its theme
tremendous in its treatment
tremendous in its impact
and excitement

Cassell's poster for the British edition of *The Man*.

roughly 1975. "I have had to walk a tight line," he wrote Korda on March 13, "conceding certain information to what it might be like ten years from now, keeping other information and background absolutely contemporary (for the sake of reality and identification)."

Even the type size was a matter for authorial concern. In chapter six The Articles of Impeachment were quoted. Wallace wrote Korda not "to destroy them and make them unreadable by use of small type! Remember, they are the cornerstone of what follows in the book."

To write *The Man* Wallace had to become a fictional legislator. Under the real federal law, Wallace's Black President, Douglass Dilman, would have been quickly removed from his job. For the sake of the story Wallace had to keep Dilman in office. "So, based on the old 1860's Tenure of Office Act, I invented my New Succession Bill. No reader may need this—but you can be sure some political pro or reviewer might miss it."

By April 8, 1964, the film studios were "whipped into a frenzy" over the book. They wanted to see it, but Evarts Ziegler did not want it to be shown for a month. Paul Reynolds had the manuscript locked in his safe and there was another copy at Simon and Schuster. "This week, in New York," he wrote Korda on May 13, "two efforts were made by studios to buy off girls in Reynolds' office for 'an overnight peek' at the first six chapters." Wallace himself gives a detailed account of the bizarre events of the motion picture sale on pages 333 to 343 of this book.

On May 13 the Book-of-the-Month Club offered to place *The Man* as its alternate selection for September. "I'm delighted and told them yes—for one major reason—it may cost us a few bucks in sales immediately—but it will help qualify the book for many outside readers who might otherwise worry that a Wallace book means Sex."

It is commonly supposed that mass-market, popular writers do not labor over their manuscripts the way elitist authors do. But the hundreds of pages of editorial letters sent back and forth between Wallace and his editorial assistants and Korda indicate that the common supposition does not apply to Irving Wallace.

Within the course of editing, each sentence is analyzed for clarity and accuracy. One example: on manuscript page 714 of *The Man* Wallace originally wrote, "He hesitated going into the bar." It was suggested at Simon and Schuster that the sentence be rewritten as, "He was hesitant to go to the bar." Wallace thought the revision was awkward and rejected it. But instead of going back to the original sentence he rewrote it as "He was reluctant to go to the bar." That seemed to read better, and so he left it in that form.

Some editing problems dealt with obscure linguistic distinctions. When writing *The Word* (1972), Wallace wanted to use the Greek letter anagram for "Jesus Christ, Son of God, Savior," which in Greek spells ICHTHYS or "fish." The fourth word of the anagram caused a problem. Checking three different sources, Wallace found three different renderings of the fourth word: *Hyios, Uios,* and *'Yios.* Which should be used? If *Hyios* were used, the anagram would be spelled ICHTHHS; if *Uios* were used it would be ICHTHUS; if *'Yios* were used, then it would be ICHTHYS. In the Greek the first letter of the problematic word is upsilon, rendered into English as a "u" in lower case letters, a "Y" in upper case. Since the anagram capitalized the initial letter of each word, the "Y" was most appropriate. But what about the "H" in *Hyios*? The Greeks did not have that letter, but indicated its phonetic sound with a rough breathing mark ('). *'Yios* indicates the rough breathing mark. But since the "Th" sound (Theou—"of God") precedes the *'Yios*, the rough breathing indicated by using "Hy" would be redundant and unnecessary. Wallace properly used the ICHTHYS spelling.

Sometimes the editing is less problematic. In a note on page 761 of *The Man* galley sheets, Wallace asked that a line be deleted: "The typesetter was obviously smashed on cheap bourbon and felt creative and stuck in a wandering line. Out, damn line!"

The Man was published on September 18, 1964. That is, it was released for commercial distribution. The reviewers had received their copies earlier. On September 15 Korda wrote Wallace about the early reviews: "Well, *Time* and *Newsweek* are BAD. We expected they might be, so there is no use worrying over them. Denver (Sunday) *Post* and Associated Press—VERY GOOD.

Both of these are worth having for their own sakes; but I hope they are indicative of the general trend to come. I think it's likely. The two weekly magazines, after all, make a specialty of savagery. Don't let *Time* and *Newsweek* worry you. They're a bunch of bastards."

The Man did very well. Simon and Schuster sold over 100,000 casebound copies, 1,250,000 in paperback. The Reader's Digest Book Club sold 2,200,000, Book-of-the-Month Club 29,000, plus the sales of seventeen foreign editions. Alice Payne Hackett in *70 Years of Best Sellers: 1895-1965* (New York: R. R. Bowker, 1967) lists it as the number five bestseller of 1964, behind *The Spy Who Came In From The Cold, Candy, Herzog,* and *Armageddon.*

Perhaps the greatest personal reward derived from *The Man* came on October 31, 1964. In recognition of his "Outstanding Contribution to the betterment of race relations and human welfare," Wallace was awarded the George Washington Carver Memorial Institute's Supreme Award of Merit and Honorary Fellowship. In the last pages of the novel a character quotes William Allen White: "The American people have finally learned what a great Kansas editor tried to teach them years ago, that liberty is the only thing you cannot have unless you are willing to give it to others." As Wallace told station KFH, "That is what *The Man* is all about."

The Man, Wallace feels today, is his most important book for two reasons:

"First, I was moved to undertake a difficult problem story, and when I was done, I felt in my bones it was close to the novel I meant to write. Second, based on my voluminous mail, that part of my audience that was white seemed to derive from the story a better understanding of their black brothers and sisters, and many felt it put a spotlight on their own unconscious prejudices and intolerance and felt the book had dramatically changed their outlook. When you write a book that entertains or absorbs the reader, that is one thing. But when you write a book that also affects the reader for better, improves him, gives him more love and understanding of his fellows, then you feel a deeper satisfaction for having produced your novel. This apparently, is the extra dividend

Irving Wallace receiving the Carver Institute's Supreme Award of Merit for *The Man*. Mrs. Mallie Robinson, Jackie Robinson's mother, presents the award. (Photo: UPI Telephoto)

First cover sketch of *The Sunday Gentleman*, 1965.

factor that makes *The Man* so important to me."

Twelve days after the first manuscript of *The Man* was completed Wallace began *The Sunday Gentleman,* a revised collection of his best nonfiction from the magazine days. Why *The Sunday Gentleman*? The big successes from *Chapman* to *The Man* meant the freedom to pursue The Dream, in fact, to live it, but the successes meant nothing without the context of the apprenticeship years. Few knew about the thirty years of Sunday dreaming— where this phenomenal "over-night success" came from. *The Sunday Gentleman* was an attempt to rectify that oversight. But more, it was a tribute to the old friends who had spent those Sundays with him. The amps in the Georgia hospital, Frank Merriwell —"Paragon of the Paperback," Dr. Bell—the Sherlock Holmes prototype, the Everleigh sisters, and fifteen other well-remembered companions. The book was a sentimental journey, a tip of the hat, an attempt to go home again.

By March 29, 1965, *The Man* was into its fifth printing. Other movie deals were closed, the New English Library had paid a $300,000 advance on the next three novels. By May 16 *The Man* had been on the *New York Times* and *Time* bestseller lists for thirty-three weeks. All being in good order, the Wallace's left for Europe on June 24.

After a hectic press tour of England, they relaxed in France. On August 26, Wallace was sitting at an outdoor table of Fouquet's Restaurant on the Champs Elysees in Paris. For years he had been thinking about an international political novel, and that afternoon the characters and dramatic action came to focus in his mind. He went back to the hotel room and began writing *The Plot.*

"The story and character outline of *The Plot* challenged me with certain questions. What is it like to be a pretty English girl doing strip-teases in French nightclubs? I don't mean what does it feel like, but what are the day-to-day problems of being a foreign performer? What is it like to be a former diplomat who is declared a poor security risk and discharged? What is the routine of an American foreign correspondent in Moscow and Paris? And, indeed, how does one find out what a Five-Power Summit Conference is really like? What is the protocol? How do the leaders actually behave behind closed doors?

"Now a great amount of my necessary material did not have to be freshly researched, because I had traveled a good deal, and had always kept a daily journal and had always had a lively memory for what I had observed, heard, felt. But still, memory plays tricks."

The research led him to an American embassy in Europe where he had an off-the-record discussion with "a well-known Ambassador who had attended high-level Summit conferences with Franklin D. Roosevelt and Harry Truman, and who was able to tell me what really went on when world leaders met, how they behaved, their private language, that sort of thing." Then there is the evening he spent backstage with the Bluebell Girls of the Lido Cabaret: "I was back stage chatting with two of the tall British girls who were part of the Bluebell Girls. Moments later the girls removed their robes—the girls go out with naked breasts. One of the most mind-boggling moments occurred fifteen minutes later. Word had got out as to who I was, and most of the girls had read British editions of my novels, and I was standing alone inside the curtain when suddenly these six-foot and six-foot-four girls, all bare chested, surrounded me, eager to tell me how they loved my work. Visually, it was like an erotic dream come true. In fact, except that I do remember it as special, it was all very natural and unself-conscious."

The Plot was formally begun on November 8 in Los Angeles. The first week he wrote forty-eight pages. By Thanksgiving he had written one hundred and twelve, by Christmas there were close to three hundred manuscript pages. There were, as there always had been, the empty days when nothing worked and not a page was written. On the good days he could write six to eight pages; on the best days there were fifteen to eighteen pages. Through the winter and spring he wrote steadily, going into a final slump on the seventh and eighth days of May when he wrote only three pages. But by the ninth the material began to flow again, and the work culminated in a one hundred and twelve page burst in the last seven days. He completed page 1369 and the first draft at 4:52 Sunday afternoon, May 15, 1966. It had taken six months and

Irving Wallace backstage with the Bluebell Girls.

1965-1966

Irving Wallace

THE PLOT

CHAPTER	STARTED	FINISHED	PAGES	BOOK TOTAL
I	November 8, 1965	January 5, 1966	346	346
II	January 7, 1966	February 2, 1966	161	507
III	February 3, 1966	February 22, 1966	125	632
IV	February 23, 1966	March 10, 1966	121	754
V	March 11, 1966	March 28, 1966	121	875
VI	March 29, 1966	April 8, 1966	111	986
VII	April 11, 1966	April 27, 1966	173	1159
VIII	April 28, 1966	May 5, 1966	87	1246
IX	May 6, 1966	May 15, 1966	123	1369

Finished The Plot at 4:52 Sunday afternoon, May 15, 1966 — on page 1369 —

Irving Wallace

Work Sheet — *The Plot.*

eight days to write *The Plot.*

The first rewrite began June 25. More than five hundred working hours later it was completed, on August 8. The second rewrite was finished in less than a month. The final rewrite was accomplished by November 17, 1966. Working over the huge manuscript a word at a time, cutting here, revising there, Wallace deleted six thousand words on the final rewrite alone.

The Plot was published on May 22, 1967. Simon and Schuster along with 20th Century-Fox helped the author celebrate with a cocktail party for three hundred and fifty at the Beverly Wilshire Hotel.

Twentieth Century-Fox had purchased the film rights a month earlier. Evarts Ziegler showed Richard Zanuck a two and a half page outline on April 16. Zanuck liked it, signed a contract immediately. That was the easy part. The original screen writer, William Fairchild, was dropped from the project in December of 1967. John Michael Hayes (*Rear Window*) was hired, but could not produce a satisfactory script. He was dropped in March, 1969. Erich Segal (*Love Story*) flew in from New Haven to give it a try, and he was also fired. A fourth writer, John Sherlock, fared no better. The project was finally shelved when 20th Century-Fox ran out of money and the Zanucks were, in effect, fired.

How did Wallace feel about *The Plot?* What were his hopes for it? "I feel lighter of mind and spirit now that the burden of that book has been removed from inside me and put in print. I also feel fainter of heart at what I reached for, dared to do, attempted to achieve, and, I am sure, never fully succeeded in accomplishing. I tried my best—I could do no better at this time— but no author, when he sees his book a reality, can be satisfied that it possesses the purity and perfection that was once in his head. My one hope is that the book will find readers who will not only enjoy it as a narrative, but will find in it something more, something that its writer felt all through the creation of it—that life is worth living, worth fighting for, worth defending against the forces of death."

The forces of life, at least some of them, were the subject

Finished on
February 19, 1968.
Irving Wallace

February 5, 1968

81 scenes

FINAL OUTLINE

THE SEVEN MINUTES

by

Irving Wallace

CHAPTER I:

1. Two men in sport clothes, Ike Iverson and Otto
Kellog, drive their coupe up Center Boulevard, turn into
Third Street, in the thriving suburban community of Oakwood,
a part of Los Angeles, California. Iverson points to a
store front bearing large sign, "Fremont's Book Emporium,"
and says, "There it is, over there." Kellog says, "Okay."
Iverson parks near the store. Kellog gets out awkwardly,
and walks casually to store.
It is a lazy, sunny May day, and this mid-morning
not many shoppers yet in street. Kellog goes to store window,
studies books on display. Largest on display, filling most of
window, is a new novel, THE SEVEN MINUTES by J J Jadway. The
full page advertisement from yesterday's Sunday paper is
posted beside books, and also a brochure announcement from
Sanford House#, the distinguished New York publishing firm.
There is a ferret-like balding man behind cash
register working on invoices, and a girl clerk with a
customer searching for some title in rear. Kellog asks man
if he is Mr. Fremont, and man says Yes, and Kellog says
his wife shops here sometimes and she in hospital and wants
some reading and told him Mr. Fremont has good judgment. She
wants some light, distracting reading, something brand new.
The one in window, is that a new book? Nothing newer says
Fremont, not officially published yet. There was such demand,
he displayed it moment he unpacked it. It is a great book,
banned 35 years, great work of art, if you like this sort of
thing. Kellog says: what sort of thing you mean? ... Well,
pretty frank about sex. Did your wife read Lady Chatterley
or Fanny Hill? ... Think she read the first one ... Fremont
says Jadway book even better, real artistic ... Kellog says
- but not dull ... Dull? Makes your hair stand on end, it is
really hot stuff.
Kellog finally buys the book, gets a receipt. Goes
outside to car. He asks Iverson if everything went okay.
Iverson says it went well (later we will learn it was all
being transmitted to a tape in the car). Kellog compares the
book to the earlier copy Iverson has on hand. The same.
Kellog goes back in store with book. He goes
straight to Fremont and says, in effect, Ben Fremont, I place
you under arrest under Section Such-and-Such for selling
an obscene book. Kellog is stunned. What does it all mean?
What's going to happen? Kellog says he must accompany them
to police station to be booked. He can enter a plea of guilty

Page one of the outline Irving Wallace referred to in writing *The Seven Minutes*.
When he finished writing a scene, he put a cross in the margin of this outline.

1969 party for *The Seven Minutes*. L-R: Irving Wallace, Sylvia Wallace, and Paul Gitlin, Irving Wallace's literary agent.

of a censorship trial in his next novel, *The Seven Minutes*. Ten years before, in 1959, he had the idea of doing a novel about the thoughts inside a woman's head during seven minutes of intercourse. An interior monologue would reveal her thoughts about the three men in her life. The lover she was with would be the one she had finally chosen to marry. He would be revealed at the end when she cried out his name. Wallace never wrote that interior-monologue novel, but he used it as the object of his fictional pornography trial. *The Seven Minutes* by Irving Wallace is about the legal debate over *The Seven Minutes* by J. J. Jadway, the imagined, interior-monologue book by an imagined author. Jadway's *The Seven Minutes* was written in Paris in the 1930's. Thirty or forty years later, roughly the present, an American publisher attempts to publish and sell the book. The censors sue, a trial is set, and Irving Wallace's *The Seven Minutes* is ticking away.

Wallace partially dedicated the book "to Fanny, Constance, Molly, who made it possible. . . ." Fanny is John Cleland's fictional heroine, Fanny Hill; D. H. Lawrence created Constance in *Lady Chatterly's Lover*; Molly Bloom is from James Joyce's *Ulysses*. Each of these fictional women, along with their creators, were also subjected to pornography trials. All were acquitted and gained literary respectability.

The idea of *The Seven Minutes* came to Wallace in 1964. Four years later he had the background research, the characters and the plot sufficiently in focus to begin the formal writing. Working seven to eight hours a day, six days a week, from February 26, 1968 to May 26, 1968, he completed an 839 page first draft. Between July, 1968, and March, 1969, he rewrote the novel six times and added one hundred and eleven pages to the original draft. Then, working with Michael Korda, Sophie Sorkin (his copy editor at Simon and Schuster), Elizebethe Kempthorne (his research assistant), and Paul Gitlin (literary agent and counsel), he revised the novel a seventh time. The five-year project ended in September, 1969. Simon and Schuster, Literary Guild, and Doubleday Book Club sold a total of 475,000 copies. The Pocket Books paperback has sold more than 3,000,000

Ad for *The Seven Minutes*. 1969.

copies to date. The movie rights were sold to 20th Century-Fox on February 11, 1969. (The full story of that deal can be found on pages 343 to 346.)

The library research for *The Seven Minutes* was in five major areas: 1) studies for and against censorship; 2) the classics of pornography; 3) books by lawyers who had been involved in censorship or freedom of speech cases; 4) studies on antisocial behavior in young people; 5) transcripts of pornography trials.

While reading through the 1163 page transcript of the California pornography trial of Henry Miller's *Tropic of Cancer*, Wallace found a reference to *The Chapman Report*. Professor Otto W. Fick, a witness for the defense, cited the Sarah Goldsmith rape scene from *Chapman* and characterized it as dishonest and sheer sensationalism because it was so *mild*. There is a certain irony in that, especially since *The Chapman Report* was banned in Ireland, South Africa, and for a while in Italy because of its alleged lack of mild sex.

Quitting the library for a first-hand account of his subject, Wallace interviewed or had interviewed hundreds of people from the Los Angeles District Attorney's office, to trial attorneys, to porno shop owners and habitués.

Past research was also helpful. In 1947 Wallace interviewed a priest named Monsignor Pucci, a Vatican expert on the Catholic Church's *Index of Prohibited Books*. Monsignor Pucci answered a long series of questions on the church's censoring apparatus in general, and the *Index* specifically. The magazine article about the *Index* was never written, the priest's comments were filed away and forgotten. More than twenty years later, while outlining *The Seven Minutes*, the material came to mind, and Wallace created two clergymen who condemned Jadway's *The Seven Minutes*, a book once listed in the Vatican's *Index of Prohibited Books*.

A character formed from long unused research was Norman C. Quandt, a producer of stag films. In 1951 Wallace planned to write an article exposing the stag film industry. He made inquiries, and through the friend of a friend of a friend got in touch with a stag film producer. The producer took him around to the "studios" (suburban bedrooms) and gave him the information about stag film production he would use in *The Seven Minutes.* The novel had its own censorship problems. Nine newspapers banned advertising because of the jacket, which featured a diffused, gauzy drawing of a nude woman.* But other than that, and a few minor flaps, the book escaped the censors.

Some censorship is more subtle. Wallace wrote in 1967 that he does not consciously censor himself when he is writing, but there is another kind of self-censorship, "a secret and niggling one that grows out of a fear of revealing to mate or friends something personal one prefers them not to know, that may have been a personal experience. And once, in the margin of a manuscript of a novel of mine that my wife had been reading, she wrote in bold hand, 'My God! think of the children!' "

Wallace also had to think of the adults when he wrote *The Seven Minutes.* He asked Paul Gitlin and Simon and Schuster's attorney, Richard H. Sugarman, to comment on the legal procedures of the fictional attorneys. Both found a number of errors, but more important, scenes which could be libelous. One section included a real judge whose bench advocacy of censorship and purity conflicted with his personal behavior. He had been disbarred and sent to jail. Wallace was urged by his legal editors to provide evidence that the judge had been arrested and convicted of the chicanery cited in the novel manuscript. Wallace provided

---

*A note on Wallace's feelings about his book jackets. On May 4, 1969, he wrote Michael Korda indicating he liked the jacket design for *The Seven Minutes,* but thought it could be improved. He added that Korda did not just send the jacket designs for his novels and ask him what he thought, but he first remarked that *everyone* at Simon and Schuster thought they were *tremendous,* and then asked what the author thought. "I can't forget that in past years you have reported to me the same unanimity of feeling about the love of a jacket—and then, not until a year or two later, do I learn that feelings were anything but unanimous. I cite the dull jacket of *The Plot* as an example. Everyone followed Nina's lead and finally loved it. Much later I learned many people at S & S thought it was as dreary as I thought it was. We can go all the way back to *The Chapman Report.* Smashing, I was told. Years later I learned many people at S & S detested it."

it, and made other revisions elsewhere to keep himself and his
novel out of the courts.

But he did go to court to keep another book out of circulation. *The Seven Minutes* by J. J. Jadway, a fictional, non-existent
book, became a very real book when Olympia Press, the outfit
Time had called the "jaunty bad boys of publishing," sought to
distribute what they contended was the actual Jadway novel.
What Olympia really did was try to pirate the fictional book-
within-a-book for a fast dollar. They hired an anonymous writer
of some pornographic talent to ghost Jadway's *The Seven Minutes*,
then printed it and put a cover on it that looked almost exactly
like the cover on Wallace's *The Seven Minutes*. Simon and Schuster and Wallace took Olympia to court. Justice Mitchell D.
Schweitzer of the New York Supreme Court granted their motion
to enjoin the distribution of the Olympia book on the ground
that it would cause irreparable injury to Wallace's novel. Justice
Schweitzer agreed with the plaintiffs' contention that Olympia
was consciously attempting to deceive the public into believing
that the "Jadway" novel was the actual book that Wallace's novel
referred to. Olympia then discarded the look-alike cover and
replaced it with another, renaming the book *Seven Erotic Minutes.*
Wallace called the incident "surreal and bizarre."

Wallace's next book came to the attention of Michael Korda
on December 31, 1969:

"Paul Gitlin is here [Los Angeles] and told me today that he
had mentioned my new book to you, and you thought it commercial but wanted to see it through before I put any more work
into it. I told Paul—and tell you—I see no necessity in doing this.
The book is *done*, parts of it written over many years. It needs
only three or four weeks of minor rewriting and editing on my
part, then retyping, which should have it in your hands by
February.

"There are sixteen chapters. Of these, nine are brand new,
written for this book and never before published—and seven were
previously published in two of my long out-of-print Knopf books.
Of the seven that were published, four appeared in *The Fabulous
Originals*, which was published fifteen years ago which I would

5.

Defendants' Book and Advertising

Defendant The Olympia Press, Inc. ("Olympia") is
a publishing firm and defendant Maurice Girodias ("Girodias")
is its President.

Just prior to the commencement of this action,
defendants caused to be printed, published and advertised
for sale the book of which plaintiffs complain - the cover
of which (Complaint, Exhs. B and B-1), and the advertising of
which (Complaint, Exh. C), state it to be "THE . . . EROTIC
MASTERPIECE . . . . . . ON WHICH IRVING WALLACE BASED HIS
BESTSELLING NOVEL". It also contains a Preface, written and
signed by defendant Girodias (Complaint, Exh. B-2) to the
same effect.

The cover and advertising of defendants' book further
incorporate and feature, in exactly the same format as on
plaintiffs' "THE SEVEN MINUTES", the following:

a) in the middle, a pinkish-colored "soft-line"
drawing of a nude woman lying on her back with her
knees raised and her right arm thrown back over her
head;

b) at the bottom, the title "THE SEVEN MINUTES",
composed of the three words "THE", "SEVEN" and

From Simon and Schuster and Irving Wallace's injunction against Olympia
Press's *The Real Seven Minutes.*

never permit in paperback (because I wanted to revive them in hardcover, in this book, at a time when I had a bigger public) and three appeared in *The Square Pegs* some thirteen years ago. All of these seven I am cutting, rewriting and reediting this coming month [January 2, 1970-February 6, 1970]. Each chapter deals with a young female who was scandalous in some different ways, although most created sex sensations.

"The temporary working title had been *The Scandalous Ladies.* Sylvia and I felt that too ordinary, and I sought another appropriate title, a now title, and I think I hit one we all like— *The Nympho and Other Maniacs.*"

Although the title promises some sexual interest, many of the women in this 1971 collective biography were deemed maniacal because they defiled conventions in other than sexual matters. To be a "maniac" is not necessarily synonymous with being a "lunatic." It also refers to an intense or exaggerated enthusiasm or desire for someone or something. The book covered a broad spectrum of maniacal ladies.

There was Delia Bacon, for example, a New England spinster and school teacher who thought Shakespeare "a vulgar, illiterate deer-poacher" who had not written the plays attributed to him. She became obsessed with the idea that a secret syndicate consisting of Sir Francis Bacon (no relation), Sir Walter Raleigh, Edmund Spenser and others had written the dramas. So persuasive was she that Mark Twain, Walt Whitman and Sigmund Freud were converts to her conspiracy theory.

Each "Maniac" qualified for the book by fulfilling three requirements: 1) dramatic impact on her time; 2) fearlessness in the face of scandal; 3) unusualness in some way. Wallace wanted only those women who had been daring enough to behave as individuals, as liberated women who went against the social standards of their time.

By applying these standards Wallace was able to include Cleopatra, Ninon de Lenclos (who founded a School of Lovemaking in seventeenth century France), and Madame de Stael (a writer, hostess, and unsuccessful seductress of Napoleon).

Other fascinating women had to be left out. One was

The Lives, the Loves
and the Sexual Adventures of
Some Scandalous and
Liberated Ladies

Irving Wallace

Dust jacket — *The Nympho.*

Madame de Pompadour, who worried that she was sexually inadequate with King Louis VI, and who insisted her physician find her more potent aphrodisiacs. Another was Adah Isaacs Menken, a girl from New Orleans who performed semi-nude as an actress in Europe, married heavyweight boxing champion John Heenan, and had love affairs with authors Charles Swinburne and Alexandre Dumas *fils*. With great reluctance he blue-penciled Nellie Bly, a reporter for the *New York World* who beat Phileas Fogg's record of going around the world in eighty days. Setting out with a knapsack and crocodile gripsack, she devoted a mere seventy-two days of 1889 to circling the globe.

Wallace's earliest inspiration for the book came during the army years. Coming across a reference to Lady Jane Ellenborough's life with four husbands, her affair with author Honore' Balzac, and her adventures with an Arabian sheik, he decided to investigate her more thoroughly. His idea was to write a biography of her or make her part of a biographical collection of similar liberated women. It took almost thirty years, but in 1971 he finished the job.

The book was dedicated to "Amy Wallace and David Wallace and A Different Drummer." Amy is the Wallace's second child, born July 3, 1955. Her father described her in 1970 as "a high school sophomore into witchcraft, anarchy and organic foods." David Wallace recently published a book called *Laughing Gas* (Either/Or, 1973), a history of nitrous oxide as comic relief in the lives of many famous users, among them Samuel Coleridge and William James. His first book, *Chico's Organic Gardening and Natural Living*, went into two printings at Lippincott and has sold 25,000 copies to date.

The "Different Drummer" is from chapter eighteen of Thoreau's *Walden*. "If a man does not keep pace with his companions, perhaps it is because he hears a different drummer. Let him step to the music which he hears, however measured or far away."

Wallace wrote *The Nympho* for a break from fiction. "In *The Seven Minutes* I had to draw upon every resource of my imagination, my passions, my feelings, to write it. When I was

Irving Wallace in front of *Le Hotel*, Paris, dictating research for *The Word* into a tape recorder. Plaque behind him states that Oscar Wilde died at *Le Hotel*.

done with it, I wanted all those heart and gut parts of me to recharge, and I was ready and eager to undertake a work of non-fiction, a work circumscribed by fact, where I had to call more upon my mind and intellect to do it well."

After the break came *The Word.* Formal writing began October 5, 1970; one hundred seven days and eight hundred forty-one pages later the first draft was completed—on Tuesday, January 19, 1971.

As with his other books, *The Word* was conceived and re-searched years before it was actually written. A personal spiritual crisis was one factor in the motivation for the novel. Another was a public opinion poll among leading American journalists. Asked what news story within the realm of possibility would be the biggest story of our time, the majority of the newspeople voted for the Second Coming of Christ.

Nineteenth century German Biblical scholars determined there was a missing Gospel, a document referred to as Q (for *Quelle,* "source"). Wallace "found" the Gospel in the ruins of the ancient Roman seaport of Ostia Antica. The effect of the dis-covery on a number of lives is the basis for the action of the novel.

The research began in 1961, took place in six countries and cost the author approximately 2,150 hours and $40,000. The expertise he gained is reflected in his response to a charge from a Salt Lake City woman who, in a letter to Robert Cromie, disputed Wallace's claim that there were no detailed descriptions of Christ. Wallace wrote Cromie:

"I'm very familiar with the Lentulus letter (cited by the Salt Lake City Woman). It gives a detailed description of Jesus. Unfortunately, it is pure fiction—a forgery that purports to be a first-hand description.

"To begin with, an examination of Roman officials of the first century will show you no such person as Publius Lentulus was ever president or procurator or governor of Judea. He was non-existent, purely invented by someone at a much later date. Secondly, the Lentulus letter has been traced—by Bible scholars— back to the 11th century where it is first found in the writings of St. Anselm, the Archbishop of Canterbury. There is no evidence

Irving Wallace and Michael Korda at Simon and Schuster's publication party for *The Word*, 1972. (Photo: Burton Berinsky)

anywhere that this so-called authentic description of Jesus existed before the year 1090. It was probably written by a forger—eager to promote the faith—to excite people about the reality of Jesus, and then picked up by the Archbishop and incorporated into his writings.

"No contemporary descriptions exist because portraits or descriptions were forbidden by Jewish law in the first century. We can only guess what Jesus may have looked like from our knowledge of the appearance, height, weight of the average Palestinian of that time. I invented a description of Jesus in *The Word* by studying the writings of early Christian historians who were alive a century or so after Jesus' crucifixion.

"Andrew of Crete wrote at that time that Jesus had 'eyebrows that met.' Clement of Alexandria said that Jesus was 'ugly of countenance.' And Tertullian, a Christian convert, implied that Jesus was lame or crippled by writing in 207 A. D. that 'His body was not even of honest human shape.' "

Reader responses, pro or con, were heated. Two representative Referendum Card comments: Thomas G. Watson, Jr., of Charleston, South Carolina, thought "the author has the ability to touch upon a unique subject and to present it in an almost nonfiction fashion. The characters have depth and purpose and their dialogue always 'moves the story along.' " F. S. Smith of Westbury, N. Y., "struggled to like it, 100 pages, gave up. (Loved *The Man* and *The Prize*.) The author is repelled by his own characters and his own theme. He is doing an assignment whose quantity counts highest and extra credit is given for sexual references, scotches consumed, and 'in' places referred to. A classic case of a writer too big to be edited? (But I'm forgetting the stockholders.)"

The professional critics were also divided. James Watkins, in the San Diego *Union*, called it Wallace's "best" work (March 26, 1972). Nancy Hart, reviewing it for the Memphis *Press-Scimitar*, recommended it with reservations: "the historical data, descriptions and explanations are so wordy and overdone that it would take more than the Wallace-trademark sex scenes to perk them up" (May 5, 1972). Bob McKnight, Sr., of the Cleveland

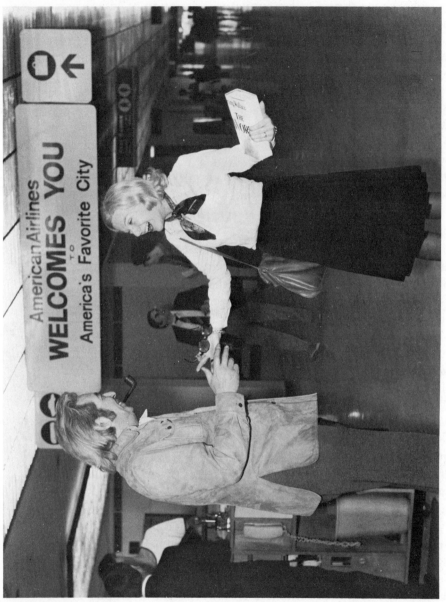

Irving and Sylvia Wallace at the Los Angeles airport. He had just returned from a press and television tour promoting *The Word*. (Photo: Hal Randall)

Press, considered the book one of Wallace's best as he "again shows his facility for authentic detail and great story-telling ability" (April 21, 1972). The New Haven *Register* cited the author's mastery of factual fiction and "the art of story telling" (March 26, 1972). Joe Pollack, writing in the St. Louis *Post-Dispatch*, called the "characterization strong, the research deep and effective, and the entire book a superior and well-written example of escape literature" (March 19, 1972). Brad Darrach of *Time* called it "an absorbing theological thriller. So absorbing in fact that readers may wonder if there isn't a misprint on the title page. There isn't. This entertaining puzzler was actually produced by Irving Wallace" (April 10, 1972). Robert Nye of the Manchester *Guardian* titled his review "Another bestseller from the man who doesn't know the alphabet" (June 22, 1972). Steven Kroll, reviewing it for *The New York Times Magazine*, thought Wallace had "no insight into what he's doing and no ear for language. What he does have is a flair for controversial, topical subjects and a good liberal's respect for honesty, justice and nonconformity. He's also very adept at those unlikely coincidences that keep a reader wondering" (March 19, 1972). Long Island's *Newsday* said "It has been a sport of critics for untold years to kick Irving Wallace around, perhaps because his writing has been simplistic if not plodding. That hasn't bothered his readers, who make every Wallace book a bestseller anyway. Yet this time he has turned out a winner—a first-rate suspense story that makes skillful use of his talent for research, with a convincing plot that moves along briskly" (March 18, 1972). Marian Simon Carmel of *The National Observer* thought *The Word* "a good old-fashioned mystery," with a fascinating international background—"Wallace is a marvelous tour guide, with a fine eye for an offbeat detail" (April 29, 1972).

Through the years the critics have generally liked Wallace's stories, but they have been less enthusiastic about how he tells them. In May, 1964, Wallace expressed some of his feelings about the critics to Zika Todorovic of Belgrade's *Politika* magazine:

"In America, it seems to me, there is a wide schism between what is wanted and loved by the professional reviewers and critics, and what is wanted and loved by the broad reading public. The critics, not all but the great majority, have shown a tendency to prefer precious writing, concave writing. The broad reading public, which for the most part ignores the critics, seems to prefer direct writing, plain writing, exciting writing, topical writing (both realistic and escapist), story writing, meaningful writing (that is, characters who bear some relationship to the lives of the readers)."

Of all Wallace's critics his most severe has always been his wife. She is the first to see his books, and is described by her husband as editorially sharp, sensitive, perceptive, unsparing." After reading his first novel, *The Sins of Philip Fleming*, Sylvia Wallace criticized it for its sexual explicitness. Her spouse listened and made numerous changes. In his latest novel, *The Fan Club* (March, 1974), Sylvia was still criticizing. For example, on manuscript page 167 of *The Fan Club* he wrote: "Yost turned several pages of the policy. 'Here we have it the way the doctor wrote it down. Sharon Fields. Height—5 feet 6½ inches. Weight—116 pounds. Measurements—38D-24-37.' "

Sylvia crossed out "Measurements—38D-24-37" and wrote in the margin, "Never!! in a policy. In a fan mag maybe." She suggested another version to be inserted after the "Weight—116 pounds" sentence. Sylvia rewrote it: "He paused. 'And right here let me throw in this little statistical sidelight I picked out of a movie magazine in the drugstore last night.' He paused to dramatize it. 'Sharon Fields' physical measurements—are you ready? Okay—38D-24-37.' "

On page 237 of the manuscript Wallace described an actress "who'd had three formally announced children out of wedlock" by the time she was twenty. Sylvia's marginal note: "Make her a bit older—or cut one or two kids. How could she have done it all?" Wallace relieved the strain on credulity by making her two years older, although he allowed her to keep the three children.

A fictional character is partly delineated by the language he characteristically uses. The fictional narrator also uses his own characteristic diction. Sometimes the author will unwittingly confuse their distinctive vocabularies. On manuscript page 637 Sylvia noted that the narrator's use of "immersed" in "The others were

Irving and Sylvia Wallace in the lobby of the Fontainbleau Hotel while attending the Republican Convention. (Photo: Jimmy Alterman)

Daniel Ellsberg and Irving Wallace at the Republican National Convention, 1972.

too far immersed" was inappropriate to the narrator. She suggested that "immersed" was another character's kind of word, and it might be changed to "The others were too far gone." Wallace made the change exactly as she had suggested.

In 1970 Wallace joined the ranks of another type of critic. Because he had always been interested in politics, and because he wanted a nonfiction break between *The Word* and *The Fan Club*, he took an assignment with the Chicago *Sun-Times/Daily News* syndicate to report the 1972 political conventions. He plunged back into journalism with what *Time* called "a cub reporter's drive and determination."

The first story, "Bit of a confrontation with Chief Pomerance," appeared on July 6. The last dispatch, "An interview with Kissinger," was published on the twenty-fifth of August. In between were sixteen other reports ranging in topic from Shirley Chisolm's affinity to Victoria Woodhull, to Billy Graham's "spiritual" presence in Miami, to what used-car salesmen thought of Nixon's political salesmanship.

The Kissinger interview noted "how different Kissinger was here in Key Biscayne from the way I had found him at the Beverly Hills dinner party several months ago. On that social occasion he had been easier, freer, and most charming. He had been eager to prove to us he was not Mr. Nixon's man, but his own man."

It is Wallace's habit to keep a daily Journal—part diary, part writer's notebook. On January 9, the night of the first meeting with Kissinger, he jotted down extensive notes on the future Secretary of State.

—"Kissinger told Sylvia that he was planning his secret trip to China to pave the way for President Nixon when he learned that Scottie Reston of the *New York Times* had been admitted to China and was on his way. Kissinger went into the Oval Office to tell Nixon that Reston was going to be there at the same time. President Nixon was very upset and said, 'You've got to prevent Reston from knowing you are there for me; it's got to be a secret that has to be maintained.' Kissinger said, 'well, maybe while I am in Peking they could put him on a slow train from Canton to Peking until I'm finished.' Then he went off to China in secrecy,

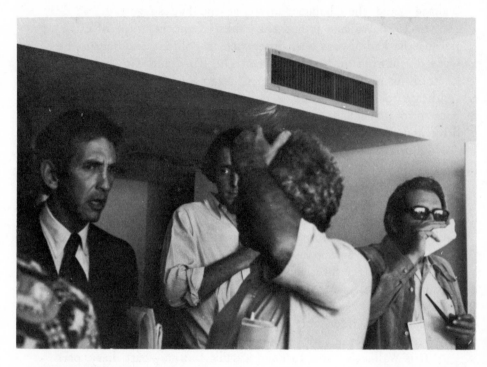

Irving Wallace's caption: "During the Republican Convention in Miami Beach, Dan Ellsberg arrived with Pete McCloskey to hold a press conference. When it was over, Norman Mailer, Kurt Vonnegut, and Joe McGinnis (*The Selling of the President*) wanted to talk to Ellsberg some more, so we all came up to our suite and held a gabfest and party for three hours." L-R: Daniel Ellsberg, Joe McGinnis, Norman Mailer, I. W.

Original sketch by Rafael Cauduro published in *El*, a Mexican magazine. This went with an Irving Wallace essay on Kissinger.

On April 15, 1968, Irving Wallace gave a fund-raising party for Eugene McCarthy. Irving Wallace's caption: "I have just finished introducing Senator McCarthy—and here I had whispered, 'Give 'em hell'—then he said, 'But you promised I didn't have to.' "

and one of the first things he said to Chou En-lai when they met was, 'Look, the President is very eager that this be kept secret from Reston, and I am very worried that he shouldn't get to Peking and see me here.' Chou En-lai smiled and said, 'that's no problem. Right now he's on a slow train from Canton to Peking.' "

—"Kissinger said that whatever happens in 1972—if Nixon's re-elected and he continues—that he won't go the entire course with Nixon as his number one foreign policy advisor, because it's not good to be identified with a single administration. He doesn't want that. Sylvia said, 'What will you do?' He said he didn't know."

Discussing their conversation with Kissinger on the way home from the party, the Wallaces agreed that he was personable, shrewd and a survivor. "He is in the business of Henry Kissinger. He is looking out for himself. He likes to think his view of foreign policy is an overview and long view, the way the Vatican looks upon human affairs and its own survival. We suspect he can't see the incompatibility of his own aggressive directing of Nixon in Vietnam, and into Laos and Cambodia, with the world peace he keeps bringing up as his crusade. We suspect he's a big balance-of-power boy, and doesn't count the bodies. We've read all about his power and influence, and his personal insecurity and intellectual arrogance. The arrogance wasn't shown to us at all, but the insecurity was—the absolute desire to not be thought of as evil or bad or the agent of leaders and happenings we plainly thought to be harmful and bad."

In the 1968 campaign Wallace had supported Eugene Mc-Carthy. When Humphrey won the Democratic nomination and ran against Nixon, Wallace refused to vote for either. In 1972 he was a strong supporter of Senator George McGovern. He took time out from the first draft of *The Fan Club* to write numerous articles for the *McGovern-Shriver Newsletter*, a campaign sheet that is historically interesting for its early documentation of Watergate and related affairs. The facts presented were then considered merely campaign propaganda and generally neglected by the press.

Wallace's research into Nixon's legal background produced

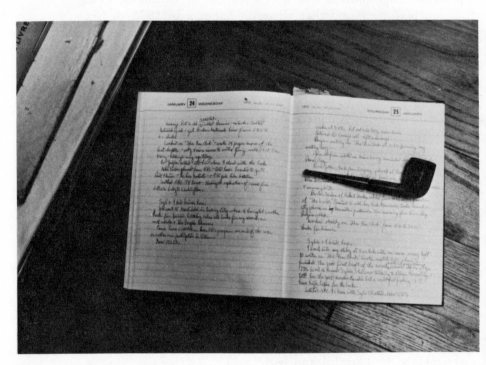

Irving Wallace's private Journal. January 24-25, 1973.

a muckraking article titled "How Young Lawyer Nixon Bungled His First Case." The case, Los Angeles Municipal Court Action Number 457600, dated December 10, 1937, dealt with a property suit. Nixon handled the case so badly that he was sued by his client's stepmother, Mrs. S. Emilie Force, for misrepresenting her stepdaughter's best interests. Nixon defended himself with an affidavit explaining his activities. The case so enraged Judge Alfred Paovessa that he suggested from the bench that Nixon might not have the ethical qualifications to practice law in California, and he threatened to turn the matter over to the Bar Association. (The full story of Nixon's first case is in *LA* newspaper, December 9, 1972, p. 12.)

The journalist's habit of keeping a daily Journal began with the personal record of the Fountain of Blood expedition. After the return to Kenosha the daily log was abandoned for six years until the Far East trip, during which he kept a typed record of interviews and observations. Between 1942 and 1946 Wallace was too busy with army duties to keep an ongoing record, but occasionally he would spend a few hours of an evening writing notes of stories and anecdotes he had heard.

The daily Journal was resumed during the Wallaces' first European trip in 1946-1947. He wrote two-thirds of it, but by the time they reached Spain he was too occupied writing magazine pieces to continue, and it was done by Sylvia. The European Journal was extremely helpful later in recollecting incidents and characters for *The Prize* and *The Writing of One Novel.*

After that trip there was no Journal for over ten years, until Sunday, December 7, 1958, when he bought a loose-leaf binder and typed in the first page:

"Once, in Mexico in 1934, I kept a diary, and from time to time, since, I have made notes on events, meetings with well known personages, anecdotes, reflections. But now I have decided—at the somewhat advanced age of 42 years and 9 months—to keep an irregular Journal of doings and thinkings."

Wallace did not write in this Journal every day, but used it as a summary Journal to record his relationship with his wife, the growing up of his children, his changing attitudes, his health, the books he was writing, and the people he had met. His final entry was Sunday, January 18, 1970, the day his mother was buried: "Services in chapel of Hillside Memorial Park. From 1 to 1:30. Then, to Court of Devotion, gathering around casket, where kaddish was read at 1:45. Then, after a while we all left."

The part-time, summary Journal was ended because, beginning December 1, 1961, he had begun a more detailed weekly Journal. Throughout the early years of the 1960's Wallace spent several hours each Friday writing about the week's events. Finally he began writing in the Journal every evening. He has kept up that red-bound Standard Daily Journal ever since.

There are twenty-six lines to each dated page, and he never fills more than one page. To write more would be burdensome and discourage him from going on with it.

"It's a private Journal. No one has ever seen a page of it. And the question remains—why do I write it? I suppose, subconsciously, anyone who keeps a diary or journal expects it to be seen or read by someone else some day, maybe even hoping that it will be read. I suppose, too, such daily records are kept as an effort to achieve mini immortality, extend one's identity after one's death. You may be gone, but with luck your Journal will be in the possession of others alive, or in a college and available to living persons, and in that way you continue to live, even for moments, hours, days again. It's really the game of literary cryonics.

"But all that about motives is guesswork. What is not guesswork is the conscious reason I keep my Journal. The main reason is that I like it as a personal record to refer to years later when I'm writing about events past in fiction or nonfiction. As a reference, it is absolutely invaluable. Even in the most minor ways. When I was writing the chapter called 'Intrigue Express' in *The Sunday Gentleman*, I tried to recollect a certain encounter I had one night on the Orient Express somewhere between Venice and Paris. And lo, I found it in my Journal under an entry made on the train on August 24, 1964. The entry refreshed my memory and I was able to write the tag to my chapter:

" 'Yes, Virginia, there is an Orient Express. You can ignore

AURORA FILMS PRESENTS SHARON FIELDS

LIST OF SHARON FIELDS' MOTION PICTURES:

FOR MEN ONLY

COINCIDENCE

PETTICOAT PRESIDENT

HOTEL FOR TERROR

THE EIGHTEEN ACTS ... Oberammergau Passion Play

LOVE NEST

THE SEVENTH VEIL ... girl reporter crashes a harem

ARE YOU DECENT? ... lady censor

THE GHOST WITH BLUE EYES

THE WIDOW'S WALK

AND THEN GOODNIGHT

BECAUSE OF SEX

SPEAK OF THE DEVIL

MASTERPIECE

THE LOST CRUSADE

VENUS DE MILD

NOTHING HAPPENS IN MONTEREY

MADELEINE SMITH

THE ASYLUM

DARLING NELL

THE WHITE CAMELLIA

THE NUDE ... Pauline Bonaparte

THE SCARLET *Harlot* EMPRESS ... Valeria Messalina of Rome

For The Fan Club list of fictional credits I prepared for my heroine — many based on old movie originals or plays I once wrote or did not sell.
Irving Wallace
Oct. 23, 1973

The clients of Dr. Bellmore

List of fictional credits for Sharon Fields movies (*The Fan Club*).
Many are based on unsold Irving Wallace movie originals and plays.

the obituaries and pallbearers. They are the lie. And one more thing, Virginia. Ignore the debunkers. Listen to me. I was up at three that last morning, in the aisle of the Orient Express as it sped through Switzerland and France—and you know what? There *was* a lady in distress. True, she was only on her way to the bathroom. But she *was* swathed in a long mink coat, a mink coat and *nothing else*, Virginia. When that happens on an airplane, I'll turn in my Wagons-Lit ticket and fly. But not before. No, never.' "

Another value in writing a brief daily Journal before bedtime is that it clears his mind of the events of the day. By putting his thoughts down on paper he is rid of them. "If it is time to sleep, I sleep, and let my Journal be the insomniac."

A train and insomnia were important to the conception of Wallace's latest novel, *The Fan Club*. On the night of Tuesday, October 14, 1969, Wallace was riding the shuttle-train between Boston and New York. Although exhausted from his Eastern press and television tour on behalf of the recently published *The Seven Minutes*, Wallace could not sleep. About an hour out of New York the coach on which he was riding had been emptied of all passengers but himself. At some stop along the Connecticut-New York state line, six railroad men came on. Two were conductors, one an engineer, the others railyard laborers. They lolled about in the middle of the coach, relaxing, leafing through the newspapers, and talking. One of the laborers noticed a headlined story about Richard Burton giving Elizabeth Taylor a million dollar diamond.

"He shook his head, and held the newspaper up for the others. 'Look at this, giving her something worth a cool million. Well, can't say as I'd blame him. If I had that kind of money, I'd give it to her, too, considering what she'd be giving me in the sack every night.'

"Then one of the others, a middle-aged conductor, said, 'Yeah, it would be worth it, all right, giving up anything I have, for just one night with Elizabeth Taylor. I'd do it, you know. But guys like us, we never get the chance.' "

Wallace's Journal for that night mentions nothing about the trainmen's conversation. It would be six months before he would

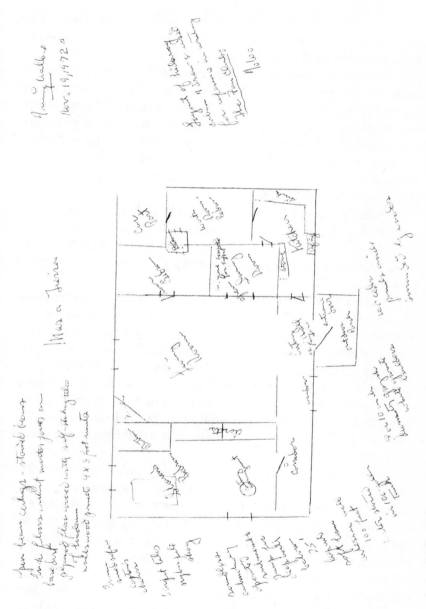

Irving Wallace's layout for hideaway cabin. He used it for reference in writing *The Fan Club.*

realize the implications of their comments for his next novel. That was on April 7, 1970, the day he drove to Beverly Hills to see his podiatrist about a shoe correction.

"Taking the twenty minute drive on Wilshire Boulevard to our home in the west part of Los Angeles, in Brentwood, I turned on the car radio to one of the all-news stations. The announcer was speaking of the Academy Awards that were to be given that very evening. Then he began to speak about Elizabeth Taylor—she had returned from Europe to give one of the awards—and he referred to her as the still reigning sex symbol of the cinema and the leading glamour actress in the world.

"That's when it happened. Mention of her name in the context of desirability and glamour instantly triggered my mind—shot it backwards to that train ride from Boston to New York and those railroad men sitting around talking about what they'd give to possess Elizabeth Taylor for one night.

"From that, my mind tripped backward into a deeper recess of the past, to 1952, and an evening when I first met Marilyn Monroe, and then my mind came forward in time again to fragments of conversations with men about Marilyn Monroe and her sexuality. Impressions, rumors, facts, fantasies. Some evenings I'd spent talking to world-renowned glamour girls, and long before, several young actresses I had known, and how much I wanted them, and what I imagined it would be like, and what it was like when we went to bed and had intimate relationships over a period of time."

The notes of April 7 were typed under the title, *The Fantasy Caper*. The trainmen and Taylor/Monroe were to be brought together in a fictional kidnapping. "Story, I think, is of how she gives up fighting and, perhaps realizing that they may kill and dump her in end, because they might be traced, she gradually applies those techniques, arts, cold ambitions she used to rise to the top—to gain dominance over the gang of six or seven whites and blacks—and how in the end she destroys them—how I don't know—gets one to murder a couple others before he is murdered, reduces one to shameful impotency, makes one sorry for her, gets at the avarice of another—until she gets them down to two and

Irving Wallace proofing galleys of *The Fan Club*.

destroys them and returns and never tells what happened. . . .
Or in end, just when she has almost succeeded, slips once on last
man, becomes real, falls for him, and is killed or in some way
destroyed . . . or gets one to finally leave ransom note for money
when she isn't what he really wanted. . . ."

Wallace's first thought for a "fan club" was a group of men
who were actually fans of the actress. When he began writing the
book he discarded that idea because he felt it would limit his
characters "to one kind of obsessive kook" and he wanted a more
representative group of middle-class men.

The Fantasy Caper was a short-lived title. Later in the evening of April 7 he recorded *The Wish* as the title in his Journal.
He was never pleased with *The Wish* because it was too similar to
The Word, his most recent novel. Yet *The Wish* remained until
he had completed no less than one-third of the novel. Then, in a
scene where Sharon Fields/Taylor/Monroe first confronts her kid-
nappers, she wonders if they are not part of a publicity stunt or
fan club gimmick. "Well, the moment I'd spontaneously written
the words 'the fan club' in this context, I stopped and sat up
straight. I said to myself—hey, what a terrific title, *The Fan Club*,
much better than *The Wish*. And later, in my first rewrite, I
planted the use of it as the cover name for their kidnapping plot."

The notion of "six or seven whites and blacks" was dropped
very early. Six or seven seemed too cumbersome for a realistic
kidnapping plot, and Wallace did not want to work with that many
characters. He quickly settled on four as being a more suitable
number, and just enough to reflect different ages, domestic backgrounds, different jobs or positions, different points of view, and
they also gave the author enough room to explore the psyches and
sex attitudes of different persons he knew and would partially use
in the novel.

Nor did he ever seriously develop the idea of black and white
men. He felt that if one of the characters had been black there
would have been an unnecessary and harmful alteration of the
thrust and theme of the book. Furthermore, he had never known
nor could imagine one who would be particularly interested in
the fan club's kind of crime. This was a story that called for sexist

whites.

On April 7 he had thought about writing the story from Sharon Fields' point of view. But when he considered the excitement and suspense that could be generated by an omniscient narrator showing the details of preparation for the kidnapping, he knew Sharon Fields' narration would not do.

"When I began writing the novel—I had it broken into three parts or acts—I meant to write the first part without the reader ever meeting Sharon or getting inside her head until after she is kidnapped and the men meet her. Then I intended to write the second part entirely from her point of view. But once I got started, I saw that didn't write very well. So I revised my thinking about the first part. I showed Sharon at a premiere, to dramatize how really famous and glamorous she was from afar. And I ended the first part of the novel by getting into Sharon's mind, playing a scene from her point of view, so that we know her before she is kidnapped, we glimpse her as a human being and not merely a symbol, which my instinct told me would also intensify the suspense and horror of what was to follow.

"In the second part, while much of it, most of it, is indeed told from her point of view, what she is secretly thinking, I had to counterpoint this by going to the men from time to time. This made the story more honest, taut, and moved it along better.

"As to having her slip up and be murdered in the end, that was just one of several options I gave myself. When I was writing, I had an ending in mind, but kept changing and modifying it as my story developed. There could have been many endings, but the one I used was the one that just unfolded naturally and without contrivance. My readers can determine for themselves if I made the right choice."

The research on *The Fan Club* was minimal compared with his previous books (except *The Sins of Philip Fleming*). There was some research on the careers of three of the male characters—research on insurance, auto repair and accounting. Wallace did further homework on kidnapping, spoke with rape victims, and spent days locating and photographing scenes that he would describe in the story. He knew Sharon Fields from his own experiences with actresses. And he knew his men. "Not one of the men represents me, but each of them, one way or another, reflects something of my thinking and my own fantasies."

After the book was through a first draft, Wallace had to face his most difficult problem: what about the explicit sexuality of the second part? While he wrote it there were only the book and Irving Wallace. When it was done there were the book, Irving Wallace, and the public. He knew that many people would label it a sex book. Throughout the several rewrites he worried that the explicit sex would obscure everything else.

"One of the three epigraphs that head up the novel is the line from Thoreau that the mass of men lead lives of quiet desperation. That is truly what *The Fan Club* is all about, at least to begin with. Most men on earth, in our society—women, too, but this book does it through men's eyes—think they've been shortchanged by life. They think someone else, higher up, has it better, the good life. So they go through life mildly unhappy, sometimes very unhappy, sometimes seething with frustration. *The Fan Club* sets out to show the fantasies of four such men—and to show what happens when they move to convert their fantasies into reality. Well, since my men covet a woman sexually—then sex has to become the machinery that makes the story go. I mean, if you are writing a story of mortal vengeance, you'd be hard put to not have murder in it. Violence would be the inner mechanism that made the crime book work. And, in my novel, sex is used merely as the mechanism that shows what happens when you try to act out fantasy for real. In short, the book is about the condition of the human animal, and sex is used to dramatize that condition. In my rewrites I toned down certain overt sex scenes that seemed to work against the characters and distract from the main point of the book. But I made no effort to be dishonest and play central bed scenes off stage or have people speak in euphemisms."

It is too early to discuss reader and critical response to *The Fan Club*, but Simon and Schuster has prepared a 100,000 first printing, it has been chosen as the March selection of the Literary Guild, and eight studios are interested in the film rights.

Following the fiction to nonfiction alternation of the last

few years, Wallace and his son David will co-author *The People's Almanac*, an idea David had in 1971 when he decided that almanacs on the market were too dull, misleading, and "square." He felt they relied too much on handouts and did not delve deeply enough for the truth, and that there was room for a new kind of almanac. So, together with his father, he wrote a 106-page outline of *The People's Almanac.*

Doubleday and Company will publish it in 1975. The 1,500-page almanac will cover over three thousand topics ranging from a series of predictions for the future, to a listing of the last will and testaments of famous men and women, to an essay on Clyde Barrow's last Ford. A staff of five are helping to gather the information, and outside contributors such as Ralph Nader, Ray Bradbury and Amy Wallace are also at work. To keep the almanac up to date, readers will be asked to contribute interesting information that is little-known, or of which they have some specialized knowledge. A revised edition is planned for every two years.

Wallace finds the almanac "extremely stimulating to the gray cells and red corpuscles. It keeps one alert and refreshed. Going from *The Fan Club* to *The People's Almanac* gave me a whole new recharge, and by the time I've done my share of the almanac, I'm sure I'll be eager to get back to a work of fiction."

Wallace will be eager to get back to many works of fiction. When he is sparked by a book idea he free-associates everything that comes into his mind about it, and then files the notes away. If he continues to get more ideas, he makes more notes and adds them to the file. At any one time he has fifteen to twenty manila folders that could become books.

Now there are three other files besides the almanac that are developing into books. One is a short historical biography he has almost completed research on and will write in the near future. The third, with the working title *The R Document*, is deep into preparation. "The background is government and politics and an absolutely unusual story, which I feel is timely yet timeless. Oddly enough, had I attempted this novel a few years back, many people might have considered it unbelievable. But with the exposé of the Watergate Affair and all the shenanigans in the Executive Branch

Irving Wallace and David working together in 1948.

They discuss *The People's Almanac.*

of government—well, all that dirty stuff in real life will give absolute credence to my fiction."

It is significant that Wallace is now working on two fiction and two nonfiction books. Although separated by almost a half century from "The Horse Laugh," they are very close to that first important tale—a combination of fiction and nonfiction. Wallace's recurring interest in fact and fantasy has continuously dominated his writing, and the same fundamental questions have been raised again and again. Whatever the setting in whichever work, they are roughly these: What are the unique and shared problems of male and female in our society? How can an individual endure the social, psychological, physical and financial pressures of modern life and still be whole? Above all, where is the order and sense of it all?

In all of his novels Wallace has tried to tell readable, enjoyable stories, integrating plausible characters and thematic relevancies. In *The Sins of Philip Fleming* he tried to show how the pressures of career and marriage can render a man psychologically and physically impotent. In *The Chapman Report* he tried to reveal how the modern woman endures a multitude of indignities which leave her unfulfilled and unhappy, and how the modern means of learning the truth about her, as by sexual surveys, cannot reach the truth and can often do harm. In *The Prize* he investigated the meaning of success in contemporary society and sought to reveal the rickety facades of public honor and the latent strength within private failures. In *The Three Sirens* he wanted to show the restrictions and inhibitions imposed by artificial custom upon the lives of modern men and women, and to speculate on how they might learn from those they call uncivilized. In *The Man* he attacked the madness of racial prejudice and affirmed the intrinsic value as well as the human weaknesses beneath the skin of every individual. In *The Plot* he dealt with the central issue of our time, the possibility of nuclear destruction, and how men and women suffering our own sense of helplessness and fear can still affirm the worth of life. In *The Seven Minutes* he spoke out against moral prejudice and tried to show how censorship is a subtle form of the fear we ought to fear. In *The*

Word he detailed modern man's lack of faith and his longing and need for that faith, and how our deepest personal problems are ineffable without a recognition of their spiritual roots. And in *The Fan Club* he described the sad and disturbing America that defines masculinity and femininity in terms of sex and power.

In answer to the question, how does a writer enforce his own willingness to work, Wallace went to the heart of his life and career. He said, "I think if you like writing enough, have something you want to say or create, you will work, providing you can afford to work."

He always had something to create, and there was never a time he did not want to do it with paper and ink. That part was *a priori*. But there were times when he played the have-to-make-a-living-or-else game with a desperate seriousness. His pursuit of freedom and independence was a pursuit by the pursued. Frightened by the real possibility of a life making change in an all-night laundromat or carrying groceries out to old ladies' cars for a Kenosha market, Wallace fled, fighting a rear-guard action. What he hoped would be a short struggle lasted thirty years. What should have been a big sale to the movies in 1941 turned into a dead manuscript when Hal Wallis would not let Bette Davis do a costume picture. What should have been a first published book in 1942 turned into another dead manuscript when six publishers lost interest because they were not oriented to Japanese history. Pursued by debt and failure, drawn by his private vision of something he knew was a Dream but he was determined to make a reality, driven by a romantic and then a stubborn conviction that he could get his foot on that ladder of success they kept moving on him, he kept on writing until he did not have to write anymore. And then he could begin to write.

Irving Wallace Speaking

Irving Wallace and I began our talk at the door of his West Los Angeles home. We continued over a couple of cokes in his living room, then while munching on a light lunch in his dining room, and finally settled down in his study for a three-hour non-stop interview.

We sat amid motley colored stacks of books that filled the majority of the room's floorspace and completely covered Wallace's regulation sized pool table. I knew that the books represented the ongoing research Wallace and his son, David, are engaged in for the writing of their Almanac. But the piles of books also stood for that constant and insatiable appetite Irving Wallace has for finding out about his fellow human beings and the world in which they live. This interview gave him a chance to tell of his findings and to report on some of his preliminary conclusions.

The afternoon wasn't long enough, though, for either of us. I had more questions to ask, and he had much more to tell and explain. We continued the conversation at long-distance. Irving worked long hours clarifying and elaborating his tape-recorded responses, while I continued to worry him with more questions by phone and through the mail. But he was eager to tell his story, and to tell it honestly and candidly.

Irving Wallace has been interviewed countless times, but those conversations seemed to always revolve around money and number of copies sold. This talk allows Irving to move beyond the glamorous façade of bestselling author to the more deeply human and committed individual that he is.

The first half of the interview deals mainly with Irving Wallace's views on writing and popular literature. The second half covers his experiences with the movies and with the Hollywood community. Abbreviated portions of this interview have appeared in the Journal of Popular Culture and the Journal of Popular Film.

Sam L. Grogg, Jr.

I

SG: Your work is characterized by a great deal of research. Is the notion of the author-as-detective a significant part of your approach to writing?

IW: Yes, but perhaps in a way that is not generally understood. To most people, research means burrowing into old books, periodicals, documents, correspondence. To me, while it means that kind of digging, of course, it also means having conversations with, interviewing, observing, perceiving living men and women who relate to a subject and to characters I am writing about in a novel.

I'm very much turned on to research. You see, I believe it helps an author to leave his interior world and explore other worlds. It gives his work variety and breadth. There are too many novelists, I feel, who are writing straight out of their navels. By this I mean that they confine their material only to what they have personally experienced in their day-to-day living. These novelists are always writing about themselves, embellishing their tribulations with thin coats of imagination. They write about the difficulties of growing to maturity, about their college years or early career years, about their first love affairs, about their marriages and their other women. And so on. Fine. Some of them are doing wonderfully well and are perhaps producing literature. They succeed because they are interesting or write interestingly. But nine out of ten novelists writing this sort of novel finally bore the reading public and eventually remain unread. Had any of them stepped outside themselves and their limited circles, and attempted to learn how other people live, they might have been stimulated to write far more exciting books.

I don't have to force myself to do research, to leave my skin and get inside the skins of others, because I am naturally curious. I want to find out about other people. And what I learn in these explorations excites me, and I hope I transmit this excitement to my readers.

Take the subject of my recent novel, *The Word*, which dealt with religion. This subject—not in an intellectual but in a spiritual sense—was absolutely foreign to me. When I undertook *The Word* ten or twelve years ago, I was an atheist. I did not relate in any way to theologians, clergymen, Biblical archeologists. Perhaps that inhibited me from writing the book when I first became interested in it. There seemed too much to learn. But gradually, as I underwent a personal spiritual crisis, I was again attracted to the religion, and finally I determined to tackle it—perhaps to resolve certain problems I had. From the outset, I told myself: All right, get out there and learn all you can about the world of Biblical scholarship and publishing, about the Christian churches, about the young man named Jesus, about his modern disciples. I told myself: Go out and travel and meet those people, and talk to them, and listen to them, and get inside their heads—not only get into their heads to acquire information (because much of this factual information you discard when you are writing fiction), but to learn their lifestyles, attitudes, feelings.

In beginning such research, I'm always curious to investigate what psychological motives bring a certain person into his field or profession. Why is a surgeon a surgeon? Why does he enjoy cutting flesh? Why is a psychiatrist a psychiatrist? Why does he like to tune in on patients' private lives? Why does that woman like to teach, and why does this man like to dig into the earth? And so—for *The Word*—why did this man choose to become a man of God? And, indeed, how much of a man of God is he truly? Is his motive spiritual, one of pure

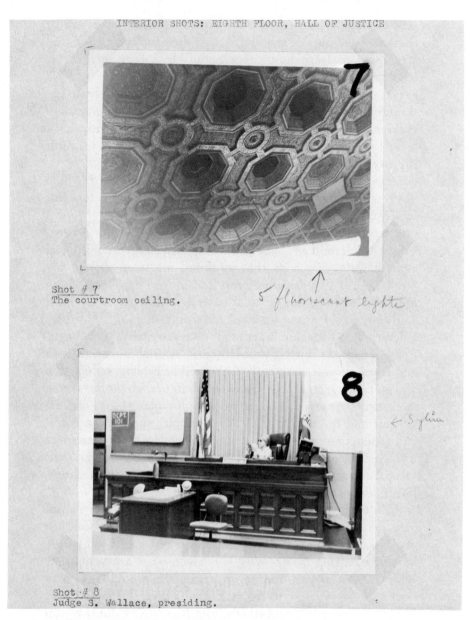

Irving Wallace had these photos taken in preparation for the court room scenes of *The Seven Minutes*.

faith, and a desire to make life more bearable, and the certainty of death more acceptable to others? Or is his motive a desire for power and authority? Or is his motive more crass, a decision to promote belief in God in order to make a livelihood or gain wealth?

Off and on for a period of ten years, seeking answers, I read, skimmed, dipped into about 500 books dealing with religion, amassed and consulted 3,500 newspaper and magazine clippings, and, most important of all, personally interviewed or had interviewed for me (when there was a language barrier) fifty-eight varied Bible experts in places ranging from the Yale Divinity School to the Sorbonne to the Vatican. By the time I was ready to write, I was writing about a subject as familiar to me as my own life. Indeed, the world of religion had become part of my life.

My earliest concept of *The Word* was to make it an inside story about the people who inhabit the world of Bible publishing. Toward this end, I think I interviewed half the leading Bible publishers and editors in the United States, England, France, and Italy. But as time passed, my approach to this novel began to change, and in the end I discarded most of this Bible publishing research and concentrated more on churchmen, theologians, and ordinary people seeking faith.

And, of course, as I wrote, I found I was writing more and more about myself. I mean, as much as you research new backgrounds or people, you still wind up writing about yourself in a novel. You have no choice. Even though Gustave Flaubert based *Madame Bovary* on a scandalous young woman he knew about named Delphine Delamare, when his book was done he was able to say, "*I* am Madame Bovary." And he was right. So a good part of me walked inside my fictional hero, Steve Randall, when he entered into the world of religion. But in writing the novel, I not only knew me, but I also knew the religion-oriented characters that my fictional surrogate was encountering.

In fact, the one novel for which I did the most research— I refer to *The Prize,* where I was delving into the psyches of

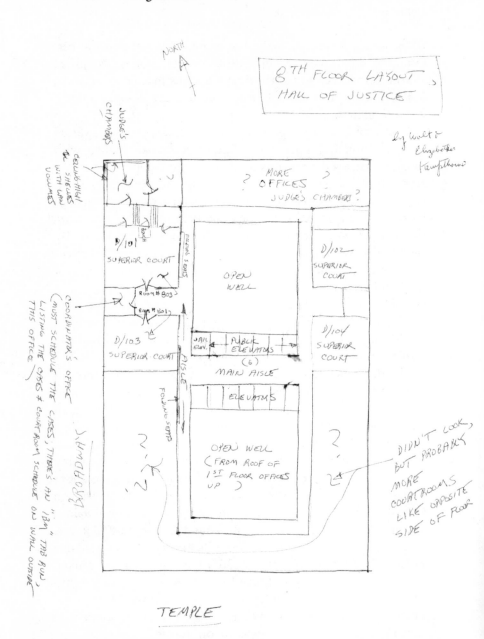

Irving Wallace used this sketch to help prepare courtroom scenes for *The Seven Minutes*.

Swedish Nobel Prize judges, and international laureates in the fields of physics, medicine, chemistry—is the novel that has the most of me in it. The protagonist is an author, Andrew Craig, and the great part of the inner Craig reflects the inner Irving Wallace, as well as many of the external facts about Craig which are drawn from my own history. In short, I'm saying an author can't help but be a character in all of his books. The question is one of degree, for I feel the author would be wise to bring in characters and backgrounds drawn from research—research in the broadest sense—and make room for them, also. This variety enriches a novel.

So, in that sense, author-as-detective—right. I play that game. And I enjoy it immensely. There's a great excitement in reading or interviewing or observing something new that will inspire something unexpected for your novel: a new character, a fresh site for a scene, even a previously unknown piece of information that illuminates a character through dialogue or that underscores plot.

I remember writing *The Seven Minutes*, a novel in which my hero was an attorney who had to become a specialist in the area of obscenity law. I knew more about attorneys— God, I live with them in business—than I knew about theologians, but I'd really never thought about their personal lives. I asked myself: Do they live differently than authors? Do they think differently? Are their aspirations different? Are their conflicts different? So I set out to learn. I was stunned to realize how little I'd known about the legal world. This research, as well as trying to find out more about the special, strange world of obscenity—going down all those mean streets with those pitiful porno shops inhabited by those poor harmless males who could not relate to real women in a love relationship so they dwelt in a safer masturbatory world—that experience was invaluable for my novel. I simply could not have written that novel without the first-hand research.

I'm reminded of an exchange I once had with Clifford Irving—yes, the fellow involved in the Howard Hughes auto-

biography hoax—at a time when our lives crossed briefly out
here in Los Angeles during 1961 and 1962. Cliff was writing
novels at the time, and not doing too well with them. On this
particular evening, we were sitting in our living room discussing literary matters. I recall Clifford Irving saying to me,
"I've been carrying around a wonderful idea for a novel, but
I simply cannot write it because the main character is an
attorney. I've never been an attorney, and I don't know a
damn thing about law, so I'm afraid I can't write the novel.
Too bad, because the idea is a good one." I remember wanting to tell Cliff, "Godammit, go out and strike up friendships
with some attorneys, get to know how they talk, think, feel,
and in a half a year you'll be able to write that novel you're
dying to write." But I didn't speak my mind, and Cliff never
got to write that novel. A decade later, when the Howard
Hughes case blew wide open, and Cliff Irving was in the headlines as a forger, I went back to my daily journals to see if I'd
noted anything of our social meetings together. I found a
telling entry I had made under the date of April 22, 1962. It
concerned an evening that my wife and I had with Cliff
Irving and his beautiful third wife, Faye, a red-headed English girl. Faye and I got off in a corner for a private conversation, and Faye complained to me about her husband. I found
that I had noted in my journal: "Faye told me Cliff is
incapable of love, he is too self-absorbed. . . . She considered him smart but immature, both as a writer and a mate.
The big problem is that he's lazy, she says, has no curiosity
and does little research." My own perception of Cliff's refusal
to get outside himself and do research was not that he was
lazy, but that he felt research was unliterary for a novel. Of
course, ten years wrought some change in him—for by 1972
he had gained world-wide notoriety for doing too much research—on Howard Hughes!

But to get back to the author-as-detective. This designa-
tion is much more applicable to authors who write nonfiction,
especially historians and biographers. That's where scholarly
sleuthing really comes into full play. Since I write factual

biographies as well as novels, I'm familiar with the dogged spadework necessary to have a long-buried personality come back to life. When I wrote my biography of Phineas T. Barnum, *The Fabulous Showman*—incidentally, the only book of mine that originated from someone else's idea, and from a movie idea at that, a bastard birth much forwned upon by the literary establishment in those days, but much more accepted these days when movie scripts are converted into books, and often successfully—anyway, with the Barnum biography I was faced with a problem. But first let me preface the problem by telling you how the problem came about. Two producers at Paramount Studios wanted to make a film about Barnum. They had read my collective biography, *The Square Pegs,* in which Barnum was mentioned in a chapter on Anne Royall, and they were much taken with my research, off-beat approach, and style. They came to me and asked me if I'd like to write a factual profile of Barnum which they could use as a springboard for a fictionalized screenplay. I'd always been intrigued by Barnum, and I quickly agreed to undertake the project. But the moment I began my research, I saw that Barnum demanded the dimensions of a full-length book, not a short profile. I asked the producers if they'd sit still for a book. They were delighted. So I holed up in my study and resumed research. And then I came face to face with the big problem.

The problem? What did I have to say about Barnum that had not already been written countless times before? Barnum, himself, had published nine versions of his autobiography. Excellent biographies of Barnum had been written by Joel Benton and Harvey W. Root, and a marvellous one had been written by M. A. Werner and published in 1923. Then, gradually, as I researched, I began to see that I might have something new to say about the gaudy showman. All previous biographies had concentrated on Barnum as a public figure. Next to nothing had been written about his private life. And I learned the reason why. Barnum had made every effort to keep his private life secret. This spurred my detec-

DAY BY DAY WORK ON "THE TWENTY-SEVENTH WIFE" ... 81 pages
had been done between July 27 and August 8, 1959. This
resumes with Chapter II:

date	pages						
SEPT. 14	0ᴿ	OCTOBER 12	6	DECEMBER 7	2	JANUARY 18	16
15	0ᴿ	13	5	8	1	19	17
16	5	14	5	9	0ᴿ	20	18
17	4	15	7	10	2	21	0'
18	5	16	9	11	3	22	0'
19	0	17	7	12	0.	23	6
21	2	19	0ᴿ	14	7	25	11
22	2ᴿ	20	1	15	2	26	4
23	8	21	5	16		27	1
24	0ᴿ	22	7	17		28	2
25	12	23	0	CHAPMAN REWRITES 18		29	8
26	0	24	0	19		30	0
28	6	26	7	JANUARY 4	8	1	8
29	0	27	2	5	12	2	13
30	2ᴿ	28	5	6	15	3	10
OCTOBER 1	3	29	1	7	6	4	4
2	4	30	5	8	15	5	8
3	4	31	5	9	0	6	0
5	0ᴿ	NOVEMBER 2	6	11	0ᴿ	8	12
6	2	3	14	12	0ᴿ	9	9
7	10	4	6	13	11	10	11
8	5	CHAPMAN REWRITES DEC. 3	2	14	12	11	14
9	8	4	3	15	15	12	12
10	4	5	9	16	3	13	

II done

Work Sheet — *The Twenty-Seventh Wife.*

tive work. After that, I got lucky. There came a series of breaks. One resource was so obvious it had been generally overlooked—Barnum's Last Will and Testament. In his Will I learned that Barnum had disinherited one of his three daughters. That was enough. I was on my way. Before I was through, I had learned that Barnum had disowned his daughter because of a scandal—she had left her husband to become the mistress of several lovers. More followed. I learned that Barnum had been a near alcoholic. Most previous biographies had given him only one wife, Charity Hallett, to whom he'd been married for forty-four years. But I discovered a second wife, whom he had married in 1894, when he was sixty-four and she—his second wife, Nancy Fish—was twenty-four. After Barnum's death, she became a French countess and a confidante of the Empress Eugenie of France. Anyway, that is detective work of which I am still proud. And I was delighted last year when the *Encyclopædia Britannica* asked me to write the Barnum biography for their radically new edition which will be published in the near future.

I think the most challenging research I ever undertook was when I decided to write *The Twenty-Seventh Wife*. The easy way would have been to tell the story of American polygamy by writing another biography of Brigham Young. Instead, I asked myself—what person or what action wrecked polygamy in the United States? Where did it really run into trouble? I learned it ran into trouble when Brigham married an attractive young actress, Ann Eliza Webb, for his last wife in polygamy. Ann Eliza hated the so-called harem, escaped it, divorced Brigham, created a national scandal, and went on one of the first sell-out lecture tours of the nation speaking against polygamy. She even got to Congress and the President, and that was the beginning of the end for polygamy.

Now the problem here was not only that this episode in American history was almost totally forgotten, but that the Mormon historians had hidden or destroyed most of the evidence. I had very little material to go by. No biography

LDS Books Club, Inc.

1188 SOUTH MAIN • P. O. BOX 400 • SALT LAKE CITY 10, UTAH

December 10, 1963

Dear Member:

We are very happy this month to be able to offer another exceptional addition to Mormon literature in the distribution of the new and witty analysis by Hugh Nibley of the Irving Wallace book "The Twenty-Seventh Wife."

Dr. Nibley — well-known to students of L.D.S. literature for his outstanding book "The Myth Makers," published in 1961, and other writings — is on the faculty of Brigham Young University, where he is professor in the departments of history and religion.

After reading Mr. Wallace's account of the life and hard times of Ann Eliza Young — a wife of President Brigham Young — Dr. Nibley decided it was high time that the record be set straight. To this end he has written "Sounding Brass" ($3.50, one bonus credit).

Where Mr. Wallace's sources have been less than accurate, Dr. Nibley painstakingly points out the facts. Where imagination has been given as literal fact in "The Twenty-Seventh Wife," Dr. Nibley returns it to the realm of imagination. Before long the authenticity of Mr. Wallace's researched book is shattered forever.

But while Dr. Nibley uses the Irving Wallace book as a detailed example of the sort of misrepresentation of which some writers are capable, the book has wider appeal. For it shows the sort of ruses most anti-Mormon writers get up to in order to make their points.

"Sounding Brass" is a clever book in that it completely exposes the nonsense that so often sees the light of day in novel or non-fiction anti-Mormon literature. Readers will enjoy Dr. Nibley's style, his wit, and his remarkable knowledge.

ALTERNATE:

Once in a while Bookcraft offers readers as an alternate a choice from a wide selection of important books. This is the case for this month. The return card lists each of these books, together with their cost.

Yours truly,

R. Richards

LDS BOOKS CLUB

The Latter Day Saints Books Club, Inc. ad for *Sounding Brass,* an attack on Irving Wallace's *The Twenty-Seventh Wife.*

had ever been written about Ann Eliza Young. However, she had published her autobiography in 1876, and a revised version in 1908—but this was largely untrustworthy, for it consisted mainly of a diatribe against Brigham and the horrors of polygamy. Its value was that it did give me some leads. For other leads, I read a great part of the literature on Mormonism. Working with these leads, furnished by family descendants I had met in Salt Lake City, I was able to acquire material on Ann Eliza through newspapers of the period in Salt Lake City and in other cities where Ann Eliza lectured. I was also able to run down a good deal of her correspondence, and the published and unpublished writings by persons who had been associated with her. Almost all of the research was dug up from primary sources. In the end, I came up with what I believed to be the complete story—everything essential about the lady except the time and place of her death (despite hundreds of letters chasing down clues that produced no facts), which I believe were erased from history by Mormon relatives. *The Twenty-Seventh Wife* was published in 1961, became a bestseller, went into three printings, and was also published in Great Britain, France, Germany, Italy, Spain, Portugal, Brazil. Although it was an extremely objective biography, the Mormon hierarchy was very unhappy about it. In 1964, Dr. Hugh Nibley, professor of history and religion at Brigham Young University, published a book called *Sounding Brass*, a book which became the monthly choice of the Latter-Day Saints Book Club, and this book was entirely devoted to an attack on me and on *The Twenty-Seventh Wife.*

But in the creation of novels—which has been my greater interest in the years since—I've been able to satisfy both this detective-as-author research side of me and the imaginative, make-believing side of me. My novels as "faction" or "factual fiction"—are usually mixtures of fact and fiction.

SG: Critics have mentioned that you have managed to weld the two together.

IW: Yes, I love to do that. My earliest books were nonfiction. But eventually I found this too restricting. The novel gave me a chance for more scope and variety. All of my novels, except my very first one, *The Sins of Philip Fleming*, and my latest one, *The Fan Club*, which will be published in 1974, have involved a good deal of research.

The Sins of Philip Fleming had no factual documentation and included no designed research whatsoever. The story, not the idea, simply was born out of my head, spontaneously, from what I'd heard from other men. On this knowledge I superimposed my own experiences, feelings, and above all, my creative imaginings. From *The Chapman Report* to *The Word*, but much more in the latter than the former, I had wholly invented and imagined characters and situations, but purposely set out to acquire factual information that seemed to belong in the narrative background and in dialogue. In *The Fan Club*, working on it in 1972 and into 1973, I went back to attempting a novel almost devoid of factual research.

SG: What about your readers—do you think they turn-on to your research? Does "faction" or the so-called documentary novel have especially great appeal to the popular audience?

IW: From my own experience, from the reaction to my novels, I have absolutely no doubts that most readers like this kind of novel. Of course, readers don't like this kind of novel merely because it integrates fact with fiction. They like it because it offers a good story—"a good read," as my publisher, Peter Schwed, likes to say—or because the subject, characters, plot, or narrative hold the readers' attention and interest.

I've never had a letter from a reader who objected to my use of fact in fiction. Quite the contrary, readers are always telling me they liked the novel, and they liked the research. They are often grateful for having learned something while reading for entertainment. Most of my mail on

The Seven Minutes and *The Word* praising the books also thanked me for all the added information on pornography and obscenity and on religion and the Bible.

There's another point to be made, too. This interspersing of fact with fiction gives most readers the feeling of absolute authenticity. I've had endless letters on *The Word* asking me if The Gospel According to James, which I had invented, really had been dug up by archeologists, translated, and where copies might be purchased. Well, I suppose it seems real because I created the text partially out of my imagination and partially out of long neglected very real gospels that were passed over when the New Testament was assembled and sanctified. Further, while creating my gospel, I drew upon the best research, archeological discoveries, theories and speculations of the finest Biblical scholars. This gave my fiction an added underpinning of realism.

I remember after I'd finished *The Prize*, there was a mild disagreement among the editorial staff of my publisher on my use of fact throughout the novel. Those who felt it was excessive believed it might slow down the narrative thrust of the story. Those who felt it was just right felt that it enhanced the believability and excitement of the book. In the end, I had to make up my own mind—and since my mind had dictated the kind of book it was and is—I allowed it to remain a documentary novel.

A minority of critics objected to the mixture of fact with fiction, but most agreed it helped the book. I've already recounted some of this disagreement in my book *The Writing of One Novel*. On the one hand there was *Newsweek*, which complained that the novel had "all the local detail of a James A. Fitzpatrick Traveltalk." On the other hand, there was Clifton Fadiman in the *Book-of-the-Month Club News* stating, "What gives this narrative its motive power is the extraordinary vividness of the Stockholm scene and the seemingly absolute authority with which Mr. Wallace details secret after secret involving actual awards of the immediate and distant past."

Who is to say what is right? It's an entirely subjective matter. Each reader makes up his own mind.

The main thing is this—I was writing as I pleased, doing the kind of novel I wanted to do exactly as I enjoyed doing it. And the vast public out there tuned in, agreed with what I was doing, and told me so by reading the book and writing me in praise of it.

SG: Why do you think this kind of novel has such wide appeal, at least as you write it? Do you have any speculations at all on what the appeal of such fact-fiction materials say about its readers?

IW: Well, I remember reading years ago in Maugham's *The Summing Up* that the purpose of the novel is not to teach, not to educate, but to entertain. Basically, I'm in accord with that. If you sit down to write a novel merely to educate or proselytize, you are not really writing a novel, and certainly you may wind up with no one out there to educate or proselytize at all.

I sit down to write a novel—let's say *The Plot*—because I'm interested in several characters, in an idea, in a fictional conflict. I'm interested in spinning a tale about some people in my head and their personal stories. I want the novel to be about something more, as well, to make a point through its fiction. But I don't have any thought about weaving facts into my fiction simply to teach. If my five major characters in *The Plot* were drawn to Paris because of a nuclear summit disarmament conference, then naturally there is going to be talk in the story about nuclear disarmament, just as there would be in real life. So I try to learn about disarmament, since my characters are depending upon me to provide them with dialogue. When I created the character of Dr. Dietrich von Goerlitz in that book—he was inspired by my long meeting with Krupp back in 1953 in Essen, Germany—I felt I should learn the facts about the munitions business as practiced in Germany today. I got in touch with the Krupp plant, asked for their catalogues and other information—and that's how I learned that Krupp will sell you a ready-made city and place it down for you anywhere in your country. All for a price. That became very useful to me in *The Plot.*

In short, I wasn't trying to teach my readers anything about nuclear disarmament or munitions making. I was simply trying to brief my characters, who should and would know about those specialties.

At the same time, I'd guess the reader's attitude toward facts in a novel is different than when he faces facts nakedly in his daily life. The reader is interested, curious, and utterly overwhelmed by the daily output of media information he or she can't possibly digest. The reader has too much to cope with in daily life to spend spare time studying, learning. The reader wants to relax or escape. So the reader might buy a novel of mine and hopefully become absorbed. In its pages he escapes, relaxes—but at the same time receives an almost subliminal input of off-beat, inside factual information. Education sugarcoated. Learning painlessly. The reader of *The Chapman Report* learns a good deal about real sex surveys. The reader of *The Three Sirens* learns a considerable amount about anthropology. The reader of *The Word* learns a good deal about the business of religion.

This is not all speculation on my part. This is the feedback I get through letters from readers.

There have always been documentary novels. But I've been credited with—or blamed for—starting the whole cycle again. I remember the first time I met Arthur Hailey at a cocktail party given by Nelson Doubleday in Los Angeles. Hailey had just written *Hotel,* and upon our introduction he said to me, "I'm trying to do just what you've been doing. The next one is airplanes. Great fun, isn't it?"

It is great fun—certainly for the writer, if he is of such a mind—and it is greater fun if millions of readers find it so, also.

I will make one exception to my statement that I don't set out to teach in a novel. Every so often, researching or thinking out the background for a character, I'll stumble upon some true incident, or recollect one, that I find irresistible. I want the whole world to share it with me. I'll never try to work such an incident into a story by force, simply for the sake of getting it in. That would be a story stopper. But if my fascinating incident belongs naturally to a character in a certain scene, I'll remember it and have the character use it. For example, in researching *The Prize*, I learned from Nobel Prize judges how anti-Russian they were—anti-Czarist as well as anti-Communist Russia—and I had factual evidence of this. Then, when I was writing the novel, I came to an important scene where a character named Gunnar Gottling, an eccentric, embittered Swedish writer who'd consistently been denied the Nobel Prize, had a confrontation with my protagonist, Andrew Craig. In this scene, Gottling tells Craig the real reason why Craig had won the Nobel Prize for Literature—not for Craig's literary genius but because Craig had once written an anti-Communist novel which had achieved a certain popularity in Scandinavia. Well, it was a perfect scene for me to go into the facts of Sweden's anti-Russian bias, which in turn led naturally into Gottling's fictional revelation of Sweden's anti-Russian bias that got Craig the award.

Another more recent example. Years ago I had heard or read somewhere the true story of a San Quentin prisoner on Death Row who blew up his cell using the explosive ingredients in a deck of playing cards. By 1972, when I was writing *The Fan Club*, I'm sure that story was far removed from my conscious memory. At one point in the book, I reached a scene where my heroine, Sharon Fields, who had been abducted and was being held prisoner, tries to think of ways to escape. There seems no way possible, and her mind— an actress's mind, impractical, full of make-believe—seizes on a memory of an exotic true incident she'd once heard while making a prison picture. It was possible to blow out the side of a room with the ingredients in a deck of playing cards. So I entered that fact into my fiction.

I enjoy the entire process, I love fact. I love fiction. In my novels I find it enjoyable to blend both, and thus have the best of two possible worlds—a synthesis that marks my fiction for better or for worse.

As to what this says about my readers? You asked that, didn't you? It says that they are as curious about the world and its inhabitants as I am. It says they want to know a truth that is truer than reality through fiction, but want that perceived truth supported by clearly factual evidence drawn from life and its histories around us. What this interest says to me also is that there can no longer be unadulterated fiction in the sense the purists would have it. The world is crowding us too much, flowing vats of information and experience into us at great speed. There are few earthly mysteries or wonders from afar. Unadulterated fiction can no longer compete with actuality. So fiction must absorb actuality, and then it must make an effort to exceed it to arrest and hold the weary through instinctive or carefully devised story-telling.

SG: Earlier you spoke of novelists who write straight out of their navels. All right, could *The Fan Club*—since you indicate that it grows out of your own experiences—be called a navel-novel? Or is the difference you've tried to articulate between the type of work you do and that of the "navelists" one that is not tied up with personal experience so much as the ability to make others' experiences your own?

IW: In answer to your first question—no, *The Fan Club* is not a navel-novel in the sense that I have defined that sort of novel. It is not a story based strictly upon an experience I lived through physically and in my head.

In reply to your second question—navelists do not usually try to make others' experiences their own. A navelist is involved mainly with his personal experiences and all other things he draws upon are secondary. On the other hand, a novelist will usually make others' experiences his own, and

draw upon his personal experiences either to supplement what he has observed or imagined about others.

Of course, no novelist can be classified as wholly one type of writer or another. We all draw upon a common pool— a pool filled with personal experiences, observations and perceptions of persons we've encountered, as well as our reading, our fantasies and day-dreaming. It is the degree an author depends on one resource or another in the pool of inspiration that invites him to be classified as a certain type of creator.

By doing research for works of fiction, I feel I am not imitating or repeating myself in successive novels. I am always into something brand new. Perhaps the protagonists faintly resemble each other—but that is because each one, in part, reflects some part of my own character that is hidden. In my latest novel, *The Fan Club*, there is no surrogate character representing me—there is no hero—there is only a heroine. And there is no research. I wanted to experiment, attempt a novel drawn entirely from my imagination, observation, experience, feelings—drawn out of my experience of years in this community—in Hollywood, in Los Angeles. In *The Fan Club*, I'm not dealing so much with my psyche as I am with my perceptions of persons I've been involved with or whose lives I've brushed against—Marilyn Monroe for one—in the movie colony, as well as more ordinary people, whose frustrations and yearnings have fascinated me.

SG: You're interested in people, aren't you?

IW: Oh, yes. For a writer, that's what it is all about. To be honest with you, I'm interested in two things, and I have an ambivalence about discussing them. I'm deeply interested in my fellow human beings. I have great curiosity about people. I am one of the few writers I know who really listens to people. Most writers, it seems, don't listen to people because —well, I suppose because they're alone so much that they're eager to talk to someone, and because their egos are so battered (if not by publishers and editors, then by critics and

Irving Wallace surveying a climactic scene for *The Fan Club*. See opposite page for his description.

Eighteen minutes after leaving the coastline, he had
finally spotted Fortress Rock in the near distance -- the
craggy, russet sandstone boulder etched against the blue
sky, so familiar from those times when he had taken weekend
excursions with Nancy and Tim, and explored the surrounding
area with them.

A minute more, and the huge shadow of the massive
boulder enveloped his truck, and he had slowed down trying
to figure out where best to park. There was a dirt promon-
tory off the highway past the boulder, but he had decided
against it. He had driven on, lost Fortress Rock in his
rear view mirror as he swung around the mountainside,
crawling along, watching for a side road. At last, perhaps
two hundred yards beyond the boulder, further than he had
planned to park, considering the weight of the luggage he
would be carrying, he had come upon a perfect side lane, a
sizable hikers' path, that angled off past a high clump of
wild bushes and disappeared. He had spun the truck onto
the path, jolted down it, and had finally left the vehicle
in a place where it was screened off from the highway.

From manuscript pages 761-762 of *The Fan Club.*

the public or lack of public) that they feel no one out there is listening, paying attention to their words, so they compensate in social relationships by talking instead of listening. They miss a good deal.

To some extent, I was prematurely women's lib. At a dinner party, I rarely went off to join the men. I stayed with their wives or female companions. I still do. I find women infinitely more interesting than men—not only because they are the opposite sex, and more attractive and exciting in a sexual way—but because they are more mysterious to me. I know less about them. I want to know more. I want to know what women are really like. That doesn't mean I can write women well, convey their true femininity, in a book. It simply means I want to understand them and write them truly. In fact, two of my novels, *The Chapman Report* and *The Fan Club*, are told essentially from the female point of view, a difficult undertaking for a male author but very rewarding when it comes off.

So one of the two things I'm interested in is people, yes—which translates into creating characters when writing. But the other thing I'm interested in—and generally even bringing this up is verboten for most writers, because it is a red flag that antagonizes critics—is ideas. I'm interested in the novel of ideas, the book that grows out of an unusual approach or notion, the book about something.

I think most novels that fail today—fail to find a publisher or, once published, fail to find a public—are born to die unread because they are usually banal. They contain nothing fresh or exciting. From the moment of conception, they are doomed to arrive stillborn. A novelist should approach an old subject—be it love, marriage, faith, murder—in a new way, with a fresh slant. Or he should tackle a unique theme. How can I illustrate this? Well, I once read a book about a man who'd reached a crossroads in his life, and was at a point where he had to relive and review it, and the author put the man on a sea voyage for this purpose. Now, had he kept the man on the sea voyage, with no conflict other than inner conflict, it might have been a good book, but it also might have been an ordinary book. Instead, the author had the man fall overboard, and the entire novel is told in his head as he treads water, tries to stay alive, suspensefully hopes to be rescued. That slant made the book gripping. Or speaking from my own experience—I always wanted to write a novel about the problem of blacks in this country, about racism and the suffering of blacks. Time and again I was tempted to tell the story of a black moving into a white neighborhood. I always rejected it because it was too obvious, too warmed over. Then, one day I was struck by the idea of a black man, a black senator, accidentally succeeding to the Presidency of the United States. That instantly excited me. It was challenging, provocative, certainly arresting, and so I wrote *The Man*, which came as much out of an idea as out of character.

SG: Well, regarding your interest in people—how do you express this interest in your work?

IW: I think that's obvious. More than most novelists, my books are populated by great numbers of men and women. Many of the backgrounds, habits, speech tricks, emotional problems in my characters are drawn from real people I've come to know fairly well or from others more casually met about whom I perceive—wrongly or rightly—certain things.

   I don't go around in an obnoxious way during my daily life looking for people, or exploring people, so that I can use them in one of my novels. But, after all, I do have a writer's mind, and all writers' minds have big blotters inside them. Years ago, when I met a man or woman—usually a woman—who interested me, I would jot notes about that person when I reached home. I had one folder, crammed with typed notes, which was called my "Damaged Women" folder —meaning, I'm attracted to bright, neurotic women to whom life, at one time or another, has been unkind. They are usually just slightly off-center, and to me very special. But I don't make as many notes about people any more—except what I write down briefly in my Journal—because I find when I am actually creating a character, I remember almost everything that I earlier used to note on paper.

Take Faye Osborn and Maggie Russell in *The Seven Minutes*. I know both of them very well. But each of them is not based on a real woman I'd known. Each is based on many women I've known or observed, as well as the dream woman—good dream or bad dream—I want her to be. Faye Osborn, the spoiled rich woman—I began going out with her when I was in high school in Wisconsin. I went out with another Faye in Berkeley, and yet another in Los Angeles.

SG: Do you provide varieties of people in various situations to show the diversity of humanness? Or do you deal with types in order to catch essences and basic qualities of humans?

IW: You pose the question very kindly. Some literary critics would pose it more harshly—do you try to write individuals or stereotypes? Obviously, I make every effort to develop an individual human being, different from any other, on paper. Yet, to the critic or reader some of these individuals appear to be graduates of one type of person.

In reality, in the world, every person is different, as different as his fingerprint. But, remember, his fingerprint isn't that different, and neither is he or she. There are many broad types of man or woman physically, emotionally, even as to heredity and environment, and within each type there are shadings of difference. And so it is, often, with characters in a novel.

For example, each of the four leading men in *The Fan Club* is different, one from the other, and each from anyone I've ever known, and I look upon them as individuals. Yet, an argument could be made that timid Brunner, the accountant, or blustering Yost, the insurance agent, are types. Of course, I think of all the salesmen I've met and while each is a different individual, still all have certain characteristics in common. In that sense, every individual is a type. I think I could make an excellent case for proving Sadie Thompson, Marcel Swann, Nana, Buck Mulligan, Anna Karenina were strikingly unique individuals, but each one of a type that had been written many times before and that has been written many times since.

I will add this. If you are writing a novel mainly about one character, you have considerably more opportunity to get beneath the skin. Your book becomes, in effect, a single filled out portrait, with little else on the canvas. But if you are writing a novel of great scope and plot, filled with multiple characters, you have less opportunity to go into every pimple and wart of each person in your cast of characters. On this kind of canvas, the human figures are less detailed, they are shown in simpler strokes, because the activity on the canvas, and the landscape as well, demand attention.

SG: Does your work present recognizable characters to your readers, that is characters that are familiar to them and who create an empathy between reader and character? Or do you try to present characters that are completely novel and unique, unfamiliar to the reader? Or is it a combination of the unique and the familiar that provides the basis for your people?

IW: I'd like to think my novels contain a combination of characters, evenly balanced between ones really unique and ones extremely familiar. Actually, I think I lean slightly more to introducing characters at least slightly familiar to the reader.

I don't think a writer deliberately tells himself he'll have this many unique characters and that many familiar ones. At least, I don't. For the most, my invention of characters is done instinctively. But, looking back at my choices, I think I come up with a pretty fair mix.

I like to have characters that I—and through me the reader—can identify with. Certainly, for the reader, a familiar character, one whose life resembles his life or the lives of others he knows, can be reassuring. You believe in a character who reacts to certain things the way you do, and it makes you feel better to read about a fictional character who secretly has your sexual hangups or perversions or who has your enthusiasms or doubts. The reader is very interested in such characters, and feels at home with them. And I attempt to create such characters because I feel at home with them.

There is one more point to be made about the value of familiar characters. I once remarked elsewhere, on this point, that we all live in the Age of Anxiety, to coin nothing. Fear and inadequacy, in every area, infect most of us. To follow characters in whom one faintly recognizes facets of one's self, be they base, shameful, confused, or complex, and yet facets not precisely one's own, is intriguing and provides a sense of relief. By standing aloof from the novelist's paper people, unseen by them, the reader may watch a small part of himself, or of someone close to him, perform—and know how it will come out, as he will seldom know how it will come out in real life.

On the other hand, I suspect most readers also like to read about characters they can't identify with, yet characters about whom they are very curious to know more.

You may choose to call such characters unique, but they are actually characters who are larger than life—certainly larger and far removed from the average person's life—the kind of characters the average person may read or hear about but will never come to meet or know intimately. Such a character might be a billionaire similar to Howard Hughes or J. Paul Getty. Such a character might be a politician similar to Teddy Kennedy or Chou En-lai. Such a character might be a legendary woman like Greta Garbo or Golda Meir. Or, indeed, one like the remarkable Marie Duplessis who inspired Alexandre Dumas *fils* to create Marguerite Gautier, heroine of *Camille*.

In short, I am interested in both familiar, identifiable

The Three Sirens

Secretary - *Tall - Flat - Face wrong - legs okay - hips wide -*

She was homely - all wrong - but three times slept with men and was the best - problem one of communicating her best to what they wanted -

Unfair that beautiful girls got almost all men - most no good in bed - made part slutty - this didn't mean conversely homely girls better - but she was one - perfect sex machine but no one knew or wanted to know —

• Reviews three affairs as often did — one boss ashamed later other never saw again other couldn't locate him

Sublimated in efficiency pity of it -

Perhaps an isle what she has to offer better than beauty — Here zest, and still more important than beauty

Ennobled - picked queen of Festival -

Determines to stay —

Something spoils it - Fellow prudish to reform her — will never want or appreciate her yet she goes because wants to belong - forgoes choice of the best -

Characterization sketch for *The Three Sirens*.

characters, and unique, exotic characters—and I suspect the reading public is equally interested in both kinds, presuming the fictional creations are handled with knowledge, understanding, and authority in a novel.

In *The Three Sirens* I made use of both kinds of characters. The central character was Dr. Maud Hayden, one of America's leading anthropologists, whom many members of the press saw as a fictional representation of Dr. Margaret Mead or Ruth Benedict. Since Maud Hayden was a renowned authority figure, the average reader might not identify with her but he might be curious about her, curious about the human story of one of the headliners in anthropology. The remaining characters were the kind that the average reader might meet, recognize, come to know quite well in daily life— or indeed mirror something of the reader's own life. My character, Sam Karpowicz, a photographer with concerns about his sixteen-year-old daughter, was meant to be a familiar person. Also, Harriet Bleaska, the ugly but warm nurse with so much love to give and no takers. Also, Lisa Hackfeld, wealthily married, bored, and frightened as hell at the knowledge that tomorrow she will turn forty years old.

Sometimes fictional characters unique and special to the reader will at the same time be familiar because they seem similar to someone well-known that the reader has read about in the press or seen on television for many years. For example, in *The Plot* one of the major characters is a former President of the United States—Emmett A. Earnshaw—known to everyone as The Ex. Many readers felt comfortable with him, because some chose to see him as a fictional character similar to or based on Dwight D. Eisenhower. In the same way, many readers saw the character of The Judge in *The Man* as someone based on Harry Truman after he had completed his presidency and returned to the Midwest. Now, neither of these characters was drawn exactly from Ike or Truman, yet they were similar to their supposed prototypes, and I was interested to know how men like that behaved after they were out of office and out of power. And so I

Irving Wallace at the White House during research on *The Man*. 1963.
(Photo: Harris & Ewing)

tried to find out more about two such men by dissecting them in fiction. And, as it turned out, readers were as interested in reading about such characters as I was in writing about them.

But this is dangerous talk. The literary tradition, promoted by professors and critics, is that the best novels grow out of character. A novel that grows from an idea is suspect—a gimmick, a polemic, and certainly unliterary. Of course, that attitude is utter nonsense. Countless fine novels have been essentially idea novels—John Buchan's *The Thirty-Nine Steps*, Lewis Carroll's *Alice in Wonderland*, Conan Doyle's *Lost World*, George Orwell's *1984*, even Thornton Wilder's *The Bridge of San Luis Rey*, to name a few. But I don't want to overdo this, either. Because basically, it is true that a novel will be better and will last longer if it develops out of character. An idea can date, be wiped out fast by changing times and mores. But a book growing out of a memorable character—be it Robinson Crusoe or Emma Bovary or Sherlock Holmes—will be timeless and survive all change.

SG: A number of your novels, at least on the thematic level, really broke ground on a mass scale. I think that's what intrigues me most. Somehow, topics which were then restricted to elitist artists—like looking at racial things—you have managed to deal with those same topics and disseminate them to the masses.

IW: That's exactly right. You see, it takes a long time for a subject that is kept strictly in the province of the elite to filter down to the masses. Now we're dealing with the subject of popularizing, of reaching the vast reading public. Of course, no one knows what will appeal, what will be accepted by the public. A writer can only write for himself, and what interests or excites him.

Concerning this question, I had a fascinating conversation in Cannes, on the Riviera, with James Baldwin some years ago. We were introduced on the terrace of the Carlton Hotel, and we stayed up one night drinking together. During the evening, at some point or other, I said to him, "Jim, you know, I think you're spending too damn much time lecturing. You're only getting to a few hundred people at a time. I know you're turned on, passionate about your message, about discussing racism, but it is taking you away from your books. I think you can perform a greater service by writing. In a single book you might get to millions of people." Baldwin agreed with me. He said, "Yes, I'm afraid I've set myself back the last few years by trying to get to people in person. Well, anyway, I'm off to Istanbul to resume on a book." Then Baldwin said, "Incidentally, Irving, what are you doing?" I said, "I've just finished a novel about a black man who becomes President of the United States." He looked at me with disbelief. "The hell you have. What credentials do you have to do that? How can you write about a black man?" I said, "The same way you were able to write about a white man in your last novel." He said, "Fair enough." I went on. I said, "I think I have every right to do a book about a black man. I can't do what you, as a black author, can do. None of us, no whitey, can write a book about blacks the way a black can—the way you or Ralph Ellison or LeRoi Jones can. But I'm sensitive enough to understand what you've gone through, and I think I can come close to reflecting what you all feel. The main thing is that I can do something about the problem that many black writers can't do. I believe I can reach a wider white audience." Then I explained to Baldwin, or at least I think I did— it may have been an afterthought—that I was fortunate at that point to have a vast following among readers, not only in the United States but abroad, around the world. As a bestselling white author, millions of readers who had enjoyed my previous books might buy my latest book, even though a black man was the protagonist, even though it dealt with the racial issue. They might buy *The Man* because they believed that they would get a good story, hopefully a story that

In a composite Nation like ours, made up of almost every variety of the human family, there should be, as before the Law no rich, no poor, no high, no low, no Black, no white, but one country, one Citizenship, equal rights and a common destiny for all.

A Government that cannot or does not protect the Humblest Citizen in his right to life, Liberty and the pursuit of happiness, should be reformed or overthrown, without delay.

*Fred*k *Douglass*

Washington D.C. Oct 20. 1883.

b174 DOUGLASS, Frederick (1817-1895). American Negro writer and lecturer. Escaped slavery, 1838. Worked for anti-slavery. Consulted by Lincoln. U.S. Minister to Haiti. AMs.S., 8vo, Washington, Oct. 20, 1883. "In a composite Nation like ours, made up of almost every variety of the human family, there should be, as before the Law, no rich, no poor, no high, no low, no black, no white, but one country, one citizenship, equal rights and a common destiny for all. A Government that cannot or does not protect the humblest citizen in his right to life, Liberty and the pursuit of happiness, should be reformed or overthrown, without delay."

Frederick Douglass manuscript in Irving Wallace's collection. He used it for the epigraph to *The Man*.

would intrigue them. In that way, my Trojan Horse of a novel might enter into homes where no James Baldwin book has ever appeared and where no Ralph Ellison book has been heard of. I do remember Baldwin saying, "I hope it works." I said, "I hope so too. I just have the feeling that I can get to people you may not be able to get to on this subject. Those readers might avoid a novel about racism written by a black because they'd feel they were buying propaganda for the blacks, from a black. Those same readers, who know me as a storyteller with no single axe to grind, would more likely buy my novel on blacks because they don't feel I'll be lecturing or propagandizing them. They know me, from the past, as a writer of suspense and entertainment, and they'll hope for more of the same, and indeed they'll get what they bargained for. But they'll get more. They'll get your message, which is also mine."

And in fact, it worked out that way. *The Man*, to my own astonishment, turned out to be my biggest hardcover seller at that time. It's never ceased selling and being read, in this country and around the world, and my mail from readers has been incredible—white readers admitting they'd been intolerant or bigoted but finding themselves caught up in *The Man*, well, it worked profound changes in their racial attitudes. That's been the most important thing of all to me, in terms of that novel and some of the others. The fact that what I've written has not only entertained people, but has actually changed them, educated them, made them better human beings by my standards.

SG: You made a point just now I'd like to know more about. You said that your readers "know" you, and that allows you to discuss issues that another writer might be unable to approach if he wished a large audience. This brings to mind several questions. How important is the establishment of a name with the audience for the popular author? Is it, in a way, some extension of the idea of the star system where people went to see movies because they "knew" the stars?

Irving Wallace's first book poster. In 1957 the New York Area Booksellers Association picked *The Square Pegs* as their choice for the summer publishing season. This poster was displayed in their windows.

And further, what do you feel are the expectations of a reader who knows Irving Wallace? How do you work with those expectations? Can they limit you in any way?

IW: To begin with, let's discuss the importance of having an established name. I can only give you the point of view of the literary agent and publisher in the marketplace. Almost every publisher considers a Name Author important. This is simply because the publisher feels the known author has a pre-sold audience. Someone once sent me a transcript of a talk Bennett Cerf gave in 1966, when he was the head of Random House, to an audience of writing teachers. Cerf said, "Just think what an agent can make out of a new book by a Truman Capote or by an Irving Wallace or by a James Jones. . . . Having Wallace as an author is like having Richard Burton and Julie Andrews together in a movie."

Speaking of Bennett Cerf, I used to hear him quoted as saying that even before Random House published a new John O'Hara novel, they could count on 35,000 hardcover copies being sold immediately. Those 35,000 book readers were buying the new novel blind, entirely on O'Hara's reputation, because he had not failed his readers before, they had enjoyed him before and expected they would again. A few years ago, I was told by the sales executives at Simon and Schuster that before a new novel of mine came out in hardcover, they could count on 65,000 copies being sold, no matter what the novel was about, sold to readers who had enjoyed my previous novels.

Well, when a publisher can bring out a novel that he feels is already pre-sold to 35,000 or 65,000 readers to begin with—before the book itself and its subject are reviewed or advertised, and when he knows that the average novel by an unknown or little-known author sells no more than 2,000 to 4,000 copies in its entire life, then you can understand the importance of the Name Author to the publisher.

In paperback, the value of a recognizable name—the name of an author who has had previous bestsellers—is even

BEST-SELLING PAPERBACKS

COMPILED BY BESTSELLERS MAGAZINE

BESTSELLER

OCT. 1970

Rank			Months on List
1	**THE SEVEN MINUTES** (Pocket Books 78508) $1.50 *Irving Wallace* Dramatic conflict over sexual freedom, obscenity and human rights in this blockbuster from the author of "The Man" and "The Plot."		1
2	**THE FAME GAME** (Fawcett M1477) 95¢ *Rona Jaffe* A savagely candid novel of today's super celebrity players who will do anything to win the fame game!		1
3	**FIRE ISLAND** (Avon W206) $1.25 *Burt Hirschfeld* Sizzling scoop on the playground of the ambitious young, the jaded old, the outcasts, the desperate and the damned.		2
4	**THE GODFATHER** (Fawcett Crest, 01388) $1.50 *Mario Puzo* A record-smasher in hardcover, this novel of the criminal underworld of the Mafia should shatter most paperback records.		7
5	**GOOD TIME COMING** (Bantam Q5480) $1.25 *Edmund Schiddel* The sensational story of a Harvard-bred young publisher, climaxing in a drug-filled sex orgy, this shocker goes the limit!		2
6	**BLACK STAR** (N.A.L. Y4333) $1.25 *Morton Cooper* Robin Hamilton; a beautiful, talented and seductive young black girl who seeks love and success in the world of show biz.		1
7	**THE LOVE MACHINE** (Bantam T5400) $1.50 *Jacqueline Susann* Gripping story of the love and intrigue of a ruthless TV network wheeler-dealer.		3
8	**THE ANDROMEDA STRAIN** (Dell, 0199-1) $1.25 *Michael Crichton* A frantic scientific search for an antidote to an outer space genocidic germ scored 30 weeks on best seller lists.		4
9	**MY LIFE WITH MARTIN LUTHER KING, JR** (Avon J100) $1.50 *Coretta King* The legend which was a spiritual sunburst for us all now transcends the headlines and becomes a very personal inspiration.		2
10	**THE DECEMBER SYNDROME** (Pyramid V2291) $1.25 *Robert Carson* Dr. Henry Brulard, handsome super-salesman of sexual rejuvenation, promised new life at his fabulously successful clinic.		1
11	**THE AMERICAN HERITAGE DICTIONARY** (Dell 0207-1) 75¢ *William Morris* "The freshest, most innovative, most useful dictionary; more entries and more illustrations than any other paperback dictionary!"		1
12	**MY LIFE WITH JACQUELINE KENNEDY** (Paperback Lib. 68-409) $1.50 *Mary Barelli Gallagher* The behind-the-scenes "know-it-all, tell-it-all" best seller from her personal secretary.		2

Movie Best Sellers
CATCH-22 (Dell 1120-1) 95¢   Joseph Heller   M*A*S*H (Pocket Books 77232) 95¢ Richard Hooker
AIRPORT (Bantam 553-08982) $1.50 Arthur Hailey   STRAWBERRY STATEMENT (Avon W161) $1.25 James Simon Kunen

New Books

THE SELLING OF THE PRESIDENT 1968 (Pocket Books, 78036) $1.25   *Joe McGinniss*
A reporter who sat in on the Nixon campaign candidly describes the "packaging" of a Presidential candidate.

MILE HIGH (Dell, 5625-1) $1.25   *Richard Condon*
Novel of a powerful Irish-American family who reproduce an entire Swiss resort village in an upstate New York palace.

IN THIS HOUSE OF BREDE (Fawcett Crest, P1466) $1.25   *Rumer Godden*
A dramatic account of the personal and religious lives of an enclosed community of nuns in England.

A PLACE IN THE COUNTRY (Avon, W211) $1.25   *Sarah Gainham*
A novel... The locale: Vienna, a city recovering from the ravages of war; The People: struggling to re-make their lives in the aftermath.

MANNEQUIN: MY LIFE AS A MODEL (Bantam, N5569) 95¢   *Carolyn Kenmore*
A sensationally frank non-fiction story of the beautiful $300 per hour girls in the modeling profession.

Best Bets for Best Sellers

SIAM MIAMI (Paperback Library, 68-441) $1.50   *Morris Renek*
A sensual novel of a Judy Garland-like singer. Her problems on the way up, her talented, tough-fragile personality.

THE WIFE-SWAP REPORT (Dell, 9558-1) $1.25   *John Warren Wells*
The uncensored story of the new sexual underground, the thousands of middle class couples who are engaging in group sex.

DO IT! (Ballantine, 02038-125) $1.25   *Jerry Rubin*
The most important statement made by a white revolutionary in America today. "The communist manifesto of our era."

ERNEST HEMINGWAY: A LIFE STORY (Bantam, Y5554) $1.95   *Carlos Baker*
A non-fiction account, spanning six decades—from Hemingway's happy boyhood in Chicago, to the tragic last years of his life.

AMBASSADOR'S JOURNAL (Signet, W4383) $1.50   *John Kenneth Galbraith*
A highly personal, witty, revealing account of the "Kennedy years," by the late President's Ambassador to India.

ARTHUR GODFREY ENVIRONMENTAL READER (Ballantine, 02039-1-095) 95¢   *Arthur Godfrey*
Seems like old times as TV and radio personality Arthur Godfrey brings to the attention of the public the urgency of our crisis.

ED McMAHON'S BARSIDE COMPANION (Pocket Books, 77215) 95¢   *Ed McMahon*
A hilarious blend of 'round the bar games, bets, spirited stunts, jokes and tricks from TV personality Johnny Carson dubbed a "lush."

The Seven Minutes — the number one paperback bestseller in October, 1970.

more important, I'm told. The average reprinted novel goes out in an edition ranging anywhere between 75,000 copies and 150,000 copies. If it catches on, there are new printings and editions. If it doesn't catch on, it has had its entire run. The first printing of my first novel in Signet paperback was 150,000 copies. But after that I had seven successive best-selling novels. So when it came to bringing out the paperback edition of *The Word*, my paperback publisher felt safe in putting out a first printing of 2,000,000 copies.

But then—what are we speaking about when we speak of a Name Author? What does it mean? What's in a name?

It means the author has a well-known name because thousands or millions of readers went out and bought his previous book or many of his earlier books and were pleased with what they read, and were ready to read more by the same author.

Which brings me to your comparison of the Name Authors in publishing to the star system in motion pictures. They are legitimately comparable, I'd say. Millions of people out there enjoy a Barbra Streisand film, as they used to enjoy a Humphrey Bogart film. Well, two things appear to happen. First, if people were satisfied by one Bogart film, they felt sure they'd be satisfied in seeing another. Second, as they enjoyed one Bogart film, and then three or four, they became involved with Bogart. His screen image, the lifestyle he projected, became very much a part of his followers' own lives. They got used to him, depended upon him, and attended him faithfully.

In a sense that also happens with authors. I remember, as a reader, the first time I read an Arthur Koestler book in the early 1940's. The book was *Arrival and Departure*. I was so taken by the novel, by the mind that had created it, that I sought out every earlier book Koestler had written, from *Scum of the Earth* to *Darkness at Noon*, and read all of them, and for years continued to buy and read each new Koestler book, fiction and non-fiction. I liked what he wrote, how he wrote, and the kind of person who could write such books. Readers become very close to the novelists they enjoy reading.

I can speak from my own experiences with readers in the last fifteen years. Hardly a day passes that I don't get at least one letter from someone, man or woman, young or old, telling me they've just read a novel of mine for the first time— perhaps a recent book like *The Fan Club* or *The Word* or a reissue of *The Man* or *The Sunday Gentleman*—and they enjoyed it so much they want to read everything I've had published in the past and everything I will write in the future. Invariably, they want to know more about me personally, about how I get ideas, how I write, about my private life, my tastes, my plans for the future.

I appreciate those letters. That's touching and being touched, communicating both ways and relating.

I can understand this whole name and star interest, even more in books than in movies. In a book, one person, one individual, creates a new planet and populates it with new people, all born entirely out of creative imagination and knowledge. This whole new world, encased in the package of a book, goes into another person's home, into the privacy of his home. And then this other person shares the exploration and the adventure of the new planet with its creator, and a friendship, a warmth, an understanding is established that links the pair—reader and author—in a relationship sometimes as close as real human friendship or love.

SG: What do you feel are the expectations of a reader who knows Irving Wallace? How do you work with those expectations? Can they limit you in any way?

IW: The reader who had been absorbed in two or three of my novels usually tells me he is looking forward to the next one in which he expects more of the same.

But more of what—precisely? I suppose the reader expects storytelling, an exciting plot, suspense, a variety of characters, a blend of fiction and fact, an unusual background and a fresh, controversial idea or theme. I mean, that is fairly much the feedback I get—when it is articulated—in my mail, or in conversations with readers.

These expectations do not affect me consciously in any way I know. For one thing, they don't pressure me to repeat myself as to subject matter or theme or story. When *The Chapman Report* was being widely read, I received an endless amount of mail begging me to do a sequel, carry on with the characters and the sex survey. This also happened after *The Man* was published. And it occurred more than ever with *The Word*. Readers wanted me to follow up *The Word*, extend it, do more of it, dramatize what happened to Steve Randall after my book ended. They implored me to go on and tell more of his quest for truth in investigating The Gospel According to James.

It's all flattering, wonderful, but I doubt if I'd ever write the same kind of book or subject twice. I'm too interested in new subjects, people, backgrounds, conflicts, to play it safe and repeat myself. I'd much rather take the risk of tackling absolutely new themes. I find it exciting and stimulating, alive-making, to go from an intense novel about censorship and pornography to a complex novel about religion to a strange and violent novel about kidnapping in which ordinary men confront reality in their relationships with women.

Frankly, what readers may expect of my writing, or hope to have from me, does not inhibit or limit my creativity in any way. I'm at a stage as a writer where I seek to please no one other than myself. I simply have to go along on the dangerous premise that what pleases me may please millions of others. If I repeated myself, out of insecurity, to please the public, the public would tire of me quickly. And I would tire of myself. As it is, I go into each new book unfettered, free and my own person, and always extremely eager and enthusiastic about the new planet I'm about to explore and the new people I'll soon meet and the sights I'll come to see.

Robert Nathan, Irving Wallace, and Henry Miller at Irving Wallace's Los Angeles home.

SG: Do you have many writers as friends? What are your thoughts on writers hanging together? Does this help them or does it make them ingrown, separate them from the reality of the outside world?

IW: I'll put it to you simply. I have a great number of fellow writers as close friends, occasional friends, acquaintances, and every once in a while I tell myself I should mix more with people in other professions. So I contrive to meet different people who are in different social circles. I get involved socially with psychiatrists, attorneys, filmmakers, physicians, sociologists, businessmen, aircraft workers—and it is always interesting—but after a time, when I really want relaxation and stimulating talk, I return to my own more familiar writer's circle and I feel more comfortable. I also count many newspapermen and bartenders around the world as friends. I find them among the most vital and stimulating persons I know.

   Howard Fast once told me he knows almost no writers socially in New York. Up in Aspen, Colorado, my friend Leon Uris isolates himself pretty much from the literary communities. On the other hand, whenever I visit Gerold Frank in New York, I find him surrounded by a great circle of literary people ranging from John Barkham to Frederic Morton.

   I remember when Dr. Allan Nevins left New York and Columbia University to move to Pasadena and do his work at the Huntington Library. He called Irving Stone and asked him, "Don't you have any informal writer groups out here who meet to drink and indulge in good conversation?" Irving Stone called me and suggested we form such an informal group to gather at one another's homes once a month to exchange ideas. I went along. So from 1959 until 1971, we had this group—Ben Ray Redman, Paul Wellman, Harold Lamb, Allan Nevins—all dead now—were in the charter group, as was Robert Nathan, and sometimes guests would join us like David Lavender or Clifton Fadiman or A. L. Rowse

Joseph Wambaugh, Robert Nathan, and Irving Wallace at a June, 1973 American Booksellers Association party. (Photo: Peter C. Borsari)

Irving Wallace and Leon Uris.

Irving Wallace and James Jones.

from Oxford. And the talk was good, damn good.

I remember one evening when we had the group over to our house for dinner. Allan Nevins was telling us how, in effect, he had been patted on the head by General George Washington. I challenged him on the tall tale, and he explained how it came about. As a youth, Washington Irving, the author, was introduced to General George Washington in the street and received a pat on the head from the Father of Our Country. In *his* old age, Washington Irving passed the pat on the head on to George Putnam, his publisher. When Putnam was an old man, he, in turn, passed the pat on to the young Allan Nevins. And now Nevins was ready to pass this historic pat on to someone else. Our daughter, Amy, then ten years old, had come into the room during this story, listened with wonder—and then Allan Nevins spotted her, beckoned her, and he laid his hand on her curly-haired head and said, "Amy, I pat you on behalf of General George Washington." She refused to wash her hair for a week, and she is still in possession of the right to confer that pat on another, who will hopefully pass it on to someone in the 21st century.

Like New York, our Southern California abounds in writers one runs into all the time, many of whom I count among my best friends—Budd Schulberg, Eric Ambler, Ray Bradbury, Christopher Isherwood, Bernard Wolfe, Max Schulman, Harold Robbins, Joe Wambaugh, Eileen and Robert Bassing, David Chandler, George Zuckerman, Carlos Castaneda —or writers coming and going like John Kobler, Arthur Hailey, Mario Puzo, even Charles Schulz, whom I consider a writer—just too many to remember, but with few exceptions they make the best companions on earth. Then, of course, when we go to Europe, there are Paul Gallico and John Collier, who live on the Riviera—

SG: You go abroad regularly, don't you? Are those trips largely for relaxing between books or for researching a specific work?

Gerold Frank, Artie Shaw, and Irving Wallace at a publicity party for
The Word. March, 1972, at the Plaza Hotel in New York.

Irving Wallace with Ralph Nader and Ray Bradbury, 1973.

Irving Wallace and Melvin Belli, 1969. (Photo: Cal Pictures)

IW: Actually, for both reasons. I find that travel breaks my routine, breaks neurotic compulsive habits, gets one off the daily treadmill. Even though I live fifteen, twenty minutes from the Santa Monica and Malibu beaches, I rarely use those beaches. But when I get away from Los Angeles, go to Europe, I'll spend part of every day in Juan-les-Pins or Cannes on the beach or go over from Venice to the Lido a few hours every afternoon to enjoy the sand and water. Both resorts are fairly much as I've described them in *The Plot*.

At the same time, I can't think of a day I've ever spent in a foreign country where I wasn't also looking for some specific material for a book or unknowingly soaking in some material that surfaced when I needed it.

I took my first trip outside the United States after I graduated from high school—went with two friends down to Mexico, Guatemala, Honduras, Colombia, Panama, Cuba—that was in 1934 and 1935. Then in 1940, with some speculative magazine assignments in hand, I went to Japan and China. When my wife and I were married in 1941, we honeymooned in Mexico and Cuba. After my stint in the army, Sylvia and I had a second honeymoon, a memorable one, starting in Sweden and working down through Denmark to Paris, to London, going on to Madrid, Barcelona, Cannes, Rome, Berne.

I went back to Europe alone on magazine assignments in 1949 and 1953. Then I stopped traveling abroad, mainly because I'd given up magazine writing and was concentrating on trying to make the transition into books. When *The Chapman Report* had its success in 1960, we resumed traveling once more, this time with our children, and except for missing two years, have gone annually since. Out of those trips, of course, grew *The Prize*, *The Plot*, *The Word*. The last time abroad, we took a French ship to Istanbul, Athens, Constanta in Rumania, and Russian cities like Odessa, Sochi, Yalta.

I'd say my favorite cities on earth, among those I've spent any time in, are Paris and Venice. When you wake up

Irving Wallace at Juan-les-Pins, 1964.

Irving Wallace at Harry's Bar in Venice.

Irving Wallace on the Left Bank of Paris, 1971.

Irving Wallace at Balzac's house in Lorre Valley, France. 1971.

Irving Wallace at the Alexander Pushkin Memorial, Odessa, Russia. 1971.

in either of those cities, it's Christmas morning every day. Always full of surprises. I think 1940 Shanghai was the most exciting city I ever visited. Now I'm rather drawn to returning to Istanbul and to visiting China again and perhaps India.

I think traveling to new lands, trying to understand alien cultures, is very useful for a writer. It opens him up. Still, traveling is not an absolute necessity for a writer. The Brontë sisters didn't travel very extensively, except in their heads. And while firsthand research is helpful—at least I find it so— it isn't a must. I recall meeting James Hilton in Los Angeles in 1947, at a time when his *Lost Horizon* was still a worldwide hit. I asked him if he'd gone to Tibet to research the book. "No," Hilton said, "not at all. I went to *National Geographic* magazine." Not having the opportunity to travel is no excuse for not writing about places you haven't seen. As I always tell beginners who use this excuse—Da Vinci didn't have to attend The Last Supper to paint it.

SG: What about your reputation as an author in foreign countries? Could you discuss it? I know you are widely published abroad. What do your books appeal to in that overseas audience? Is the foreign readership different in any way from the domestic?

IW: I can only report to you what my foreign publishers and agents report to me and what I read and hear about foreign editions of my books in the press and from foreign readers.

Some or all of my books have been published in about every nation on earth where books are published and sold. I've had my greatest readership abroad in Great Britain— including South Africa, where my books are either banned or Number One on their bestseller lists. I seem to have an equally wide following in Spain and Mexico, where every one of my books has been published by the same publisher in one country or the other, depending on Spain's Censorship Board. My Spanish editions are constantly brought out in hardcover, paperback, and now in leather-bound sets sold

German ad for *The Seven Minutes*.

Irving Wallace

AS TRÊS SEREIAS

contemporânea | portugália

Ad for Portuguese edition of *The Three Sirens*.

door to door. I'm widely read in two languages in Yugoslavia, and well read in West Germany, Netherlands, Portugal, Japan. My novels, to date, have had only a fair audience in France, which irks me because I love France so deeply that I want to be loved by everyone there.

How can I gauge my reputation abroad? My novels are steady bestsellers in numerous foreign nations, so the verdict of the reading public is favorable. I'm discussed to a degree that surprises me by newspapers and magazines in Stockholm—where I'm a dirty word—and Moscow and London and Paris and Belgrade and Tel Aviv and Mexico City and Rio de Janeiro and Taipei. In the foreign press, I'm usually discussed in popular terms—the number of copies my books have sold, the amount of money they've earned, the controversies they've kicked up. The critics abroad have been mixed about me.

Take England. I'll get a lovely review from Cyril Connolly, and a savage review from Auberon Waugh. I'll read two reviews from London on *The Prize* and they invite schizophrenia. One review, from *The Times* of London, will tell me that my bulky novel "seems better suited for stopping doors than for reading." Yet, in the same mail I will find a review on the very same novel from the *Illustrated London News*, and this review reads: "This week has produced a novel of such outstanding excellence that it deserves high precedence. Irving Wallace . . . has now produced *The Prize*, a long, enthralling story. . . . This book is quite the most brilliant example of this genre that I have ever read; indeed, I cannot recall any novel published since the war of which I can speak with such undiluted enthusiasm. In all its 754 pages, I could not detect a phrase or even a word—let alone an incident or a development— wrongly placed or ill contrived."

As I've said before, what is one to make of such contradictions? You learn that you lose a few, you win a few, and pray that they spell your name right. You learn very fast to become philosophical.

The window of a large bookstore in Mexico City. 1972.

You've wondered what my books appeal to in that overseas audience, and, indeed, if my foreign readers are different in any way from American readers.

Well, you know, when my earliest books were published, there was only one audience for me, and that was the audience in the United States. It mattered to me most how people I knew or could see or understand regarded my work. The earliest foreign sales affected me as they affect most of my friends who write books—as something exotic, remote, a few more pounds or pesos or yen to be used toward writing another book, and best of all, a foreign edition as a trophy and conversation piece on the shelf.

But then, speaking for myself, all that changed drastically—my attitude changed—with the publication of *The Chapman Report* in so many foreign editions and with my annual trips to Europe. For one thing, my novels began to be read so widely abroad that reactions from the press as well as readers began to pour in. For another, in traveling regularly to Europe I began to know more and more Englishmen, Frenchmen, Germans, Italians, and so many of them knew me from successive foreign publications of my various books and from the exposure of my books in the leading foreign periodicals. Now, for the first time, I saw foreign readers as people I could relate to, I looked upon them as important to me as any audience back home.

Now I follow the reception of my books outside the United States with as much nervous interest as I do in the United States itself.

And now I can see that what there is in my books that appeals to foreigners is probably the same as what appeals to American readers. One can't know exactly, but from what I hear it would seem that readers in foreign countries are as interested as American readers in storytelling, unusual plot situations, varieties of fictional characters, and the interweaving of authentic fact with imaginative narrative.

However, the foreign readers differ from the domestic readers, at least to a degree, in several areas. Letters I receive

Irving Wallace autographing French edition of *The Man* at Le Drugstore, Paris, 1965.
(Photo: A. Chaptel, U.S.I.S.—Paris)

British hardcover edition of *The Chapman Report*.

from readers in India, from those in Spanish-speaking nations, show great interest in engaging me in long philosophical discussions on my themes or on a human problem posed in one of my novels. Many British readers are prone to emphasize, in correspondence, the decisions and actions of my characters. Also, British readers often pluck some facts buried in my fancies, and with erudition usually elaborate upon them. American readers, on the other hand, tend to simply tell me how my book was one of the best they'd ever read, that they couldn't put it down, that they hope I have another one coming out soon—and to thank me for the insight in the novel that has resolved some confusion or conflict in their own personal lives.

SG: Do many of your readers comment on the sex passages in your books?

IW: Perhaps one-fourth of the readers who write me will discuss a particular sex scene or a character's attitude toward sex in one of my books. Of the small amount of unfavorable mail I receive, most of it is concerned with the fact that I had written something explicitly sexual. This was particularly true in the responses to *The Word*.

But most of my mail is embarrassingly favorable, and those readers who refer to sex—seven out of ten of them women—are grateful for my treatment of the subject, for the openness and honesty. Whenever *The Three Sirens* is reissued I get a fairly large number of letters thanking me for it—at least a dozen readers have told me the novel had been recommended to them by their psychoanalysts or psychologists—and they appreciate the book as one that aided them in getting rid of their inhibitions.

SG: What about your own inhibitions, Mr. Wallace? Obviously, you are uninhibited when you write about sex. But, if I may ask, are you equally uninhibited in your own life?

IW: I'll handle that one gingerly, remembering the last time I even touched upon the subject in print. The Publishers Hall Syndicate asked me to write a feature article discussing the question you've just posed. When my article appeared in major newspapers throughout the country in February, 1970, I thought I was going to be lynched. Newspapers coast to coast were inundated with angry letters from Constant Readers.

Let me read you from the article. I began it—

"How does an author who writes a book advocating freedom—wide-open freedom in reading, viewing, speaking, in behavior with other people—live up to those printed words in his day-to-day relationship with his family, his friends, and, indeed, with himself?

"What is it like to practice what you preach?

"It's not easy. In fact, it's hell."

In this article, I admitted that in *The Seven Minutes* I had advocated freedom to read anything for everyone, and that I had shown two young women indulging in premarital affairs. As a result, I had then been bombarded by indignant parents who had asked me if I would permit my children to read the dirtiest book around. I had answered, "Yes, I would, rather than censor it and thus force them to go behind the barn to leer at it secretly." I had been asked if I would permit my daughter to engage in premarital sex. I had answered, "I doubt if I'd have anything to say about it. But if I did, I would accept it, if it resulted from deep mutual love."

I then described the long, tortuous route I'd taken since adolescence to arrive at this attitude toward freedom. I confessed, "Not until grammar school was I entirely certain what an adult female looked like anatomically. One afternoon, in manual arts class, some more advanced contemporary permitted me to peek at a photograph of a nude woman. The veil fell from my eyes. . . . And yes, there were bad girls and good girls. Just before I graduated from high school, a very 'nice' girl was expelled from school because a teacher discovered she had been distributing her favors too freely among her male classmates. Suddenly, she was a 'bad' girl.

"In short, in my formative years, that part of love that is sex was generally considered a synonym for sinful. That's how all of my friends were brought up—in fact, how most of Depression America's adolescents were brought up. And that wasn't very long ago.

"But somewhere along the way, something drastic happened. Psychoanalysis, the emancipation of women, two world wars, Kinsey surveys, scientific studies like the Masters and Johnson report on sexual response in humans, all these events liberated a new generation from puritanism. And these events shook up my generation. Most of us have changed a good deal, become healthier, but we haven't been able to change enough."

Well, anyway, to be perfectly honest with you, that's where I'm at right now.

My attitudes toward sexual relations, toward women, are beautiful, healthy, clean, loving. I can have my characters act this out on paper without any problems. But when I'm put in a position to act out these attitudes in my own performance and behavior, well, sometimes I can be as free as my characters and sometimes I can't, because a small part of me is inhibited by my early upbringing, environment, and the social mores surrounding my early years.

Now, of course, besides my wife, I've known a fair number of other women intimately. Most men have, I'm sure. Most writers certainly should. Because while you can write about many human activities without experiencing them first-hand, I would say sex is not one of them. As I told an interviewer once, "It would be difficult to write a love scene if you were a virgin." For the writer, sex is one act where being there, doing it, enjoying or suffering it, feeling it, must be experienced, first-hand. If your experiences are good, you know the best of it. If your experiences are poor, at least your wish and imagination can define and color the rest of it.

Of course, for the married writer, marriage in itself is a

Irving Wallace with Art Buchwald. Paris, 1961.

tremendous inhibition. I've been involved in discussions on this any number of times with novelist friends. If you write a kinky sex scene knowledgeably, and your wife knows you didn't have that scene with her and it reads too true to be imagined, then you're in trouble as a person. If you don't write the scene, self-censor it, then you're in trouble as a writer. It's a no win situation.

Which reminds me of a hilarious breakfast I had once in Paris with Art Buchwald—it was after I'd had several international bestsellers and Art had reached the peak of his fame writing in Paris, before moving to Washington, D. C. "Remember the way it used to be," he said to me, "all those years before we were married, ready, eager, able and willing, and none of the girls would have us because we weren't exactly what you'd call the most handsome guys in the world." Art shook his head. "And now look at us," Art said with disgust, "now suddenly we're successful, we're handsome, and now the most beautiful girls in the world, the Copa girls, the Lido girls, are throwing themselves at us—and we can't do a damn thing about it—we're married!"

But that's not what's important, really, having every girl in the world or not having her. That has nothing to do with writing. Nor does a mate have anything to do with not writing.

All that is important in writing about the opposite sex, presuming a minimal amount of experience, is to understand what it is to love and be loved, to understand human needs and feelings, to be able to give of one's self as well as to receive.

If you are capable of love, and can communicate it, then you can survive your inhibitions, both as a human being and a creative person. I'll say that now as I've said it before in my novels.

SG: Then let's take one of those novels. The whole cultural effect of life in suburbia and the sexual thing were especially important in *The Chapman Report*.

21 July 61

Dear Mr Wallace,

Thankyou for your letter pointing out the error in my SUNDAY TELEGRAPH article. I shall write to the Telegraph, and expect the editor will publish my apology for the mistake. It seems to be a very widespread idea over here; I have read it in several newspapers, including a full-length pre-publication article, published (I think) in the Sunday Express. So it is hardly surprising if this is a generally held notion in this country.

I sympathise with your irritation on the point. I have suffered myself at the hands of TIME magazine, and nothing would give me more pleasure than to see that malicious rag go bankrupt. In my case, in fact, I think I have rather more to complain of than you. Your book was a best seller, and while it was amusing reading, I dont suppose you meant to write another Crime and Punishment when you wrote it - or even Lady Chatterley. My own books, after the OUTSIDER, were fairly serious in intent; but TIME produced cheap personal abuse of me, with the nastiest sneers they could dig up, and made no attempt whatever to discuss my books. I've had the same treatment from Newsweek too.

Please dont suppose I am belitting THE CHAPMAN REPORT, which was brought out over here by one of my own publishers; I read the American edition (un-hacked) before English publication. I found it interesting reading, although it struck me that you gave the theme less extensive treatment than it deserved. It could have been made a real investigation of the sexual impulse on a level as serious as Lawrence and Wedekind - particularly if you had introduced a character who represented the mystical element of sexual experience, a kind of Lawrence figure, to offset the rather shallow women. As it was, I felt that, towards the end of the book, you lost even your human interest in your characters, and threw in rapes and murders ad.lib for the sheer fun of it. The consequence was that, taken as a whole, the book produced in me a kind of distaste. (I hope you take these comments in the spirit in which they're offered, which of one practitioner to another.) I have myself written a long novel on the sexual impulse, dealing with sadism, which was a modest best-seller over here, and am planning an even bigger one - so there is no sniffy literary distaste here.

Apologies again for the error.

sincerely

Colin Wilson

Colin Wilson on Irving Wallace's use of sex in *The Chapman Report*.

IW: It was first published in 1960, at a time when open discussion
of sex as related to women, the entire idea of the free and
liberated woman, was still somewhat taboo. I had always
wanted to write a book about some married or once-married
young women I knew in my community, in Brentwood, a
western suburb of Los Angeles. These were, for the most,
young women who thought that marriage, that financial
security, would fulfill them completely. But after they had
their men, their money, they were surprised at how unfulfilled they remained, how restless and bored and unhappy.
I wanted to dramatize, as well as make a commentary upon,
the lives of women, of marital relationships, in a typical
upper-middle-class American community. But another book
about suburbia? No, I decided not to touch it until I discovered an unusual springboard that would plunge me—and,
hopefully, the reader—into the story. And one day I found
it, it happened. I was hit by the notion of a group of sociologists moving into my neighborhood to do an intimate sex
survey of married or once married women. And that did it
for me.

　　After I'd written *The Chapman Report*, I still had the
niggling feeling that I hadn't said everything I wanted to say
about the sex lives and love relationships of women in our
culture. There was much more to be said. Many readers
urged me to write a sequel. But I didn't want to write about
these particular women anymore. I'd written all I wanted to
write about them. So, after writing two more books, *The
Twenty-Seventh Wife* and *The Prize*, I still felt *Chapman* had
left me with some unfinished business. I decided to get the
rest of it off my chest. So I wrote *The Three Sirens*. In
truth, I had meant to write it right after *Chapman*. But the
press outcry about *Chapman*, the attacks against me for having written so frankly about sex, that and three censorship
trials abroad unnerved me, and I put *The Three Sirens* aside.
With the public and critical acceptance of *The Prize*, I got my
confidence and nerve back, and finally tackled *The Three
Sirens*. The book proved a big bestseller, but not quite as

Publicity and public relations: *The Three Sirens* used this poster to promote the 1963 novel.

big as *Chapman* or *The Prize*. The reason was clear to me. The book was perhaps a half dozen years or so ahead of its time. It was too daring and, to some people, too threatening.

What I had set out to do in *Sirens* was to take these same suburban-type Americans who'd inhabited *Chapman*, and obliquely dramatize their hangups, and in a larger sense the overall hangups in our American culture and society. To achieve this, I created a group of nine varied men and women, anthropologists and lay persons, who take a field trip to study a unique and long-hidden Polynesian society, which has preserved a culture utterly different from our own. The Americans arrive on this remote South Sea island to study these primitives, to put them under a collective microscope— and what they find is that the uninhibited and unusual practices in the Sirens society concerning sex, love, marriage, children, justice force the Americans to look inward, study and reevaluate themselves and their own society.

Well, a fair number of persons in my circle who'd read the book were upset by it. They felt it was just too frank and radical at that time. A lot of critics fell on it because they thought it was just another exercise in overt sexuality, an effort to exploit *The Chapman Report*. So I lost some points, but I gained them all back with my next book, *The Man*. But now, more and more today, as *The Three Sirens* is continually reissued in paperback, I hear from new readers —in fact, numerous psychiatrists have been recommending the novel to their patients—saying this is a marvelous book that's plugged in to today. I thought it was always plugged in, but apparently in the beginning too early to shed light. Fortunately, the times finally caught up with the book. For all the earlier criticism, as I've said, it became a bestseller, although I suspect it was read largely for the wrong reasons.

SG: A number of your books deal with very new things. *The Chapman Report*, in the movies, at least, ushered in a whole new age of dealing with sex and sexuality and a candid and frank attitude concerning those things.

IW: Again, you must remember how early that was. The climate of the times, when the book was published in 1960 and motion picture released in 1962, was much different from today. In that period we were on the cusp—on the border between the restraints and repressions of the past and entry into a new age of liberation and a time of new freedoms.

Except for certain major city libraries banning the book and the USIA refusing to distribute it abroad, *Chapman* was not really banned in this country. But, as I've mentioned, the book ran into terrible trouble abroad. There was a real flap in West Germany. In April of 1961, the Ministry of the Interior in Stuttgart labeled the book "youth-corrupting." At a hearing, the ban was rescinded. In March, 1962, the Senator for Welfare and Youth in Bremen proposed banning on the grounds that *Chapman* was "dangerous to youth because it arouses sexual fantasies of juveniles." At a hearing before the Federal Examining Board for Juveniles, the book was cleared a second time. As I learned later, the German translator had deleted most of the book except the sex. *Chapman* was already in its third printing—and a smash best-seller—in Italy, under the title *Foeminae*, when the State Attorney in Milan ordered all copies seized on the grounds that the book was "of an obscene nature which, under the pretext of a survey of female psychology, describes sexual abnormalities and lurid episodes." The trial of the Republic of Italy versus Longanesi, my Italian publisher, took place in Milan during January of 1965. My publisher obtained affidavits from me describing my intent in writing the novel, and giving evidence that it had been praised by Dr. Margaret Mead and Jacqueline Kennedy (who'd called it one of her favorite books when she'd been First Lady). Fourteen other foreign publishers of *Chapman* also supported the book at the trial. In the end, Longanesi and the book itself were acquitted, and the book was reissued.

While the book was banned outright in Ireland and in South Africa, it underwent a curious trial in England itself. I'd originally sold British rights to Longmans, Green, of

London, my regular publisher in England, in 1959. Longmans had the book set in type, ready to roll off the presses, when censorship groups brought pressures against Longmans, threatening to boycott their textbooks and religious lines if they went ahead with *Chapman*. Longmans was intimidated, backed off, decided not to publish. My agent then sold the book to Arthur Barker, Ltd., of London, who acquired the plates from Longmans and went ahead and published—and had themselves a bestseller.

The Zanuck movie version of the book also ran into heavy waters. The film was emasculated by the British Board of Film Censors before they allowed it to be released with an X rating. And for a while the movie was banned in Italy.

SG: Later, when you did *The Seven Minutes*, you were dealing with kind of the same situation.

IW: Well, in fact, it was my experience with the censors over *The Chapman Report* that inspired me to create *The Seven Minutes* a decade later. And the very events I dramatized—indeed, foresaw—in *The Seven Minutes* are coming to pass today, thanks to the idiocy of the Nixon Supreme Court—the same arrests, confiscations, trials are taking place, and will escalate.

I mean, honestly, what in the hell is obscene? Some things we know are obscene—like injustice and crime promoted by the White House, like mass murder on the ground in Vietnam and from the air in Cambodia, like ignoring the impoverished and the minorities and the elderly while playing footsy with the wealthy multi-national corporations. That's all legally okay. But to have free choice to see or read about a nude body, lovemaking, the diversities of love, that's filthy and criminal. It's really madness, I tell you, for anyone to think they can legislate men's minds. Our reaction to a given book, film, work of art, is so personal, so subjective—and so different from our neighbor's—that it would be impossible to rigidly apply one standard of what is clean and what is dirty for everyone.

As to people who say a little censorship might be a good thing, I say—there can no more be a little censorship than there can be a little pregnancy. Like cancer, once censorship starts, there's almost no stopping it. And ultimately—well, I think George Bernard Shaw put it best when he said—the extreme form of censorship is assassination.

SG: And what is the link between obscenity and social action? Do pornography and violence influence?

IW: Of course, that is the key issue, one that has not and may never be resolved. Does pornography provoke antisocial behavior? I'm satisfied, from all the findings I've seen—and I've seen most everything that exists—that there is no link between pornography and antisocial actions. At most, pornography can lead to masturbation, which hurts no one and won't even give a person pimples. There is no evidence it sends men out on sprees of raping—the great American puritanical obsession. The few rapists or murderers in the past, who'd been found to possess a book of pornography, were learned to have been mentally ill long before they bought a dirty book.

The only comprehensive survey on the subject I've seen was taken by a sociologist at Northwestern University and by a psychoanalyst at Chicago University, who announced their results in 1969. I corresponded with them. They polled 3,400 psychologists and psychiatrists nationwide—and 80% of those polled replied that there was absolutely no connection between reading pornography and antisocial behavior. More interesting, I think, is that 87% of the experts polled believed people who want to censor pornography have deep sexual problems of their own. It was a Frenchman who said—of all sexual aberrations, chastity is the strangest.

Anyway, until scientific evidence proves the contrary, free choice to read or view pornography—including pornography found in the Bible—should be afforded all persons.

SG: An even broader area of what you're dealing with is what effect do the popular arts have on people and their actions. Is it a situation where the popular arts are reflecting attitudes that are already in the culture or do the popular arts have the power to influence and initiate attitudes in culture?

IW: I hate to admit that life can imitate art, but I'm inclined to believe it does. In the matter we've been discussing, I repeat I find no evidence that a work of popular art can motivate a man to rush out, crouch in the bushes, and jump the first passing woman he sees. In that sense, art does not generate certain activity or behavior in real life. Art can affect one's fantasies, ambitions, attitudes and, even to a degree, one's behavior—but I doubt if it can make a non-violent person into a violent one.

You know, when I was doing research for *The Seven Minutes*, I used to mingle with the masturbatory set in those hardcore pornographic bookstores. I could see that reading or viewing pornography was an extension of their lives and a fulfillment. Those were people who could not relate to the opposite sex or their own sex in a love relationship. And so they achieved pleasure second-hand by reviewing this hard-core fantasy material. Well, I still see nothing wrong with that, not at all. It's sick, but harmless. I daily see more sickness in more public places, high places—in government, in business—

SG: That does affect people—

IW: You're darned right. As to life imitating art, I can think back to a time when I was a youngster in Kenosha, Wisconsin, a limited, small town world, when movies and books represented the great outside world to me. Certainly, going to the movies every Saturday affected my attitude of what I wanted to do, to be, and the image of myself that I wanted to create for other people. I imagine that I probably started smoking a pipe at thirteen or fourteen because of the young Clark Gable. I can't trace the precise moment of imitation exactly, but I recall leaving a movie theatre after seeing Gable and Claudette Colbert in *It Happened One Night* and thinking Gable looked great, just great, manly, virile, cool, smoking that pipe, and that maybe I should take up pipe smoking.

I was always going to be a writer, as far back as memory reaches, of that I'm positive. Hell, I drew picture stories before I knew how to write words. But if I ever faltered in my single-minded ambition, then surely there was popular art to influence me in my ambition and prop me up and carry me along. A great influence was the fact that I had read a popular novel called *Young Man of Manhattan* by Katherine Brush, about a dissolute young sports writer who wanted to write a great novel one day—and later I saw the movie based on the book—the movie starred Norman Foster and Claudette Colbert, I believe. For me it glamorized a sports writer's existence, and this was about the period I was just beginning to write short stories and articles, and I was so stimulated that I said to myself, Wow, that's the life, that's the kind of writer I want to become. That book, that movie, may have been the final inspirations that turned me into a professional writer—although I can't imagine having become anything else.

I know for certain that many friends around me were influenced by motion pictures in many ways—certainly in their unrealistic, romantic attitudes toward marriage and family relationships—a rotten thing the way they were misled. Of course, the traditions of sex relationships and the institution of marriage were not invented by movies or books, since the traditions and institution were pretty awful before that, but false expectations and unrealistic attitudes were either implanted or solidified by those early, glossy, overblown M-G-M movies, which had no connection in reality to what true life love and sex and marriage and child raising and working was all about. Those slick movies of the 1930's shot through rose-colored lens, committed a fraud on my generation.

In fact, it's kind of ridiculous when you look back on

YOUNG MAN
OF MANHATTAN

By
KATHARINE BRUSH

Irving Wallace

FARRAR & RINEHART, INCORPORATED
On Murray Hill, New York
1930

Title page of *Young Man of Manhattan* given Irving Wallace by Harriet
Schlager, a high school girl friend, in 1934.

the hoaxes perpetrated by hundreds of Hollywood motion pictures—filled with false values and lies about life—on several generations of Americans. And not on Americans alone, but on generations of other people around the world, people who looked at these movies and believed that this was honestly the life in little golden America, and not realizing how rotten American culture and life were at the core. The American standard of living reflected in those Hollywood films was so dishonest, so blobbed over with whipped cream, that it was not only ridiculous—it was downright harmful and dangerous.

SG: But that harm and danger is okay. I mean, it has somehow been made okay by majority vote. So we let it go. Sexual pornography is a minor vote getter, as we were saying in reference to *The Seven Minutes*, and its harm and danger attracts all the public (or at least the official) concern. Isn't it odd that we give so much concern to such a minor facet of our culture and its arts?

IW: Right. I agree with you one hundred percent. But pornography is zeroed in upon as the primary influence because it makes such a marvelous political issue with which to manipulate the electorate. After all, who doesn't, at some time or other, want to clean up something dirty, that he thinks is dirty—who doesn't, to one degree or another, have sexual hangups or inhibitions or fears or concerns? That's why politicians single out pornography and beat it over the head constantly. That's why neurotic weirdos like Richard Nixon, Ronald Reagan, Strom Thurmond feel that prosecuting a book or film is more important than cleaning up a ghetto or fighting social injustice or stopping killing abroad.

But I suspect it is just not politics that motivates the Nixons and the rest in their determination to clean up art according to their standards. Those male biddies are products of our old society, the inheritors and torchbearers of the old Calvinistic and puritanical America, laced through with guilts and the work ethic and the notion that nudity and sex are dirty. They are trying to superimpose their inhibited upbringings upon a way of life that no longer exists.

One evening, at a dinner party, Dr. Henry Kissinger told me—or confirmed the fact—that President Nixon's favorite movie was that epic of violence, "Patton," that movie as well as musicals. Well, the musicals I can understand. Nixon is a product of the age of leering. But how he can find the violence of killing acceptable in art, and the human body and human lovemaking unacceptable—well, it boggles the mind. I've always intended to send a memo to the Oval Office of the White House, a memo containing a wonderful quote from Gershon Legman—"Murder is a crime. Describing murder is not. Sex is not a crime. Describing sex is." What about that? But the politics of pornography, I'm afraid it will continue, although many people are beginning to see through it.

SG: What kind of criticism should the popular arts, and your novels in particular, inspire?

IW: I won't play games with this question. I'll try to answer you as directly and honestly as possible. The big critics in this country, the important ones, are the ones who contribute to *The New York Review of Books*, *Sewanee Review*, *Partisan Review*, and a dozen other intellectual publications of limited but opinionmaking circulation. These critics set up the chain reaction that determines which of the authors in the United States are writing literature. These critics find a writer— oh, maybe a Barth, Nabokov, Pynchon, Bellows—and the word filters down to the universities, where the English Lit professors promote the authors further. The disciples, graduate students writing papers or even undergraduate students, perpetuate the word—that this author is a good bet for posterity, that he is worthwhile and will endure.

Now, there is no author on earth who wouldn't like to be perpetuated in that way in his lifetime or in the hereafter. But the judges who confer these immortalities are members of a closed and very biased club of cultists. Very few living writers who happen to be popular—meaning widely read, very widely read—are ever considered eligible by the club, picked up and promoted by it. In our society, it is difficult to have it both ways—be a darling of the top critics and the academic community and also be a bestseller. A handful have had it both ways—William Faulkner, Truman Capote, William Styron, John Cheever, Lawrence Durrell once, Katherine Anne Porter once, maybe Mary McCarthy, Norman Mailer, John Updike. And most recently, most deservedly, Kurt Vonnegut, he is a good person, a brilliant writer, who's been accepted by the public and the cult critics alike.

One problem for the popular writer is that the cult critics like to discover someone the public doesn't know, they like to plant their flag on an unknown, and be credited for making their discovery. This is their substitute for creativity, and is their ego-gratification. The other problem for the popular writer is that cult critics are suspicious of any author who's read by millions of people. Not many authors are so widely read, but a few dozen are, and they are under a cloud. If so many people read you, you must also be catering to the masses, writing by formula, writing dishonestly. The last is, of course, utter nonsense. I've never met a novelist—and I've known many—who does not write as well as he can write, and write what pleases him and what he can live with. I'm sure there are some of the others, writers trying to slant their wares, although I can't imagine how anyone can know what the reading public wants. But for every dishonest or unworthy bestselling author, there is also a dishonest or unworthy pontificating critic. I'm here reminded of Channing Pollack's remark: "The critic is a legless man who teaches running."

As a matter of fact, this rejection of widely read authors by the Name critics and college instructors is retroactive in judgment, going back to our literary past. I think it is clearly evident that Charles Dickens is not totally acceptable in the halls of academe these days.

SG: That's changing, though. In 1928, when Edmund Wilson wrote the essay on the two Scrooges, that made Dickens acceptable. But he wasn't until then.

IW: Yes, but nevertheless, I believe there is still resistance to Dickens. There was a big Dickens exhibit in Los Angeles several years ago, and a university involved solicited Dickens manuscripts and letters. I had a few items, and loaned them to the exhibit. The sponsors told me they were having a tough time interesting their campus colleagues, and were really trying hard to bring Dickens back into the schools. I love Dickens, but he was so goddam popular—all those people standing on the New York docks waiting for the next chapter of one of his serials coming over from England—and he knocked out all those pages, and went out promoting, and liked the money. Of such things are literary lepers made.

Or take W. Somerset Maugham. He's a better example. Now, no matter what you hear tell, Maugham is a writer's writer. For the last twenty years, I've heard professional writers, respected ones, speak in undertones of the marvel of Maugham. But these same authors keep their praise muffled. Many of them say to me, "Sure, we love him, he was not only a craftsman but one of the finest storytellers in our time, but we can't speak of this too much in interviews because Maugham is *persona non grata* with the literati." I used to ask myself why. Then I knew. Maugham wrote too much, sold too well, had too many of his books filmed.

Concerning Maugham, let me tell you one experience I had. Back in 1946, during my first visit to Stockholm, I was interviewing some Nobel Prize judges, which subsequently led to the writing of my novel *The Prize*. One judge in particular, Dr. Sven Hedin, was especially outspoken. He was on three Nobel committees, voting on three different awards, and one of these was the Nobel Prize in Literature.

"Seriously, I have long learnt the lesson that when I have a book to write I must give it the first place in my life, and my undivided mind. I have become content to set the pains and care it requires against the pleasures of society . . . and to put my fictitious companions in the upper place at feasts"

Charles Dickens

On my wall when I wrote "The Square Pegs"

Irving Wallace

Quotation from Dickens Irving Wallace kept on the wall by his typewriter when he wrote *The Square Pegs*.

When I asked Dr. Hedin why certain authors had never won the Nobel Prize, I mentioned omission of Maugham. Why hadn't Maugham been voted the prize? Dr. Hedin gave me a few lame reasons and finally the real reason. "Mr. Maugham," he said, "was too popular." So there you have it. Incidentally, I had reason to convey this to Maugham when he was living at Cap Ferrat, some years before his death, and he wrote me that he was grateful to finally learn the truth, and he seemed quite amused by the Nobel judgment.

However, the relationship between the critical community and the popular author has changed a little, not much, but a little, in recent years. A number of new things have been happening. For one thing, it used to be that if a living author sold three or four of his novels to motion pictures, he was frowned upon. But now movies are becoming more acceptable in the academic world, they are taken seriously as an art form, studied, expounded upon in learned journals—and no longer is the author who sells the movie rights to his book considered with suspicion.

SG: It's interesting, though, that only since the movie audience became limited is this new interest the case. Movies never would have been studied back in the thirties.

IW: You mean the M-G-M and Paramount kind of glossies made in the hey-day of Hollywood? But you know, now they're dragging all that popular stuff out of the vaults, showing it at festivals and on television, and some of it really stands up and is kind of interesting. You people at Bowling Green, and, indeed, others at a number of universities, are deep into that, and I think it's a healthy thing.

I don't know many critics personally, but the few I do know I've talked to and the others I've read and do read. Some are honest enough to respect public taste, or at least be curious about it and treat it seriously. I read an essay about myself in *Atlantic* recently—it was really a discussion of the popularity of *The Word* and what I was all about—and

VILLA MAURESQUE,
ST. JEAN - CAP FERRAT.
A. M.

22nd July, 1962.

Dear Mr. Wallace,

Thank you for your charming
letter and all the nice things you
say, and for sending me your book.
It was extremely kind of you to think
of me; I was touched and much pleased.

I am shortly starting off on a
journey, and shall take it with me.
I look forward to reading it with
great pleasure and interest.

Once again so many thanks for
your really delightful letter.

Yours sincerely,

W. S. Maugham

Irving Wallace heard from a Nobel judge that Somerset Maugham was "too
popular" to be considered for a Nobel Prize. He wrote Maugham about the
judge's comment and received this letter in return.

the fellow who wrote it, while his skepticism as to my merits was all too evident, seemed honestly interested in speculating about my connection with the public, and he was confused to the point of almost being nice. Plainly, I wasn't his kind of writer. Plainly, too, *The Word* wasn't totally the pre-marketed package he'd expected. He just seemed to be trying to work out how my kind of writer and my kind of novel were being read by millions of people. Fair enough. At least he read my book, and wanted to speak about it—about my book, not my income, my motives, my lifestyle—and recently I've been getting more and more of that from critics here and abroad. They've become curious about the phenomenon of literary popularity, and now, instead of condemning without reading, they are taking off time from Nabokov, to read some of us—read Simenon or O'Hara or Michener or Wouk or me—and trying to analyze us publicly, sometimes to beat the dead horse again or to serve themselves, but more often to honestly try to find out what the public sees in us that they don't see, what the merits of the popular novel are that they've hithertofore refused to examine, and what value the popular novel may have in sociological if not literary terms. They are addressing themselves to the question: What is there about the popular novel that is appealing? That's a small step, but a good step.

SG: You mentioned the word appealing. As we discussed earlier regarding your desire to go beyond in looking at things, in your detective work, perhaps the appeal is in that. That is, Americans, since Daniel Boone, have always been curious about what's over that next hill and perhaps your readers feel an immediate kinship with your unrelenting curiosity. What function or purpose does your writing serve?

IW: Are you asking—why do I do what I do—or why do people read what I'm doing?

SG: Both.

IW: Very well. Why am I doing what I'm doing? First of all, I love writing. I'm going to get right down to the basics. I love storytelling. There's all too little of it in fiction today. Maybe that is because it's too difficult for many writers to structure a story—tell it truly, yet with a minimum of contrivance—in such a way that the reader is forced to compulsively turn each page in order to find out what happened next. So storytelling is central, yet that's not enough, at least for me. Something more is wanted, again for me. In my book, the storytelling has to tell something—something meaningful, something that supplements pure entertainment.

I once had a big rap with someone, a noted novelist and critic, at a university in Paris about that. Because this is a controversial critical issue in France—the whole idea of the so-called committed writer, the writer who takes sides, who says something. Sartre is put down in some literary circles in France because, as a creator, he's not a purist, because he polemicizes. Well, why not? There are no rules. You write as you please and hope someone will be interested. For myself, I'm on Sartre's side. I'm for commitment.

I've said I love writing. It's true. I find the novel is fun to write. But that's too easy an answer, an oversimplification. Actually, writing a novel is a tough, wearing, lonely, and sometimes hateful occupation. At least, in the early stages and toward the end. Like running the marathon, I imagine. But like running the marathon, it is also exhilarating. I'm really saying there are happier things to do than write, because a good deal of actual writing is tense and difficult. But then, not writing, rattling around, is even worse, more tense-making and difficult. So given the choice, the lesser oppression is the act of writing. Also, on the good days, it's a way of getting lost, getting out of yourself, emptying your mind. And there is a sense of satisfaction when the words get down in a fashion that approximates your fantasies and imaginings.

But more than that, make-believing on paper is a good platform for a lot of my thinking and feeling. That doesn't mean political thinking, necessarily, or trying to change the world or the people in it—although there is a lot of Messiah complex in most authors. No, I'm speaking of something broader—the opportunity to explore other human beings, the human condition, through my own psyche and within my limitations. I'm usually very involved with myself when I write, but the personal part of me is masked in my books, probably much more than other novelists who are right up front with themselves in their characters. Only a few people can know when I'm really writing about myself in three different characters in a novel—my yearnings, failures, joys, problems—or when I'm writing from an experience that has happened to me. All of these factors have to do with why I write.

One thing I know for certain—the money factor, the drive to make money, at least for many years, has been the smallest part of my motivation. The money factor—which has been the motivation laid on me and on all so-called popular authors by book reviewers and journalists—has next to nothing to do with what compels me to create. When I read that I'm writing for money, I realize how little, how very little, the critics know of a creative person's psyche. I remember when I quit magazines and movies to do books full-time. I remember swearing to myself that if I couldn't support my family through books—well, I'd go back to doing anything to support us and write books during nights and weekends. My motivation wasn't simply to produce books, but to write as I pleased, on my own terms, to be independent and free. That I made money with my fifth book, my second novel, was important—in that it freed me to write more books—but it was incidental to the main purpose—the opportunity to write what I wished without diversion.

SG: It's almost as if for some reason the money and the fact that you want to make a statement are irreconcilable.

IW: When I go east, as I did last year to do interviews, I find I run into the money question head on. The reporters who come to interview you are interested in discussing your earnings because they've been conditioned to believe that a bestselling author's income is one of the few things that make him newsworthy, especially in off-the-book-page stories. Well, I suppose, considering the indoctrination toward the material in our society, that is understandable. Money is one of the objects that seems to fascinate almost everyone. And if an author has made two or three million on three books, that's rare, that's news, and the press and public want to know the secret—as if there were any.

I've learned, through grim experience, you have to be careful when you talk to the press—as I learned after *The Chapman Report* when, naively, I was frank about what the book had earned, especially from films—naively, because I equated the money that the marketplace paid as evidence of a successful literary enterprise. Until then, I had never known that kind of money. I was a fellow who had always struggled, like most people, to make a living, and, indeed, I had once been poor. I was proud I'd done something so many people were eager to pay for. So when I admitted honestly what the movies had paid for my book all the stories about the book or about me dealt not with my style, characters, plot, but with big money. And boy, from that time onward those articles, those clips, were available in newspaper files, and I went through years of interviewers writing about me only in terms of money, money, money. And to the critics who read these stories, well, as I've said before, they equated money with dishonesty. That's the important thing I learned. If an author is earning a lot of money, that means he is catering to the public. If he's catering to the public, he's not being true to himself and he's not being honest. And once this starts, there's no stopping it. Say what you will about your real reasons for writing, and the critics will still not believe it. Yet, I can't see how a creative person can just write for money, mainly write out of a desire for money, and make it. Maybe a few writers do that successfully, but I can't imagine how, and I've never met one, not one.

SG: If you only have the bestseller formula . . .

IW: Well, that would solve everything for publishers and writers, wouldn't it? In the sense of success and survival, I mean. But there is no such thing as a formula. There's no formula, no foolproof subject—certainly it's not writing about peace of mind, it's not sex, it's not religion, it's not violence. We never know what the public wants. The subjects that catch on are often so unexpected, and public taste is so mercurial.

Of course, for a writer writing about his time, you have to be tuned in. Although, tuned into what I'm not sure. Perhaps to cultural changes. But that's not it, either. My work doesn't reflect the headlines. I'm way ahead of the headlines, inventing and make-believing ones that don't exist.

If someone tied me down and demanded to know what I thought the public wanted, I couldn't tell them. There are some clues, perhaps. I get public response in my mail from readers. I get something else. My publisher, Simon and Schuster, is one of the few that polls book buyers, places a self-addressed stamped card in every tenth book, asking the reader's opinion of the book, why he bought it, what he liked or didn't like about it, and those cards are very revealing. But they only tell you what readers *had* liked, not what they will like. Their value is historical and past tense.

So in the end you write only what excites and pleases you, and hope there are a lot of your clones out there, all on your wave-length. That's inelegant. Let me do better. Back in 1962, *The New York Times Book Review* asked me why I believed *The Prize* was popular. Let me read you the summary of my answer to them: "I can only speculate that in some measure I am one of many storytellers who accidentally or instinctively voices the muted feelings of a body of American readers. I will never be sure, although some critics are, of my exact point of contact with the public. For me, the mystery remains, and I can only continue on my dream journeys with the hope that I will often have numerous good companions to accompany me along the way."

II

SG: To the public at large, you are known as a novelist. Too few people know you once had a movie career.

IW: My skeleton in the closet. Or at least it used to be. When I first became known as a book author, I rarely discussed my years—ten years, off and on—as a screenplay writer. Back in 1960, the literary critics would have considered that an impurity, and would have equated my books with formula films. But as time passed, and the old Hollywood assembly-line disintegrated, movies became more and more acceptable as an art form. And as that transformation took place, I became less reluctant to open the door to my personal closet and show the critics and public my Hollywood skeleton. Hell, my friend Leon Uris, in each novel, lists with pride not only the previous books he's written but his screen credits.

My movie career was very much like that other skeleton in my closet—Irving Wallace, the ghost-writer. Yes, in my early magazine writing days, in the 1940's, just about the time I planned to get married and shortly after I got married, I ghosted articles for a host of celebrities for *Liberty* magazine and several other publications. I ghosted articles for a diverse collection of Names—for Boris Karloff, Gracie Allen, Bob Hope, Red Skelton, for Donald Douglas, head of Douglas Aircraft, for Kid McCoy, Jim Thorpe, for Avila Camacho, President of Mexico. That was another career I kept hidden after I went into books. Finally, about 1967, I began to discuss that career, just as I did my motion picture past. You want to know what opened me up on that?

Okay, it was W. C. Fields. Some years ago, there was a great Fields revival. He became a genuine folk hero among the young. My children and their friends went to see W. C. Fields retrospectives. The kids spoke of Fields with awe, as if he were a legend. One day, overhearing them, I interrupted and said, "Did you know I once knew Bill Fields? In fact, I even ghosted an article for him." My son, daughter, their friends, looked at me as if I was batty. Eagerly, I dug out the old *Liberty* article and showed it to them, but it didn't go down. It was signed "by W. C. Fields." Nowhere did my name appear. The kids nodded over it, but I could see they were not impressed. I sensed they felt the old man was becoming senile and ought to be humored. They plainly didn't believe I'd written it. I realized I'd have to prove it. That night I doggedly rummaged through old cartons of my earlier work and mementos, and I'd just about given up, when—lo, there it was, a dusty framed photograph of the legend himself. It was a sober, dignified picture, full-length, of Fields wearing white shirt and tie, white slacks, black and white golf shoes of the Bobby Jones-Walter Hagen period. Across it in black ink was scrawled: "to my friend/Irving Wallace/with appreciation and thanks/W. C. Fields."

The following day, when the youth clan was again gathered in our house, I appeared with the autographed picture and unveiled it. Sensation! Until then, to that gang, to my children, too, the fact that I was a bestselling author as far off as Timbuktu meant nothing at all. I was just somebody's father. But now—W. C. Fields' friend, "Irving Wallace with appreciation and thanks." I had *known* the great man, actually worked with him. Overnight, *I* was a legend. Now I was somebody, a prophet with honor.

They wanted to know what he was like, and I told them. When I got the assignment to try to do a Fields byliner, the Universal publicist who handled Fields—Bill Edwards was his name—said Fields would not cooperate with any member of

W. C. Fields.

the press unless his interviewer drank with him, matched him drink for drink. I had misgivings because a dear lady friend of ours, who had accepted these conditions for an interview with Fields, got so smashed during the first twenty minutes of the interview that she forgot to take notes, afterwards remembered nothing, and wound up without a story.

Nevertheless, I decided to accept the challenge. I went into spring training. I was a two-drink man. Manfully, in a week, I upped my capacity to four drinks, and found I could still write my name. I was ready. I accompanied the publicist, Edwards, to the comic's mansion in the Los Feliz district of Los Angeles. There he was, W. C. Fields, in his study behind his desk, already pouring booze as we entered. The collaboration began. Four drinks later, I knew I was in trouble. My notebook pages resembled the Rosetta Stone. And Fields was pouring again. After that, at wit's end, I contrived any means to survive. I sipped, asked for the bathroom, got rid of the fifth drink, filled half the glass with water. The sixth and seventh drinks—I was able to dump two-thirds of them in a nearby rubber plant. By the time we'd reached our eighth drink together, although Fields had probably had as many before my arrival, I was still hanging in there. I looked up to ask Fields the last of my questions, when I saw an odd sight. He was no longer seated facing me. He was slumped over his desk, head in his arms, eyes closed. He had passed out. Moments later, Bill Edwards returned with a nurse, and together they half-carried the great man off and put him to bed. And I staggered out into the sunshine and returned home with material for the ghosted story, which a sobered Bill Fields okayed a week later.

After that, I had no trouble parading my ghostwriting past and my screenwriting past and, in recent years, when asked, I've been able to admit that I wrote motion pictures for James Cagney, Doris Day, Natalie Wood, Dan Dailey, Karl Malden and many others.

Now I have nothing to hide. I can be honest.

SG: Then you don't mind talking about your movie career? Very well. As I understand it, your career as a screenwriter started with the army . . .

IW: Yes, that's where I learned how to write a screenplay. But to put it in proper perspective, let's go back a little. I came to Los Angeles from Berkeley in December of 1935. I had quit college after less than a year to get into writing full time. I moved down to Los Angeles because I had an opportunity to write a weekly syndicated movie gossip column for the Thompson Syndicate, which serviced small town newspapers. But it didn't work out.

I was holed up in a cheap movie hotel, a little movie hotel in the very center of Hollywood where broken-down character actors lived. It was called the Re-Tan Hotel, and it was filled with wonderful has-beens who remembered the glorious silent days, and with a handful of tennis-anyone types on the make.

Since the syndicated column hadn't worked out, I continued writing articles and short stories to eek out a living, spent time on an unfinished nonfiction book, and turned out one-act and three-act plays for little theatres. But there I was in Hollywood, at a time when it was the center of the film business and when the air was filled with glamour. So naturally I gravitated toward getting into movies. I was fascinated by them—not so much, in retrospect, by the art of the film, by the medium, but rather by the jackpot mentality it inspired in creative people.

Yet, I did not jump into movie work. I merely put my toe in the water, tested it, to see what was possible. My abiding interest was still books. I had written three or four nonfiction books earlier, none of which were published, and I actually researched and wrote the first part of a collective biography of the early Roman emperors entitled *Portraits in Black,* which was so thoroughly rejected that I remained disheartened about doing another book for three or four years. Also, I began to write more and more plays—one, *And Then*

Goodnight, had a long run in Clark's Little Theatre, and while it didn't earn me a dime, it got me some small recognition as well as a five-year love affair with the leading lady. Also, I decided to go back to college, and I attended Los Angeles City College for a term, and then finally quit formal education for good. Meanwhile, I began to toy with making it big in the movies. I started writing motion picture originals— really novelettes written in the present-tense and broken up into scenes. My first ones were rather poor—good ideas, but I had too much interest in narrative and dialogue and not enough in what was visual. These ran from 20 pages to 50 pages each. Screen originals were selling to studios for fairly high prices in those days. I'd read *Daily Variety* at the corner newsstand, and dream of glory, and hurry back to the hotel and write another movie original.

My first one, I remember, was called *Oddity Hunter,* about a Ripleyesque character whose knowledge of strange facts helps him solve a murder mystery. It was 7 pages, and I was absolutely ecstatic when the prestigious William Morris Agency agreed to handle it. But despite their confidence, the story was amateurish and it did not sell.

I continued to write these movie originals in my spare time, and after three years—it was in 1941, the year I married a bright and pretty fan magazine editor, Sylvia Kahn—I was on the brink of a breakthrough and success. On speculation I wrote an original film story called *Madame President,* based on the life of Victoria Woodhull, who ran for President against U. S. Grant in 1872. A publicist friend of ours, a great raconteur and confidant of many of the stars, Jerry Asher by name—he died a few years ago—was very close to Bette Davis, who was at the peak of stardom at Warner Brothers. Asher asked if he could show my original to Bette. The very next day she telephoned me personally and told me she was mad about the story, just loved it, and wanted to do it. I was out of my mind with excitement. Here, at the age of 25, I was about to become rich and independent overnight, and stop struggling, and be liberated to write books. I walked on clouds for one week—and then came the fall. Bette Davis phoned me a second time, distressed. She had shown my story to the head of the studio, Hal Wallis, and he had said flatly No because he didn't want her doing a costume picture.

The next great Almost came later in 1941. I wrote a 37-page original story designed for movies called *Meet Mr. Miller*, an adventure comedy based loosely on the few known facts about the legendary Joe Miller. A powerful agent, Charles Beahan—he was married to the actress Sidney Fox—headed the A & S Lyons Agency literary department. My Miller story was brought to his attention, and he thought it unique and salable. At that time, Jack Benny was in his prime, one of the kings of comedy. Well, Beahan got my story to Benny, who loved it, wanted to do it, but was over-committed in films and radio and kept trying to find a period when he could take off and do it. For weeks, months, negotiations continued—and I was back on the clouds—and then, once more, a tumble. Benny simply could not find the time to do my story in the foreseeable future. Subsequently, I went through the same negotiations and high hopes with Bob Hope, but after endless suspense the package fell through.

Finally, because I was in a financial bind, struggling, I said to hell with movies, and forced myself to concentrate on bread and butter pieces for magazines, even during my three-and-a-quarter years in the army, when I sometimes wrote evenings and weekends to supplement my income and because I wanted to keep my hand in. But actually, to be totally truthful, I never quite kicked writing those movie originals and trying to hit the jackpot. I must have written from 30 to 40 of them in the 1940's. It was not until 1944 that I sold my first movie original, *That's My Baby*, a 29-page story. I sold it to Republic Pictures for $2,500, and it was produced that year starring Richard Arlen and Ellen Drew. When the film came out, *Daily Variety's* review said, "You can't make a motion picture without some semblance of story," while *The Hollywood Reporter* said, "Blessed with a solid story line."

It was not until January of 1950 that I sold my second movie original, and in some ways this was a turning point, financially and in terms of confidence. I wrote a 13-page screen original entitled *A Young Wives' Tale,* a really moving and honest drama about four army wives all widowed in a single day when their husbands are killed in a plane crash, and how their lives are changed by the return of the only survivor, a bachelor, who'd been with the husbands when they died and unwittingly brought back a legacy for each widow. This movie story was less contrived than anything I'd written for the screen before. It was much closer, in characterization, in natural story development, to the novels I write today. Well, I believed in it and so did everyone else. My agents, Lewis and Molson, got six studio bids. They finally sold my story to Dore Schary, head of Metro-Goldwyn -Mayer, for $20,000, to include my services at the studio for 10 weeks developing my short original into a detailed screen treatment. I moved into Metro. Arthur Hornblow, Jr., was assigned to produce my tale. I wrote a 108-page treatment for him. It was one of the best pieces of fiction I'd written to date. But then, with the expansion of the Korean War, the story was felt to be commercially wrong and was permanently shelved.

But to go back to the 1940's. I was really terribly discouraged about breaking into movies, and I devoted most of my time to magazines, as well as two completed books that were never published. It was my determination to keep away from movies, to give all my energies over to the printed word, my first and truly only love in the field of writing. But then there was Pearl Harbor, and we all caught the fever, had the desire to do our share, and after trying to get into the Marines as a combat correspondent and being rejected for being color blind, I enlisted in the Army Air Force on October 6, 1942—the date is emblazoned in memory. Well, here I was, a strange duck, a published writer with a high IQ, and the Air Force didn't quite know what to do with me. Finally, they sent me to see Lieutenant Ronald Reagan—yes, the Governor himself—who was recruiting for a new outfit, the First Motion Picture Unit of the Army Air Forces, which had leased the old Hal Roach Studio in Culver City, California, where they were to produce air force training films. So that's where they placed me late in 1942, and that's where I was forced to learn to become a screenwriter. There were some great film producers and directors in that air force unit, and officers and enlisted men who were renowned film writers, and I learned screen techniques fast from them.

Then, I think it was early in 1944, the U. S. Army Signal Corps Photographic Center, with a branch in the old 20th Century-Fox Studios on Western Avenue in Los Angeles, headed by Colonel Frank Capra, was looking for an army writer who knew something about Japan. This Capra unit had been assigned to make orientation films for our troops, and one of these was *Know Your Enemy Japan,* and they had no one in uniform who knew the enemy and who was also practiced as a screenwriter. Then they found me. By then I had some experience at screenplay writing. Best of all, for the Signal Corps, I had recently been to Japan doing magazine stories from Tokyo, mostly political, for *Esquire, Liberty,* and many other periodicals. That had been in 1940, when I barely escaped with my life after an interview with Foreign Minister Yosuke Matsuoka of Japan. He had told me, presumably off the record, that if the United States continued to provoke Japan with economic sanctions, then Japan would attack the United States, and I had dared to have the story sent out through International News. Anyway, I was well informed about Japan and Japanese culture, and the Capra unit grabbed me and had me transferred out of the Air Force to the Signal Corps. I couldn't have been happier or more relieved. I hated writing technical training films on flying—felt very insecure doing them—and even more, I hated flying, was petrified about going up in planes. So the change was a good one for me, if anything can be good in the army.

So there I was in a really exciting unit, assigned to collaborate with the only other enlisted man writer in the out-

Irving Wallace at the First Motion Picture Unit of the Army Air Forces, 1942 or 1943. This photo was found in army files by Don Dwiggins while he was researching a biography of Major Paul Mantz.

fit, Carl Foreman, who eventually became a well-known screenwriter and producer in England. Our army producer was a civilian hired by the Signal Corps, a fascinating Dutchman and radical documentary filmmaker named Joris Ivens. And we got right to work on *Know Your Enemy Japan,* a top priority hour-long feature designed to teach our troops about the mysterious enemy's culture and psyche. This was more like it, the kind of writing I enjoyed, and it was here, working with Ivens and Foreman, with Frank Capra and John Huston and Theodore Geisel (better known as Dr. Seuss), that I really began to learn the techniques of screenwriting and moviemaking. I learned an awful lot in those army years.

SG: What were some of the things you learned?

IW: I learned how to write for the eye. More importantly, for my self-interest, I learned things that would prove to be priceless when I turned to writing novels 15 years later.

I'm going to tell you flatly that I think writing for movies can be useful for most novelists. A remark like that is literary heresy, or at least it used to be. Years ago, the literati regarded movies as canned, contrived, glossy junk, the opposite of pure creativity. It was acceptable for a novelist, like Scott Fitzgerald or William Faulkner, to come to Hollywood to pick up some eating money, as long as he didn't take movies seriously and as long as he got back as fast as possible to his prose. But that's all changing now, as I said earlier. Movies are no longer an anathema to the literati. With the death of the big studios, after television, movies became more freewheeling, creative, a burgeoning art form. So I guess it is less heretical for me, as a novelist, to say now that novelists have something to gain from movies other than money.

I'll tell you what a stint as a screenwriter can do for a novelist. For one thing, in working on screenplays, you learn to write a scene, to dramatize a confrontation, a conflict, or even a romantic meeting. You learn you can't have it happen off-stage, or condense it in exposition, or dust it off in past tense. You know what I'm saying? Too many novelists, faced with a big obligatory scene in which—well, for example— the protagonist is about to enter his bedroom to tell his wife that he wants a divorce—too many authors would avoid the actual scene. This is understandable. The big scene is hard to write. It challenges, it demands, it invites failure. Too many authors will simply come to the edge of the scene, "Hanson's mind was made up. It had to be done and there was no turning back. He was going in and tell her it was over, and then it would be over. At the bedroom door, he hesitated, then firmly took the knob, pushed the door open, and went inside." End of chapter. Next chapter. Beginning. "It was strange coming awake, alone, uncommitted, free, for the first morning in twenty years. He lay there and remembered last night, himself and Lucy and the truth." Then the author will recap, in several paragraphs, several pages, in narrative not dialogue, the crucial scene, and go on.

That's no good. That's copping out and cheating the reader. And it is simply something that could not be done in writing a screenplay. In the screenplay, the novelist would have to go into the bedroom, the camera trucking behind him, and face it out, dramatize it before the lens, the big showdown with the wife. There's no way to avoid obligatory scenes in movies. You can't start a big climactic confrontation and dissolve out before it begins. No way.

So that is something many novelists might learn from a few months devoted to adapting or creating a film. This knowledge might improve the honesty and dramatic effect of their future novels.

Another equally important thing can be learned from movies. Too many novelists don't know a thing about story structure. Granted, many fine novels can be written without story. But most novels promise story growing out of char- acter, and then wander and wobble all over the place, and lose readers quickly. This is because the authors have never learned to structure, to plot, to build narrative. Some novelists have an instinct for storytelling, building to a climax, but most novelists don't. On the other hand, nine out of ten movies—no matter how strong on characterization or mood—demand sharp, spare, forward-thrusting story lines. Unlike the legitimate theatre audience, the movie audience can only see what is shown on screen. The movie audience has no options to see something else, only what the film shows them. So the film had better arrest them, hold them, excite or move them. A motion picture has to have motion, not only visual but story motion, and a moving picture has to move. And that is another thing novelists can learn from film. I would suggest that most young novelists, if they have the opportunity, try to get themselves involved in making one or two movies at some stage early in their careers. No more than that, and never more than a year in movies. They'd find their film experience serving them as a graduate course in the novel. They should learn what is useful to them, and then get out of cinema and stay out and stay with the novel.

But there's another side to the movie experience for a fiction writer, and I can speak from first-hand knowledge. There's a dangerous side to having given too much time to screenplays, and then trying to withdraw to write novels. It happened to me. When I quit movies for good in 1958, and plunged full-time into books, I ran into trouble with my first published novel, *The Sins of Philip Fleming,* and to a lesser degree with my second one, *The Chapman Report.* After ten years, off and on, in film studios, turning my back on them to devote myself to a novel, I found myself clumsy in handling scenes, since I had only words to rely on. I no longer had a camera as a collaborator. In the studio, the writer's tool and his crutch is the camera. He doesn't have to write out a visual scene or an action scene. He need merely indicate that the camera should show it. Temporarily, the screenwriter-turned-novelist has lost his power to describe and dramatize in straight prose. That power in him has atrophied. He must learn to write, dependent only upon himself, again.

Another harmful thing about spending too much time

writing for movies is that the author loses his keen awareness of the need to create inner dialogues, introspections, work inside a character's head. There's no room for that in a film script, because inner feelings, thoughts, remembrances are too difficult to translate into shadows on the screen. A director supervising a screenplay will tell the writer to leave out any writing of feelings, mood, and just stick to dialogue. All of this interior writing must be relearned when the movie writer returns to the novel.

However, on balance, I feel an experience with film writing can do an author far more good than harm.

And let me add one unspoken, uncreative asset that any prose writer can gain from movies. He can gain discipline.

I am a fairly well-disciplined writer today. I wasn't when I started out. I was as obsessive a pencil sharpener as any that exists. I first learned discipline while writing in the army, when you received an order—an order or command, mind you —to be creative and deliver a certain number of pages on a certain day. My disciplinary muscles were further strengthened when I first went on salary as a studio screenwriter—hours 9 to 5 every day, with the week's pages, 15 or 20 minimum, to be turned in to the producer every Friday—this at Warner Brothers, beginning in June, 1948, when I was hired to write my first original screenplay, *The West Point Story.*

The continuity of work time demanded by the army and studios stood me in good stead when I began to write novels. I had been spoiled in my younger years, my school years, by impractical instructors—just as kids are often crippled by their Creative Writing and English Lit professors in college today—who insist you must only write when you feel like it, when you're inspired, when you've been visited by the Muse. Well, hell, you may be visited by the Muse only twice a year. If youngsters who've been brainwashed to believe that romantic nonsense, that you write only when you're in the mood, would do as I finally did—read the letters and journals of popular writers all through history—Dickens, Tolstoi, Balzac, Dumas right to Hemingway and Maugham—

the beginning writers would see that most of those giants went to their desks every day or at least on some regular basis. They wrote regularly. It was their way of life. If what they wrote any single day was bad, they'd throw it out. If what they wrote was fair, they'd keep the best of it and rewrite the worst. If what they wrote was good, they'd achieved another fine day of creativity. But they wrote steadily because—well, because a novel has a life of its own, a life that must be sustained through continually attending to it.

This effort to maintain continuity by writing daily on a three-hour or eight-hour schedule is what produces books, and always has; books no better or worse than those written by authors who could only create when they were "in the mood."

I must credit my own discipline to my movie career, where businessmen's hours were imposed on art.

At the same time, when I cut myself off completely from screenwriting back in 1959, when I no longer had a Colonel Capra or Jack Warner over me demanding pages, I found that I needed a boss. But going into books fully, free-lance and for myself, left me without an outsider to force me to write. I mean, I'd learned the discipline of going in to work daily. But no one was demanding pages. So—since there was no boss, I invented one, an invisible, non-existent boss who expected a day's work in hand at each day's end. This helped, but it wasn't enough, because I knew it was a game and I was the only referee. But finally, there was something else that compelled me to write. I was driven to write because I had so much to say, and I realized if I didn't say it then, I wouldn't say it later, either. Also, hanging overhead, the sword of survival. No one would give me a dime unless I gave them something in exchange. At last, after my first two novels, I learned something important. I found I had to force myself to start a book, really force myself, because I was faced with blank pages, uncertain I could be as exciting on paper as I was in my head, afraid of forming characters I didn't know yet and put down words in a style not set yet. So the beginning, the first ten, twenty, fifty pages was always tough. But then, from my short experience, I learned something else. Once part of a novel was going down on paper and going fairly well, at a time when you were pushing your pencil, some mysterious thing happened—like the pull of gravity, and suddenly you weren't pushing the story but being pulled into it, pulled along with your characters as if you were one of them. And after that, despite a bad day here and there, a novel was no problem. So I learned to go along until I got into the field of creative gravity with each book, the place where I was pulled, and after that the going was easier.

I might add, this was something I also experienced in writing screenplays. Those first scenes, first twenty pages of a script, were always difficult—and suddenly there were people on paper, and I knew them, and they were talking and behaving naturally, and the screenplay was rolling of its own momentum. Although, as I recall, not always quite that simple because of interruptions. You'd hand in a third of the script to the producer or director—the first act, as they call it in Hollywood—and while you were lost in the second act, you'd be stopped to go backwards and discuss changes in the first act that the producer wanted because of budget or the director wanted because he didn't understand it or the star wanted because she didn't feel comfortable with her lines. Those interruptions, that unnatural starting and stopping, was one of the things I detested most about movies created under the studio system.

SG: Let's get back to the army, to your beginnings as a screen-writer. What was the best and worst of your army writing experience?

IW: The best of it was that we were all well-motivated. We felt, rightly or wrongly, we had a cause to fight for. We believed Hitler, Mussolini, Fascism, were menaces to our freedom.

Now, of course, long after any war, from the historical perspective of time, we always learn the obvious reasons for
fighting were the wrong ones, that other less pure factors are
behind armed conflicts. But this is no place to get into that
kind of sophisticated discussion about economics and power.
In 1942, for Americans, there was a visible enemy, a horrible
one, unlike the recent war in Vietnam, where there was no
real cause for American troops to fight.

Those of us in the Army Air Force felt our training
films were important. And when I was transferred to the
Signal Corps, we all believed as one that our orientation and
propaganda films were important. True, as time went by,
many of us were disillusioned, saw less value in our contribu-
tions to some kind of victory and settlement. But for a large
portion of the war, we were well-motivated and worked long
hours to do our jobs.

Selfishly, too, I felt at the time that I was fortunate to
be devoting those long years at what I loved to do most—
write—and in writing I was learning a new form, which was
screenplay writing. Furthermore, I was involved with some
of the best movie people in the business, perfect mentors for
someone new to movies. In the First Motion Picture Unit of
the Army Air Force I was involved with Major Paul Mantz,
the movie stunt flyer—I was actually assigned to ghostwrite a
flying manual for him, but it never came off because he was
too impatient to concentrate on a book—and actors like
Lieutenant Ronald Reagan and Sergeant Alan Ladd. Other
fellow GIs and officers included glamour photographer George
Hurrell, songwriter David Rose, producer Owen Crump,
and screenwriters Norman Krasna, Robert Carson, Jerome
Chodorov, Edwin Gilbert, Stanley Rubin, George Oppen-
heimer, and numerous others. And later, in the Signal Corps
Photographic Center, both in Hollywood and Long Island,
New York, I was able to learn from Frank Capra, John
Huston, Ted Geisel, Leonard Spigelgass, Gottfried Rinehardt,
Stanley Kramer, John Cheever, Claude Binyon, Carl Foreman,
Herb Baker—well, the list is too long to detail here. I do

remember we also had William Saroyan and Irwin Shaw as GIs in our Long Island branch.

SG: It seems odd to hear these names mentioned with the army propaganda films. It must have been a very odd climate for you.

IW: In the end, it was an impossible climate for me—and that's what I was about to say was the worst of it. In the army I was being asked to be a creative person, a free-wheeling creative writer, and at the same time endure military discipline and serve as a soldier, the absolute antithesis of creativity.

You know, I think I was the only soldier in World War II who served in both major cinema branches of the army. I've never heard of another person who served time in both branches. Creatively, they were as different as day and night. In the Air Force, most of the films we wrote were technical. In the Signal Corps, the films were documentary and popular. But both branches were one and the same in demanding soldierly discipline. After breakfast, in uniform, you stood inspection, for periods did calisthenics, sometimes did brush ups on gun drill and so forth. In both branches, you were instructed and chewed out by old line army Master Sergeants. You ate in army messes, came under the eye of MPs, had leave only with passes. Yet, at some time during the day, you were asked, as I was, to suddenly go into an office and sit down at a typewriter and write "Fade In." It was mind boggling. In those units, it was more difficult for the writers than for the directors and cameramen, who often went into the field. I worked with John Huston on two pictures after he'd come back from shooting *The Battle of San Pietro* in Italy. He had been in the center of action, so that his soldier being and his cinematic being merged, and he was less schizoid than the rest of us who were bound to our desks.

Also, as the war went on, and we were bogged down in our paper projects, I was filled with guilts and self-recriminations. There were men I knew who were overseas, some of them wounded or killed, but all of them doing something that produced immediate results, or at least results that could be seen. I felt, as the war continued, that I was doing nothing. Several times I applied to be shipped overseas, but was turned down. Then, after three years, when most of the war was over, I did an about face and was afraid I'd be shipped out and be stuck somewhere in an occupation force and be forgotten.

To give you an idea of our frustration, I want to tell you of an experience I had in the Signal Corps. Recently, Frank Capra wrote his highly praised memoirs, and in it he included the story of how he, or we, did the "Why We Fight" series, which was the glory of that branch of the Signal Corps. In fact, before being discharged from the service, we all got commendations for participating in that series. I worked on the rewrites of *The Battle for Russia* and *The Battle for China* and on the two-parter *War Comes to America,* for Major Merrill White, a brilliant film editor. But my main assignment was *Know Your Enemy Japan.* Here we were at war with Japan, and our country had no policy toward Japan, and Carl Foreman and I were to write the big documentary instructing our troops about Japan, so that the GIs in the field would understand why we were fighting and whom we were fighting.

Well, our commander-in-chief, President Franklin D. Roosevelt, and Stimson and Knox and the rest of the cabinet, and even the generals like Marshall, had never put together a coherent policy about our enemy Japan. They did not know how we should treat the Japanese, except to beat them in the field. There was no determined ideological attitude. I'm serious about this—it was early in the war—and Foreman and I were writing in a vacuum, without instruction. Unofficially, our immediate commanding officer, Frank Capra, was being asked to set the nation's policy through this orientation and propaganda film.

The real problem—when I collaborated on the movie about Japan with Foreman, later with Huston, and with

28 April 1944   Edgar Peterson
                                                Sgt. Irving Wallace

                                                [signature: Irving Wallace]

                        SYNOPSIS

                   KNOW YOUR ENEMY JAPAN

     We open on the traditional picture Americans, including
GI's, have always had of Japan and the Japanese. Opening on
the striking of a gong, we see shots from Gilbert and
Sullivan's "Mikado" with a chorus singing "We Are The
Gentlemen of Japan." As the song continues, we see quaint
paper buildings and graceful geisha girls, soft landscapes
and cherry blossoms. And, majestically, peaceful snow-
capped Mount Fuji in repose.

     Suddenly, we go to shots of the massive volcano in
terrifying eruption. Smoke and fire. The earth trembling
and cracking. Destruction everywhere. And through this
we dissolve into rousing action shots of fanatical Japanese
soldiers fighting, charging, killing. For this is the
real Japan, and these are the real gentlemen of Japan. This
is the enemy -- superior, cruel, murderous -- the Japan
behind the traditional facade of Tourist Bureau hokum. We
show graphic animation of Nippon's Pacific conquests, with
Nippon's attacking warriors superimposed.

Page one from a synopsis of *Know Your Enemy Japan.*

civilian documentary makers like Joris Ivens and Edgar Peterson, and finally when I worked alone—the real problem was our boss, Frank Capra himself. This may come as a surprise to many who know Capra only by reputation, as the famed filmmaker of *Mr. Deeds* and *Mr. Smith* and the rest. The problem was Capra because he was essentially an instinctual man, a primitive. He was a person who'd come from an Italian immigrant family, from economically poor beginnings, and through talent had risen to the very top in beautiful every-man-can-be-president America. He was totally unsophisticated when it came to political thought. He knew only one thing, America had been good to him, America was beautiful. And anyone who wanted to mar America was a heavy. For Capra, war and peace, enemies and friends, were simple to discern. He wore invisible glasses that saw everything and everyone in black and white, no shadings.

So when we had story conferences with Capra, we tried to formulate an attitude toward the Japanese for our film. That was the key to making the movie. For Capra it was not difficult. He came up with a simple foreign policy toward Japan. It added up to this: the only good Jap is a dead Jap. He did not say it in those words, but that was what his words added up to.

You can believe me when I say that Foreman and I fought this terribly, persistently, because it was all wrong. Foreman and I used to leave those meetings with Capra and say to each other—we can't allow Capra's attitude toward the enemy to be our government's policy in this picture for our troops, because while Capra doesn't understand it, the direction the film is taking is utterly racist. How could we indict an entire people in our film? How could we tell our troops that all yellow-skinned Japanese are equally guilty of war crimes and equally deserving of extinction? How can we weight and distort Japanese history and culture toward making such a statement?

And most difficult of all, how can we tell Frank Capra he is wrong? This was the army. Capra was a colonel.

Carl Foreman and Irving Wallace, April 29, 1945, at the Signal Corps
Photographic Center, Long Island.

Foreman and I were, in that period, mere corporals, the lowliest of the low. It was rough. As writers in a story conference, we'd start swinging verbally. But then someone in the room would remind us we were speaking to the commanding officer—and we'd turn back to Capra and have to say Yes, Sir, Very Good, Sir—but Well, Sir, and so on.

It seemed hopeless until Foreman and I hit upon a subtle scheme. We told Capra and the other officers under him that the Japanese film we were writing was so complex and involved that we needed outside advice, the advice of the leading American experts on Japan, in and out of the army. After enough nagging and enough memos, Capra or his underlings finally agreed. Bringing in experts made sense. It was what they had often done when they worked in the Hollywood studios and were stuck on some point.

Now I knew a lot about Japan and the Japanese mentality—not only from my recent time as a correspondent in Tokyo, Kobe, Nagasaki, but from extensive reading and interviewing. Still, I didn't know enough, and as an enlisted man I didn't pack any power. So we proceeded with our ruse. Outside experts were summoned, and we hoped they'd shed some light. The first expert, if I recall it correctly, was the last Ambassador to Japan, Ambassador Grew, who'd been imprisoned after Pearl Harbor and just been freed through an exchange of prisoners off Africa. Grew was a lovely man whom I'd met in Tokyo and who gave me American pipe tobacco out of Embassy stores when my pouch was empty. Anyway, Ambassador Grew flew out to see us. Then came others. One I remember in particular. He was Colonel Carlson of Carlson's Raiders.

What evolved out of these sessions was that Capra and his aides received an education on Japan from authorities they respected, and Capra gradually began to see what was right. And finally Foreman and I were allowed to establish the official United States position toward Japan. It was this— let's separate the Japanese people from the Japanese military —let's say the majority of people were led into the war by

General Tojo's Fascist military clique—let's remove the people and their symbolic leader, the Emperor, from the real aggressors—and in that way we can have someone to deal with and work with after the war. Furthermore, by this separation, we do not condemn an entire race of people.

Later, it was my impression, Colonel Capra lost interest in this film project—or perhaps he was diverted into newer projects. Anyway, he assigned one of his best officers as our producer. The officer was Theodore Geisel, better known to the public today as Dr. Seuss. I worked alone with Ted Geisel on one of the last narration scripts of *Know Your Enemy Japan,* and he did the final draft after I'd been given other assignments. Geisel had been with the New York experimental newspaper, *PM,* and he was a wonderful rad-lib officer, a great guy who was also in charge of the animated cartoons and newsreels we produced for the troops.

When the war was over, and our troops marched in to occupy Japan and Okinawa, our film on the Japanese was finally finished. It should have been shown to our men at least two years before they occupied Japan. By the time most of them saw it, they'd already met the Japanese firsthand and formed their own impressions, many often erroneous. Now the film is in the government archives—and now the Japanese are occupying the United States, at least economically. How ironic. Anyway, none but a handful of us know the true story behind that film and about the American policy that General Douglas MacArthur brought into Japan—the story of two lowly enlisted writers who, with some outside help, overcame Frank Capra and his circle of aides to create a historic foreign policy. In retrospect, so typically snafu, a script really for Chaplin and Buster Keaton or maybe Jacques Tati.

SG: We had never known anything about the Japanese people, and apparently we didn't want to know anything.

IW: Well, you see, I suspect the attitude of most Americans has always been—a colored person is not a person. I'm over-stating it, but Western whites have always felt superior to colored people. Indira Gandhi said it right when she said, after Nixon massively bombed North Vietnam while Kissinger was still negotiating peace with them, that America would never have ordered a Christmas bombing on a Caucasian European nation if we had been opposing them. We wouldn't think of such utter brutality mounted against whites at the very moment we were negotiating for a peaceful settlement. Against brown-skinned people, that's different, against blacks or yellows, that's different. That's also sad, our inherent racism, our feeling that white is superior.

SG: I suppose there were many other crazy stories connected with making movies in the army?

IW: I could tell you endless stories. I won't. It was so weird and unnatural, the whole scene, this mismating of the military and the filmmaker, that life became a kind of Catch-22. My friend, Joe Heller, ought to write it, but I don't think he experienced my kind of army life.

I'd always intended to write an autobiographical book about those army film years. I got the idea just before my son, David, was born in 1948, and I was going to address the book to him and call it, *What Did You Do In The Big War, Daddy?* But I never got around to write it. I know one wild incident I'd have put in it for sure.

SG: What was that?

IW: Well, early on when I was in the Air Force Motion Picture Unit, we received a directive from Washington, D. C., to make a realistic picture about VD—venereal disease—to be shown to our troops, a precautionary film. Instead, we made a film that must have scared the troops into temporary impotency.

As I recall it, after the script had been written, the officer-producer set out to cast the VD film from personnel

1947

"WHAT DID YOU DO IN THE ~~BIG~~ BIG WAR, DADDY?"

by

Irving Wallace

One day I am going to have a son, and one day after that, when he is old enough to look at those *flammable* picture books bursting with the Battle of the Bulge and the assault on Tarawa, he is going to ~~look~~ *stare* up at me ~~with those big brown eyes and he is~~ going to ask the question I will have been hiding from all those years. "Daddy," he will ask, "what did you do in the ~~great~~ *big* war, ~~daddy~~? *the little animal*" And there will be no avoiding it, for ~~he~~ will persist, ~~the little animal.~~

So let's face it.

I fought the war you never read about, and my son will never hear about. Thank God for the anonymity, but it does make those 3½ years ~~I spent in that ill-fitting suit~~ hard to explain. What did I do? Well, there's a story in it, and some awfully big names, and in the blue days when it was worse, this was the story I promised to tell out of school. I'm out of school and this is it . . .

Induction ... FMPU, *gielfish mother* purpose, what it was like ... meeting Oppenheimer ... Anecdote on his three-way deal ... Mantz, the phoney, and Haglund ... Reagen's problem ... Some of the guys ... Assignment to Washington ... Chodorov, Krasna, Carson ... Alan Ladd ... General and his book ... saluting GIs in costume ... short-arm picture ...

Transfer to Capra out fit ... Assignment on Japan ... Joris Ivens ... Spigelgass ... Rosten ... Frank Capra, first estimate and last ... Vieller ... Rinehardt ... Binyon ... Tiomkin and his stories ... Geisel ... Screen Mag, Snafu, Japan, New Mexico, Jolley, SFrancisco ... Transfer to NYC ... Long Island ... Lincoln, Royalton ... Georgia ... d'Usseau, Cheever, etc ... Mrs. Wolfe ... Fort Dix.

I was part of one of the war's greatest failures: orientation. Look at polls today. Reasons: capra with Marshall, FDR, no knowledge of men who hiss and boo. Training good, not pix. Stuff glamorous, tricky.

Irving Wallace never went beyond this page of *What Did You Do in the Big War, Daddy?*

on the post. All the men were assembled for the casting session. We put our best profiles forward. Then, to our amazement, we were all asked to drop our trousers and after that our shorts. Then the casting director began inspecting us. What he was looking for was the star of the film—the right kind of penis to suffer the agonies of VD!

What a bizarre hour that was. This one was too long, that one was too short, that one too gross. The leading player had to be just right, not too much so as not to put down the audience and not too little so as not to relate to the audience. The star had to be just average, something every GI could identify with. And at last the right one was found, and the picture was cast and began to roll. That, too, was picture making.

Another bizarre thing happened on that film. We had to find a leading lady, so we went off the post to hire a beautiful, sexy, promising young starlet. I forget her name, and maybe just as well—because the role she played in the film was that of an enticing and available young woman whom soldiers picked up, slept with, and from whom they contracted venereal disease. Well, let me tell you, the army released that film, and it was seen by literally millions of soldiers around this country and around the world. And you know what? I was told years later that the young starlet in it never got work again in studios—and she was never invited out on dates. Because the young men who came home to civilian life, and who met her, had some vague subliminal remembrance that this girl, or someone very much like her, was a carrier of syph —and no one wanted to have anything to do with her, forgetting that they had merely seen her playing a fictional part in an army VD film. So you see, life can be destroyed by art.

SG: Funny. . . . All right, you were discharged from the army. Did you go right into Hollywood films?

IW: No. I wasn't interested. I wanted to resume writing prose, and I wanted to see something of the world. My wife, Sylvia,

Irving Wallace in Stockholm (above) and Paris, 1946.

had been Western editor of Dell Publications, mainly *Modern Screen* magazine. She quit her job and off we went to Europe—our first time—for the good part of a year, eight months actually. I had an armful of magazine assignments—*The Saturday Evening Post, Collier's, Reader's Digest*—and we started our Grand Tour in Stockholm, worked our way down to Copenhagen and Amsterdam, then moved on to Paris, which really became our base. We also spent time in Madrid and Barcelona, and after that, drove to Cannes, Monte Carlo, Pisa, Rome, and made several trips to London.

The drive from Madrid to Cannes was a story in itself, but someone else wrote it. I guess I was too close to what happened, too involved, to see it at first. In Madrid, Sylvia and I had met a young, attractive correspondent named Rita Hume. We became casual friends. When we were about to leave for the Riviera and Italy, Rita said she was making the same trip and suggested we accompany her in her car. Well, that was quite a trip—I don't know how to explain it—but there were the two women, and there was I, and it got to be somewhat flirtatious and early Noel Cowardish. Somehow, I survived the journey with my marriage intact. Anyway, when I got home, I related the adventure to my friend, Zachary Gold, merely as an amusing incident, and then I forgot about it. Well, one evening about five years later, Zach said to me, "Take a look at the new issue of *Woman's Home Companion*. Remember that story you told me about Sylvia, and that other woman, and yourself driving together all those days from Spain to Italy? I used it. I hope you don't mind." I went out and got the September, 1952, issue of the magazine, and found the short story a little too close to home for comfort but fun to read. And I didn't mind. It was Zach's last short story before his death. As for the prototype of the other woman, Rita Hume, she later married John Secondari, the network correspondent who wrote *Three Coins in The Fountain,* and sometime after her marriage she was killed in an auto accident abroad.

Overall, that first long trip to Europe was a valuable

Rita Hume and Sylvia Wallace in Pisa, 1947.

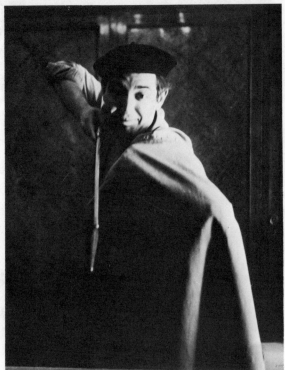

Sylvia and Irving at the Ritz Hotel, Madrid, in 1947. Irving Wallace's caption: "Death in the Afternoon."

Tea time at the Madrid Ritz, 1947.

Irving Wallace in Pisa, 1947.

one for me. A lot of input. In Stockholm I accidentally got involved in talking to a Nobel Prize judge and the seed was planted for a novel I'd write 15 years later, *The Prize*—I've told the whole story in *The Writing of One Novel,* which was brought out in 1968 and is still being published by Pocket Books in paperback.

It was on that trip, also, that I met and had part of an afternoon with Pablo Picasso. A Hungarian photographer, Brassai, took me up to Picasso's studio at 7 Rue des Grands-Augustins in Paris—that was on November 29, 1946. Picasso's vestibule was crowded with visitors, but he was out. When he returned, he was near tears. Nush Eluard, the wife of one of the artist's best friends in Switzerland, had just died. Picasso's secretary, Sabartes, shooed all of the visitors out except Brassai and myself. After a while, Picasso pulled himself together, regained his composure, and beckoned the two of us into his inner studio.

Picasso was surprisingly short and stocky, and I noted that he looked "like a prosperous Italian shoemaker wearing a beret." In the cluttered studio, Picasso took me on a tour, pointing out oils recently finished and a great number of unfinished ones still in progress. He was extremely communicative, discussed his sculptures at length, Brassai's photographic record of his art, and answered my questions about how he worked and how much he produced every week. He was very professional. That was one of a handful of memorable occasions on that first trip to Europe. I did not see Picasso again until twenty years later when I happened to be seated next to him at Felix's outdoor restaurant, a block from the Carleton, in Cannes, and he didn't look a day older.

Before I'd gone to Europe, and immediately after I returned to Los Angeles, I was inundated with offers from producers and studios to go to work as a screenwriter. Apparently, my stint in the army had impressed a number of producers. I turned all of them down and concentrated on magazines. But finally, the lure of big money became irresistable. I had told my agents an idea I had for a feature

Irving and Sylvia in Paris, 1946.

Irving Wallace at Warner Brothers Studio, in his office on the second floor of the Writer's Building.

The Warner Brothers writers celebrate Christmas, 1954. (Irving Wallace is front and center.)

picture—the story of the Army's CID. Buddy Adler, the head of Columbia Pictures, liked it. He offered me a job to go to Washington, D. C., and New York, to research some of the CID's criminal cases. The agreement was that if Adler liked the research, I would be retained to write a fictional screen treatment and a screenplay. It was good money, a good change of pace, and my own idea, so I was happy to accept it. That was in March, 1948, my first civilian movie job, the beginning of ten years of off-and-on working in films.

However, I've never really considered it my beginning in feature films because the job never worked out. I returned from Washington with some wonderful factual research, but apparently Adler couldn't translate it into a movie in his mind, so he canceled the project and I never got to do the treatment or screenplay.

My real beginning, I suppose, was at Warner Brothers in June of 1948. A producer there, Lou Edelman, felt that there had not been a real West Point musical comedy since *Flirtation Walk,* and he was eager to make one. He was looking for a writer who had published nonfiction to go to West Point, live there for a while, and come up with a story. Edelman had read some of my articles in *The Saturday Evening Post,* was impressed, and offered me the job. I went to West Point twice, did my homework, and based on what I saw and heard I got an idea for a story. I developed it into a long screen treatment. Edelman and Jack Warner read it and were enthusiastic. They retained me to do the screenplay—my first for a feature film—but since they felt I was relatively inexperienced, they gave me a collaborator, a studio contract writer, Charles Hoffman, a charming and amusing man with whom I was immediately sympatico. We collaborated on many versions of the screenplay, and finally completed a draft that the studio accepted.

I left the studio while Edelman set out to cast the picture. Then, to my surprise, I learned that James Cagney, in semi-retirement, had read it, liked it, and wanted to play the lead, that of a cocky song-and-dance man a la his earlier role in *Yankee Doodle Dandy*. Well, we had not written the leading man with Cagney in mind, so the part had to be rewritten once more to suit his personality. Cagney preferred to have a well-known playwright and author, who knew his style, do the job. John Monks, Jr., who had written the successful *Brother Rat* for Broadway, was hired, and that's how he came to share credit with Hoffman and myself.

The *West Point Story* starred James Cagney, Doris Day, Virginia Mayo—remember her?—and Gordon MacRae, and the music was written by the top team of Julie Styne and Sammy Cahn. I saw it at a preview on November 7, 1950, and enjoyed it immensely. It was somewhat silly and improbable—although it was based on a true incident—but Cagney was great, as ever, and the movie was relaxing. It did very well at the boxoffice, and was nominated by the Screen Writers Guild as one of the five "best-written American musicals" of the year. The reviews were mixed. *Daily Variety* and *The Hollywood Reporter* loved it. *The New York Times* loved only "a bright young thing named Doris Day." *Time* magazine hated it. You can still see it on television, and decide for yourself, although I imagine it's fairly dated.

Anyway, it was my first major movie screenplay credit.

SG: Why do you say your first *major* credit? Did you have any others before that one?

IW: Well, I'll let you in on a secret. Yes, I had one. I feel secure enough now to own up to it. Back in my early Army Air Force days, a lot of us, the enlisted men, were broke, we needed money. We had heard that the army had no objections to enlisted men moonlighting at something else, as long as it was done on our own time, after hours, or on weekends. So three of us at the post let the word out—another enlisted man with connections served as the conduit—that we'd be happy to do a commercial screenplay for anyone who wanted a cut-rate, quality job.

Well, there was one small studio, strictly a low-budget

James Cagney and Virginia Mayo in *The West Point Story*.

operation, PRC Pictures, Inc., that was interested. They asked the three of us—two professional Hollywood writers who were friends of mine and also in uniform, Walter Doniger and Malvin Wald, and myself—if we had any ideas for a musical. Overnight, we had a half dozen ideas. Leon Fromkess, the head of PRC, went for one, and we got the job. We concocted a story and a screenplay during our spare time in May and June of 1943. And believe it or not, it was actually made. It was called *Jive Junction*—yes, I know, but that's what it was called—starring Dickie Moore and Tiny Thayer. It was a bit of fluff, but incredibly, three out of four reviewers liked it. The *Los Angeles Times* actually said, "Has completely and delightfully captured the teenage spirit." Actually, that was over-praising it.

That movie served its purpose. It earned us some outside money. We received a flat sum, and we divided it four ways. The three of us who did the screenplay had shares, and we gave the fourth share to the other GI who had set up the deal. My share was—I've still got it written down—$369.43.

So that was the unmentionable film that proved to be my first screen credit. Satisfied?

SG: Satisfied. Now to go on. I'm interested in screenplay writing in the fifties. When I was going through your manuscripts, I noticed in *Split Second* there was a morality clause where the studio was going to beg off if any public disgrace came to the writer—a sign of the Joe McCarthy era and the black list? Also, I'm interested in the fact that in *Split Second* you used as a story basis—the first time anyone had done so for the screen, I believe—the threat of nuclear war.

IW: Yes, *Split Second* was a first, but I'll tell you, I had a hard time getting that one sold and on the screen. I was struck by this original notion: What if a group of ordinary people were trapped on a nuclear bomb testing site in Nevada, and had to live through the explosion of an atomic bomb? I thought that this might give audiences some idea of what the people of

January 25, 1951

Irving Wallace
8729 Holloway Drive
Hollywood 46, Calif

Dear Irving:

Congratulations!

Your fellow writers in the Guild have nominated your screenplay of THE WEST POINT STORY for the best written American musical.

Ballots for the final voting already have gone out. The winners in each category - and I sincerely hope you are among them - will be announced at our 3rd Annual Awards Dinner, Ambassador Hotel, February 20th. NBC will network the decisions, Alan Campbell is building a big show full of entertainment to follow and we are sure of a complete ticket sellout of 1100.

If you haven't done so, we'd all appreciate your sending in your check for as big a table as you possibly can handle.

Again, Hope you win!

Best regards,

Allen Rivkin

AWARDS COMMITTEE
Allen Rivkin, Chairman

h

Notice that *The West Point Story* was nominated for the Best Musical Award of the Screen Writers' Guild.

Hiroshima and Nagasaki had been through. Also, a suspenseful film might turn people's minds toward nuclear disarmament and peace. Besides—because a message isn't enough, shouldn't be—it was a helluva melodramatic springboard.

So I set out to develop the characters, the plot, and write an original story for the screen on speculation. It was a story about three hoodlums on the lam in Nevada, one of them wounded. To escape, they pick up several ordinary persons to use as hostages. They hole up in an abandoned shack in the desert to await a doctor, little realizing they are on an atomic bomb test range and that an explosion is scheduled for daybreak. I called the 49-page story, *I'll See You In Hell.* Later, I switched the title to *Zero Hour,* and finally settled for *Split Second.*

My agents had trouble selling it. Then, one day, a friend of mine, Ben Medford, also an agent, said he'd shown my story to Chester. Erskine, a well-known writer-director who'd directed Spencer Tracy in *The Last Mile* on Broadway, and had made a fortune on the film version of *The Egg and I* at Universal. Erskine loved the story. He told me that Howard Hughes was very much interested in him. Hughes had just bought RKO studio and was looking for properties. Erskine felt that he could sell *Split Second* to Howard Hughes if it were rewritten. He wanted to revise it with me, try to restructure it somewhat, make it more cinematic. It was a great opportunity not only to improve the story but to learn something from a well-known director. I agreed to the collaboration. Erskine and I had several long story conferences, worked out a tighter story line, and then I went away and rewrote my story, created an 83-page original.

The next step was Howard Hughes. He had just bought RKO, as I've said, and he had a big studio but no properties to shoot. Well, Chester Erskine kept his word. Somehow, he got *Split Second* to Hughes. Then we waited. We'd hoped for a decision within a week. But the week passed without news. Then a second week passed, and a third, and by the fourth week I was discouraged. And suddenly, late one morning in February, 1952—I was working on an assignment at Universal—the phone call came. Mr. Hughes had bought *Split Second* for $27,500. Of this, $10,000 went to Erskine for his part in the original story, and $17,500 went to me for my half of the story and for ten weeks developing a screenplay alone.

I was quite high about the whole thing, because I had real belief in the story, which was tightly structured in the middle, playing off various character conflicts, very much like Sherwood's *Petrified Forest,* long one of my favorite old plays and films. I moved over to RKO and into the empty Writer's Building. At almost the same time, two other writers checked in to develop properties. One was Zachary Gold, one of my closest friends, a brilliant young short story writer, who was fated to die two years later. I dedicated my novel, *The Three Sirens,* to his memory.

The other writer who checked in was a New York novelist whom I'd admired for years but never met. He was Jerome Weidman, and we developed a friendship that exists to this day. He had one of the most agile and lively minds I'd ever known. We found that we had much in common—a mutual love for writing, storytelling, the novel, good puns—and later we collaborated on several movie originals and plays. Our first joint effort, a short movie original called *The Holy Grail,* sold overnight to Universal. The collaboration had been so effortless, talking out the story, writing it, that we thought we were on our way to riches as a team. We were wrong. We never sold another movie original, although we did sell a three-act play to BBC of London. But no collaborators alive, I'm sure, had more fun working together, either in person or through correspondence across the country.

But back to *Split Second.* During my second week at RKO, some new tenants occupied the floor above me, and they made so much noise I was constantly distracted. I wondered who in the hell was making all the racket upstairs, and so I investigated. Then I learned what was going on. A ballet troupe, a whole goddam ballet from Paris, had moved into RKO and taken over the floor above.

What had happened was this—I don't know if it was true, but so it was alleged to me by Howard Hughes' lieutenants—Howard Hughes had seen a newspaper photograph of beautiful Jeanmaire, the premier ballerina of Roland Petit's troupe, which was opening in Los Angeles. Hughes dispatched two or three of his lieutenants down to the Philharmonic Auditorium to observe the ballet as a motion picture possibility. But more importantly, he had requested his aides to scout Jeanmaire as a potential leading lady. Hughes' aides returned with unanimously favorable reports on the ballet. "Okay," said Hughes. "Then buy it." So RKO bought the whole ballet and moved the troupe upstairs in the Writer's Building, where the floor had been converted into a rehearsal hall. And there they were, for weeks, months, readying themselves for the camera—until Hughes' real purpose became clear. He'd bought the ballet because he wanted Jeanmaire for a girl friend. He did not succeed in winning her. Perhaps he didn't really try. She was in love with Roland Petit, her choreographer, whom she subsequently married. I tell you, that was a weird period.

Anyway, I got *Split Second* done. It was a darn good screenplay, one I've always been proud of. Later it was rewritten slightly, first by the novelist Harry Brown, and finally by an excellent screenwriter, William Bowers. The rewrites were instigated after a director had been assigned. The director was none other than the actor Dick Powell, undertaking his first assignment behind the camera. The completed picture, starring Alexis Smith and Stephen McNally, opened in March, 1953. For a low-budget job, it was a big hit, and it received critical acclaim. The *Los Angeles Times* called it "a tight, taut thriller." *Daily Variety* found the script "terse in dialogue, tough in action." *The Motion Picture Herald* labeled it, "One of the most effective melodramas of recent years, or remote years." And *Time* magazine came very close to home with, "Seems to be a dramatic chip off Robert Sherwood's play, *The Petrified Forest*."

SG: What about the morality clause in that RKO contract?

IW: All writers' contracts had them, in some form or other, in those days. It was nothing special. Studios were very paternalistic, and big on keeping up their good names in that era. And they wanted to make sure that they could fire a writer who disgraced himself publicly as an alcoholic, homosexual, criminal, or Communist. I don't think it was a special clause inserted during the Senator Joe McCarthy witch hunt period.

Of course, the witch hunt was very much in evidence in Hollywood. There were more blacklists than scripts. Studio heads were always mounds of Jello when it came to standing up to the kind of small monsters represented by Senator McCarthy, Martin Dies, Richard Nixon and the committee he was on that hounded Alger Hiss. I was a member of the Screen Writers Guild when the Hollywood Ten were persecuted—one of the most shameful episodes in Hollywood history. And, of course, as it turned out, my former army collaborator and friend, Carl Foreman, was one of those branded Communist and driven out of the country.

I was astonished. I mean, when I learned that Foreman had been an active Communist cell member. Close as we had been, I had never known that. I'd known he was very radical, but then, so was I. Foreman had never spilled a word of his Communist interests to me, not even a hint. And I guess he'd never tried to proselytize me because he must have read me as being hopeless—maybe a capitalist somewhere in the recess of my soul, and a maverick and non-joiner. I recalled a birthday party for Foreman at his apartment, and remembering it years later, I realized that all the guests had been members of the Hollywood Ten or Twenty, all save Sylvia and myself. I'd simply been too naive to know what was going on at the time. At any rate, when the Un-American Activities hearings were held out here, I publicly backed Foreman. That gang on the Un-American Committee was far more dangerous than any cadre of Communists.

It was a frightening period. The rightists had their reign of terror. Some of the best film writers who ever lived— Dalton Trumbo, Albert Maltz, Lardner, others—were thrown out of work, into the streets, drummed into exile, forced to write underground using assumed names at bargain basement fees. In fact, anyone who had joined anything or signed any petition even faintly liberal was suspect and in trouble. I had actually signed a pro-Loyalist petition once during the Spanish Civil War. Almost everyone who had signed that petition was blocked from work during the terror. I wasn't. Somehow, my name had been overlooked or that particular page had been lost.

But during the time I was working in the studios, that kind of Un-American business didn't dominate the working day. As a writer, it was considered much more serious and subversive if you tried to get a little honest sex or realistic talk into a scenario.

The only time I ever had a regular job in my life, and the first time I got a Social Security number, was when I signed a seven year contract at Warner Brothers—one year guaranteed, with options and salary raises for six years. Well, no sooner had I signed the contract than I regretted it. I had fractured my independence—the one thing I cherished most in life—and after a year or so I wanted to restore it, be whole, my own man again. I hated having to take assignments that didn't interest me. Writing *one* horse-opera was an entertainment. But being forced to write two was depressing. Also, as a contract writer, you were expected to pick up the leavings of other writers who had come and gone.

I'll give you an example. When I was at Warners in 1954, the studio decided to do a remake of its 1938 hit, *Four Daughters*. The 1954 version was to be a musical, *Young At Heart*, starring Frank Sinatra and Doris Day. After the screenwriter, Liam O'Brien, had completed his script, left the studio, and the film began shooting, the two stars decided that they wanted some of the scenes and dialogue rewritten. Since I was a contract writer, on the lot and available daily—

in the bullpen, so to speak—I was called upon to make the changes.

Well, being brought in on someone else's screenplay like this, when you don't know it, don't feel the flow of it, and being asked to change bits and pieces of it while the cameras are ready to roll, is very difficult. Also, as I learned, this kind of rewriting on the set requires not only writing but diplomacy. Frank Sinatra was no problem for me. We hit if off right away. We were into sports and politics right from the go. We spoke the same language.

"Look," Sinatra would say to me, "I'm kind of nothing in this scene they've written. Can't you give it a little zing?" We would talk about it, and I'd go off and rewrite for an hour, and bring it back. Sinatra liked everything I did, and the studio was sufficiently impressed to ask me to do an updated version of the old movie *Angles with Dirty Faces* to star Sinatra. It was to be called *The High Fence*. Sinatra was to play the role Cagney once played. I don't like rehashes, but I went at it with enthusiasm because it was for Sinatra. I worked on what came to a 56-page narrative treatment. Three times, in the weeks I worked on it, Sinatra phoned me to find out how I was doing and to discuss it with me. By the time I finished it, and the studio had given it to him, his interest in this had waned and been diverted elsewhere.

Doris Day, on the other hand, whom I like personally, was much more difficult to work with on changes. I would walk around the set with her, and she'd try to articulate why she couldn't read certain lines in the script or why she felt uncomfortable in a scene. But she was never able to put her finger on what was bothering her. I had to sort of divine what she was groping for—and then trudge back to my office, hoping I was guessing what was on her mind, and try to rewrite a scene to her liking.

Only once did I approach with enthusiasm the task of redoing the work of another writer—and that was because I was also allowed to play director. This occurred while I was still under contract to Warner Brothers. I was very restless about doing all the fill-in work thrown to me. Then, one day the late Steve Trilling, Jack L. Warner's assistant, called me in and said, "Look, I've heard you'd like a chance to direct. Well, we can't let you direct a feature, but we can give you an opportunity to direct a small segment of a picture. Jack Warner would like you to do it."

I was suspicious, but I listened. It appeared that Jean Renoir had written a period screenplay based on an episode in the life of General Boulanger, France's Minister of War, who conspired to become dictator of France in 1887. The story also involved his love for Marguerite de Bonnemains. Jean Renoir was going to direct it himself—it was called *Paris Does Strange Things*—and Renoir had commitments from Ingrid Bergman and Mel Ferrer to star in it. He asked Warner Brothers to finance the project blindly, and they did. Then, Renoir went back to Paris and shot the film.

Well, now the 86-minute film was done, and Jack Warner had just viewed it, and he couldn't make heads or tails out of it. The picture made absolutely no sense to him. He found it incomprehensible. To rescue it, to save ·the studio from a financial disaster, Warner got the idea that I should write a prologue for the film that would explain what it was all about—can you imagine that?—and also write a narration to be interspersed between dialogue scenes in which Mel Ferrer would clarify what was happening on the screen.

I saw the movie and read the script, and Warner was right. It was a dreadful and murky film. I can't imagine how a talented man like Jean Renoir could ever have created such a cretin of a picture. Even Ingrid Bergman, for all her beauty and talent, was lost in it.

It was hopeless, but a challenge. It was a real challenge because, for the new exposition prologue, they couldn't hire the actors back. So I contrived a new opening where the camera panned over inanimate objects in Boulanger's study—books on his shelf, framed paintings, a memento on his desk. The camera held on each as Ferrer's voice-over explained the characters and events about to unfold. And then I added five

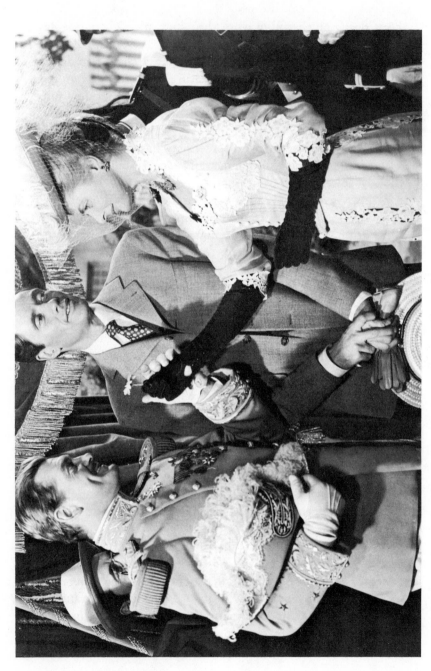

Jean Marais, Mel Ferrer, and Ingrid Bergman in *Paris Does Strange Things.*

pages of explanatory narration to be artfully interspersed throughout Renoir's picture.

Finally, I had to go out on the sound stage and direct the new opening sequence. I'll confess I was scared witless. I'd walked on a hundred sets before, but never in the guise of director. As a youngster, I used to be an extrovert. But over the years I'd become an ambivert. Socially I was and am outgoing, but at work I don't like to deal with other people. I'm very much a loner and into myself. In fact, it was not until 1969 that I consented to go on television for the first time, and to this day I refuse to make public speeches or deliver lectures. I decline at least 100 invitations a year.

Well, there I was that morning in 1957, walking on the studio set about to direct a prologue to a Renoir picture. And there were all the stagehands—cameramen, grips, electricians—staring at this—this *writer*. You must remember in what low esteem writers were held in the studios. Away from their typewriters, they were considered utterly ineffectual by crew members. So there I was and there was the crew, waiting. I stood on the set, kind of dumb, not knowing where to begin. At last someone said to me—where do you want to set the camera for the first shot? what's the angle? how do you want to adjust the lighting? I had no answers. I'd been so involved in the script, I hadn't thought out exactly how it would be shot. So there we all stood, immobilized, and at last I said something about placing the camera here or there, and then dollying in on the first object in Boulanger's study, and then the cameraman, a well-known one, moved in, snorted, shook his head, gave me a half dozen reasons why it couldn't be done that way. He began to tell me how it should be done, and before I knew it he had taken over almost completely.

We spent the morning and part of the afternoon shooting the sequence, and I don't know if I got more than two or three of my ideas into it. The cameraman and the technicians did it all. I left the set wringing wet, vowing to myself I'd never stray from my typewriter again.

The picture, *Paris Does Strange Things,* was released a month or so later, in March of 1957. In all these years, I've never met a single person who's ever seen it, not even in an Ingrid Bergman or Jean Renoir retrospective. The only happy part of the experience was that I received no screen credit.

However, to get back to the point I was making. I wanted out of my studio contract for the reasons given, but mainly because I wanted to be on my own again and devote more time to writing books. It wasn't easy getting out of a studio contract. The minute you went in and told Jack Warner or Trilling you wanted to quit, they looked at you suspiciously. A writer wanting to get out of a contract when most writers were begging for steady employment? There must be something else going on. When I first brought up quitting with Trilling, he said to me, "Why? Has M-G-M offered you more money?" I was making $1,000 a week at that time, and I didn't need more money. I said to him, "No, I promise you, this has nothing to do with money. I just want to be on my own and devote more time to writing books." Trilling looked at me as if I was crazy. "Books? What can you possibly make writing books?"

Finally, after several meetings, I convinced him that I was sane and sincere. Besides, there was an unspoken argument on my side evident at every meeting—unspoken, but understood by Trilling—which was that if I didn't feel like writing movies I wasn't going to be very effective for Warner Brothers. At last a compromise was reached. Trilling said to me, in effect, "Okay, we'll let you out of your contract if you write two more pictures for us. We've just bought film rights to a book written by a man who we understand is a friend of yours. The book is called *Too Much, Too Soon,* by Diana Barrymore as told to Gerold Frank. We've paid $100,000 for the property, more than we've paid for a book in years. Now part of the deal is that Gerold Frank comes here from New York to work on the screenplay. But he's never done any screenwriting. You've written some successful movies for us, so you know what has to be done. And you're close to Frank and can get along with him. So if you'll collaborate on the adaptation with him, and after that do a new storyline and screenplay for a second movie, we'll tear up your contract and let you go free. How's that?"

That was fine with me. So Gerold Frank came out to collaborate with me on the film version of his Diana Barrymore autobiography. Of course, Gerold and I were dear friends and we had no problem working together—except one. As author of the book, every scene and bit of dialogue was precious to Gerold—I understood it then, and understand it even better today, now that I've written so many books—but I had to explain to him that what reads well in print does not always play well on the screen. It took weeks for Gerold to gain some objectivity about his book, and the need for dropping some material and merging other material. Once he began to see Diana Barrymore's story as a visual drama, our screenplay improved and progressed wonderfully.

In terms of story, our major difficulty was in finding a way of dramatizing Diana's illness. Her illness had manifested itself in two ways—alcoholism and nymphomania. Since a woman's addiction to alcohol had just been the central conflict in a successful film—the Lillian Roth story, *I'll Cry Tomorrow,* starring Susan Hayward, also based on a Gerold Frank bestseller—we decided to concentrate on Diana Barrymore's nymphomania, her search for love, her need to be loved by a man. I interviewed psychoanalysts on the subject of nymphomania—its roots—and that was an eyeopener.

You know, the word 'nymphomania' has always been a sexist, turn-on word in our society. Men hear that a woman is a nymphomaniac, and they leer at her, and think of fun in bed. But, actually, it is a sad word and the manifestation of a deep illness, and there is nothing joyous about it for the woman or her lovers. I remember an incident that occurred a few years later when I had written my novel *The Chapman Report* and it was being read everywhere. One Sunday morning the phone rang, and there was a long-distance call from Atlanta. A young lady on the other end introduced herself. She told me that her psychoanalyst, who was one of the two authors of *The Three Faces of Eve,* felt that she should do a very personal and human book about her unusual illness. Her analyst was too busy to help her write the book, and besides he wasn't sure he was the right person for the job. He said he'd just read *The Chapman Report*, and he felt the author of that could do the best job for her. So here she was, calling me, asking me if I'd help her write the remarkable story of her illness. I said, "What is this illness you have?" She said, "I'm—well, I'm what they call a nymphomaniac."

I encouraged her to tell me a little of her story. I thought, or must have felt unconsciously, it would be titillating. So she started telling me about herself. It wasn't titillating at all. It was sick, and sad, and she was little girl lost and pitiful. Even if I'd had the time or inclination, I knew I couldn't have done it, get involved in publicly parading the deep illness of another. I told her I couldn't do it. Then her tone changed. She became flirtatious, full of sex promise. From anyone else it might have been provocative. But from her, knowing her history, it did nothing to me.

I left the phone somewhat depressed. I knew I didn't want any more phone calls like that. In those days I had a public number. I'd always felt having an unlisted number was some form of snobbery. But that day I was very tempted to have an unlisted number. Finally, four years later, when *The Man* was published, I was forced to get an unlisted phone number. Some psychotic racist phoned me from Palm Springs and said he was coming into Los Angeles to get me—because I wanted to make a black man president of the United States. He was very threatening. At first I treated it as a joke, and then, thinking about it, I found it chilling. I called the police. They said that they couldn't officially act until the man who'd threatened me acted first. I said, "By then it'll be too late." They said, "Sorry, those are the laws." So then, after two more threatening calls, the last of them from Los Angeles, I got hold of a politician friend, who spoke to the police, and, unofficially, they sent two detectives out to hunt down this psychotic. They had some clues from me as to his where-abouts. They found him—learned he had a criminal record—and warned him to stay away from me. Then the detectives came to me and showed me a mug shot of the man and said, "If you ever see anyone like that around here, get out of sight fast, and call us." I never saw the man, but for weeks, whenever I was outdoors, I found myself looking over my shoulder. At last, I called the telephone company and told them to give me an unlisted number. No more calls from potential killers or provocative nymphomaniacs.

But back at Warner Brothers, Gerold Frank and I tried to portray the deep suffering Diana Barrymore endured in her compulsive relationships with men. The script was not delib-erately sensational—was, in fact, written with restraint—but in that period anything like that was shocking.

The studio had Carol Baker in mind to play the Diana Barrymore role. Carol had just had a big hit on the screen in the title role of Kazan's *Baby Doll*, and she was a star over-night. She was also, studio hands told us, very temperamental and difficult. However, Warners thought our script perfect for her. They gave it to her. She read it, gave it back—threw it back, I should say. "You want *me* to play a *nympho?*" she was alleged to have exclaimed. "What do you think I am, anyway? Are you trying to wreck my career?" This, from the woman who'd just come off *Baby Doll*. Well, it turned out that la Baker now had a new image of herself and wanted to do only Ibsen and the classics.

As a result, the script was shelved. Gerold returned to New York, and I was kept on to do my last picture for War-ner Brothers, the contract-breaker. Anyway, Warners later hired two television writers to do a new version of *Too Much, Too Soon*. Violence was substituted for sex. The film was made. It went into release and died quietly.

My last contract picture was *Bombers B-52*. Now, you can't get the humor of that unless you know me, or knew me at the time. Here I was being ordered to do a film in co-operation with Strategic Air Command about our bomber crews and flight lines, and here I was probably the only writer in Hollywood who did not fly. I had an absolute phobia about flying, and did not get into a plane once in all the years after I'd been discharged from the army. For almost thirty years I traveled exclusively by automobile, train, ship. And here I was assigned to do *Bombers B-52*.

I took the train to Omaha to meet the top officers of SAC and to do background research. I met the commanding general there, and after the amenities, he said, "All right, first thing, let's take you up in a B-52." I said, "Sorry, sir, no can do. I don't fly." His eyes widened. He couldn't believe his ears. And when he did, he stared at me as if I was some walking anachronism out of the 17th century. He picked up a phone and called Jack L. Warner at Burbank and said, "What's going on here? You've sent me a writer who refuses to fly!" Warner said, "I know. So let him stand and look. He has a good imagination. That's enough."

And you know what? SAC let me do it my way, and I did it. They built the mock-up of an interior of a B-52 at Warners, and sent officer advisers to make the whole Rube Goldberg machinery comprehensible to me. In all, the shooting of the film was a pleasant farewell experience—my good friend, the late Richard Whorf, was the producer, and two other more casual friends, Karl Malden and Natalie Wood, were the stars. In November, 1957, when the film was released, *The New York Times* did well by me, stating, "Irving Wallace's dialogue is excellent. Furthermore, his unpretentious scenario is credible and persuasive in training sequences and especially in the hearth scenes."

After that, I took only two more jobs in studios. One was a circus picture at Columbia, based on an idea by the producer, a very stilted, contrived idea, yet the picture was a huge boxoffice success. The other job was that of doing the original story and treatment at Paramount for a big film on the life of Barnum, out of which grew my Knopf biography of Barnum. And, too, in 1958, I did a number of live and filmed television shows, mostly routine, although two or three

"NO SLEEP TILL DAWN"

Page one from "No Sleep Till Dawn," Dell comic's adptation of *Bombers B-52*.

were pretty good.

As must be only too evident to you, I was glad to get out of screenwriting. For one thing, the salaried screenwriter was always the low, low man on the totem pole. He had no autonomy, no power to protect what he had written. In the big studio days, the front office and the producers dominated the scene, followed by the star and the director. At a later period, the director gained ascendency, and to this day remains top man. But at no time was the writer a key figure. With a handful of exceptions, the average studio screenwriter was only a small part of the celluloid assembly line—talking over the story with others, writing it himself, being called in to be told by the executives, the producer, the director, the actors, what had to come out, what had to go in, what had to be changed. In my darkest period, I felt more like a secretary taking dictation than a creative writer.

Once I fully understood the screenwriter's position, my disenchantment with moviemaking was complete. I only wanted out. But since I needed the studio money to stay alive, I couldn't risk getting out until I was sure I could eek out a living at books. During the years between 1953 and 1959, to keep myself from going crazy, to give myself some hours of satisfaction and happiness, I'd come home from eight hours at the studio, and write on my own, write books during evenings, as well as weekends and between jobs. It was exhausting beyond belief. And rough on my wife, but she was good about it. She knew it kept my head together and was my only salvation.

Then the saving miracle happened. As you know, I got lucky. I threw everything over to concentrate on my second novel, with no dream that it could possibly be a success, and it became a success beyond any dream I'd ever had. After that, I knew I'd been liberated. I knew I would never have to go back to moviewriting, and I never have, although I've received some fantastic offers.

But I'll tell you a funny thing that happened along the way. In the years that followed, when I'd put movies far

behind me, devoted my life to writing all those multi-char-
actered, complex novels—*The Prize, The Man, The Plot*—and
enjoyed doing each and every one—well, at some point I
reached a curious dead end. I was tired of being alone so
many months of each year, for so many years, with only my
typewriter and make-believe characters to keep me company.
Also, looking back, I must have been utterly fatigued. So,
for the first and last time since I'd left the studios, I entertained the idea of going back to do a movie. What attracted
me was not filmmaking but the excitement of people and
outside activity, among other things.

My mood coincided with a very attractive studio offer.
Now, ever since I quit Hollywood, I had been getting offers
to adapt my own novels into screenplays. When Dick Zanuck
bought screen rights to *The Chapman Report,* he wanted me
to do the screenplay. I had refused. Later, the director,
George Cukor, had asked Zanuck to phone me in Venice,
Italy, to do the final rewrite. Again, I had refused. And in
the years after, I refused to do screenplays on *The Three
Sirens, The Man, The Plot.*

Readers of my books often castigate me, in the mail,
for allowing my stories to be changed in the film versions.
They can't understand why I don't go along with the book,
write the screenplay, and at least to see that the film is faithful to the book. They feel the movie is an extension of the
book. I always write and tell them that it isn't, that the book
is a separate thing, and my full and final statement. It would
be too difficult for me to take materials I've lived with so
many years in one medium, and attempt to condense and
adapt them to another medium. Further, if I went along
with each film, it would cost me, through loss of time,
another book, and yet another. I prefer to stand on my book.
The book represents me. The film is a different matter. I
want the film to be good, of course, but if it is disappointing,
it has nothing to do with me. The book is me. The film is
them.

Yet, here I was, after ten years devoted solely to books,

considering going back. The latest offer, if one wanted to go back into film, was almost irresistible. A major studio—I don't recall if it was Paramount or another—approached my West Coast agent, Evarts Ziegler, and said that since all of my novels had sold to movies, I might be one of the best qualified persons around to make independent pictures. The studio was prepared to set me up in an independent unit, let me produce three pictures, one of them based on one of my next books and the other based on two other books they'd let me buy. And the studio promised to let me make the picture in any way I wanted. Temptation, I'll tell you. Temptation because, first of all, again, I was tired of being alone. Temptation because, also, there were all those baubles a studio could offer—suites of offices, limousines, pretty starlets. I could well remember seeing all that in studios. And now, as a well-known novelist, I could have it all. Temptation, and yet indecision.

One day I was sitting brooding about the Faustian offer—very ambivalent about it—when my wife put indecision to rest. She said, "How can you even consider it? Don't you remember? I do. Once you got into movie making, you spent ten years trying to get out. Now you are out. You're on your own, beholden to no one. No one on earth is more independent than you. So how can you consider going to work for somebody else?"

I said I wouldn't be working for anyone else. "The offer guarantees that I'll have complete freedom."

Sylvia was exasperated. "Oh, you know better than that. If you make a movie, you can't have complete freedom. No matter how high up you are, there is still someone higher. After all, there is someone who is putting up the money. They'd be above you, and sooner or later they'd shackle you." Then she added, "And think of all the unwritten books it'll cost you, all the books you want to write. They'll never be written, never."

In seconds, indecision fled. "You're absolutely right," I said.

She was right, of course. The aberration had been temporary. It has never returned. I doubt if it ever will. Satan is behind me. And ever since, my enthusiasm for being my own person, working alone on my books, has never diminished, in fact has grown.

I'm satisfied to let studios buy film rights to my books and for myself to stay away from the picturemaking process completely.

SG: Then even if you're not writing directly for the studios, in a way you are still writing for the studios. Every bestselling book of yours they snatch up, or most of them become movies.

IW: But I'm not writing my books *for* the movies. I don't have movies in mind at all, not at all, not ever. I sometimes read a review of one of my books in which the reviewer says I prefabricated the book for films or had an eye on films when I wrote the book. That is such utter nonsense it is hard to discuss sensibly. It is nonsense because the reviewer knows absolutely nothing about movies, about the mentality of movie producers, or about my own deepest motivations and yearnings.

When I gave up films to devote myself to books full-time in 1958 or 1959, I blocked out movies completely. After I finished my novel *The Chapman Report*, I never imagined it could be a motion picture. The central subject was taboo in the film industry. The book was far too sexually explicit. The whole storyline was too difficult to convert into film. Yet, I should have known better—because I knew the producer mentality so well. The studios sniffed a potential bestseller when their people read the book in manuscript—and studios like presold properties. They're afraid to make judgments on their own, understandably, considering the amount it costs to make a movie and how many of them flop. They like a sensational and unusual story—and certainly *Chapman* was both—no matter how difficult it would be to get on the

The four women of *The Chapman Report.* L-R: Claire Bloom, Glynis Johns, Jane Fonda, Shelley Winters.

screen. But, I repeat, movies were not on my mind when I wrote *Chapman*. In fact, the novel was a revolt against all the stereotyped stories I had been forced to do in studios. It was almost as if I was defying the studios—saying, here is one thing you can't get your sticky fingers on, won't want to touch. Well, you know what happened.

SG: What happened exactly?

IW: I kept an occasional Journal in 1959 which noted some aspects of the deal, although it is scanty and incomplete since business is only marginally interesting to me. But referring to the Journal and my own memory, let me try to reconstruct what happened.

I finished the 136,750 words of *The Chapman Report* on May 16. Reynolds had flown out here on his second trip and liked it; Weybright in New York liked it but wanted some rewrites. He flew an editor, Walter Freeman, out here to work with me three days. Meanwhile, Evarts Ziegler, my Hollywood agent, read and liked it and decided to put it on the movie market in manuscript.

Seventeen copies of *The Chapman Report* went out to studios by messenger on August 18, 1959. At once we had expressions of interest or requests for prices from Dick Zanuck, Martin Manulis, Marty Jurow, Columbia, Warners, Stanley Meyer, Feldman, Hyman, and several other studios and producers. On Tuesday noon, August 25, Ziegler sent a wire to all parties asking $175,000 against 5% of world gross and a penalty of $100,000 over five years if the picture was not made in thirty months.

Sylvia and I were lunching at home on hot dogs when, at 12:30, the 25th of August, Ziegler called to say Stanley Meyer, an independent filmmaker and millionaire, had met the offer. We were in. Bidding closed the next evening at six o'clock. Zanuck and Warners also met the offer. By 6:30 that evening, Ziegler, his partner Hal Ross, and I decided to sell to Zanuck—who was phoned immediately. At least from

The Chapman Report on the Champs Elysees, 1963.

a standpoint of financial security, a new life had begun for
me.

After that, every novel I wrote, from *Chapman* to *The
Seven Minutes*, immediately sold to movies; every novel
except *The Man*, which took eight years to reach the screen.
And that one I wanted most of all to see on the screen, because my message would then reach a larger audience and because it would turn more people onto the book.

SG: What about *The Man* as a film? What happened?

IW: That was a long, long haul getting that one made. A saga of
despair. Early in May of 1964 Evarts Ziegler put 24 copies
(each copy 1,200 mimeographed pages in three ream boxes)
of *The Man* on the studio market. Ziegler liked to submit my
books in manuscript. Psychologically, he felt, it gave each
potential buyer a feeling he was getting an exclusive look.
When a producer gets a book in galleys or hardbound, he
knows it is being shopped around all over the place. So *The
Man* went out in manuscript form.

By the end of May, six firm requests were in Ziegler's
hands. On June 3, 1964, he sent telegrams to those six and
fourteen other studios and producers requesting half a million
dollars for the film rights to the novel. The buyer would
have until six P.M. on June 5 to comply.

Not one of them did comply, and Ziegler, refusing to
settle for less, took the book off the market to wait until
publication date. A number of producers I've gotten to know
since then told me what happened. They wanted the book.
It was not the asking price that bothered them. What worried them was the subject. Several had made inquiries among
theatre exhibitors in the South. As one, those exhibitors said
they would not show the movie. Don't forget, that was the
year 1964. The producers feared boycotting and trouble.
Only a few Black movies were being made at that time, and
they were low-budget, token films, usually starring Sidney
Poitier and some nuns. They were simple, gentle pictures,

Evarts Ziegler, Irving Wallace's West Coast agent.

not very angry. But *The Man* was an angry book, would make an expensive, controversial film—the idea of putting a black man in The White House was a bit too much in those days—so the studios and producers backed off.

But the book continued to sell, stir interest, and was constantly being resurrected for films. One resurrection among many came in late January, 1965. Milton Green, the photographer and former partner of Marilyn Monroe, Sammy Davis, Jr., and their attorney, Irving Stein, purchased the motion picture rights of *The Man*. They agreed to pay an end sum of $200,000 plus 5% of gross after the film had grossed $3,750,000 in black and white version. Sidney Poitier would play Douglass Dilman, my black President. I happened to be in New York when the deal was made, and I met Sammy Davis and Milton Green for the signing.

Five months later the contract fell through. The reason for the investors' failure to follow through on the deal was that Irving Stein was killed in an auto accident. Sammy Davis and Milton Green played lesser roles. But Irving Stein was one of the big attorneys in New York, and he was the key to the whole project. I met with him a couple times and thought him a lovely man. But, after he died, Sammy Davis lost all interest in his company and the project. So *The Man* reverted back to us. Again, the property was briefly side-tracked.

In September, 1967, Mel Shayne and Monte Proser of New York formed an independent film company to make the novel into a film. They called their company Promel Productions. A month later they sold the film rights to Eddie Fisher and Burton D. Chait.

Chait and Fisher hired Richard Attaway, a black writer, to do the screenplay. Attaway did three screenplay drafts. They were powerful, but the producers felt they were too long and too rough. Rough they may have been, but he was damn good—he had passion. And because he was black, he understood those characters in the book. He came out here to Los Angeles one weekend to talk over the script. He said

Sammy Davis, Jr., Irving Wallace, and Milton Green signing the film rights to *The Man*, 1965.

to me, "Irving, you've got the White point of view perfect but only some of the black. Now let me give it the full black point of view. Let's give the movie balance." I thought he was an excellent choice to do the script.

While Attaway was writing, Chait and Fisher were reassigning the film rights. In some kind of sell-off or trade, they transferred the property to Argo Internacional of Madrid, a production company actively making low-budget pictures in Spain—Spaghetti Westerns or something.

In mid-April, 1968, a few days after Argo picked up the rights from Chait and Fisher, Argo asked Ziegler for a deferment of the $140,000 payment for film rights to *The Man*. As compensation, they agreed to forward $15,000 on Ziegler's acceptance of the extension, and that $15,000 would be applied against the eventual $140,000 purchase price for the film rights. Ziegler agreed, and in September the Argo people, headed by Jack Lamont, took over the rights completely and paid $15,000 for option extension to August 1, 1969. Argo paid another $15,000 in May of 1970, but later that year they could not (or simply did not) make the final $110,000 payment, and the film rights reverted back to me.

So the film rights had gone from the Sammy Davis group to Promel Productions, then to Chait and Fisher, to Argo, and then back home again to me. I was becoming discouraged that the film would ever be made when, in April of 1970, Hal Ross, Ziegler's partner, called and told me ABC Television had purchased *The Man* for a two hour film-of-the-week and for international theatrical release. That is, it was to be shown on television here, as a feature film in Europe.

In August, 1970, I noted in my Journal that "Gethers was dropped when ABC demanded vast changes. Rod Serling assigned to write a new screenplay." Gethers was Steve Gethers, a producer-writer working for Lee Rich Productions —the outfit that was doing the film for ABC. What happened to Gethers and his screenplay, at least as I heard it from him and from my agents, was that Gethers had written a straightforward, honest screenplay adhering faithfully to the story of

Marquee of *The Man* in Westwood (Los Angeles).

Huge lighted billboard of *The Man* above Sunset Strip.

my novel, and ended his script as I had ended my novel, with the impeachment of the president. But in that fall of 1970, President Nixon had the then powerful Vice-President Spiro Agnew out doing his dirties—laying it into the media, trying to intimidate the press and television. Also, there was a movement on in the east to try to impeach Nixon during his very first term, even before it was fully known what he and his White House gang were up to. Well, the TV networks were fighting back against the administration, but they were very worried, and a certain amount of self-censorship was going on, and perhaps this had some effect on the timid lions at ABC.

Now ABC would probably never corroborate this, but after reading Gethers hard-hitting script, I was told they called him in and said words to this effect: "It's good, but we can't have the impeachment as the climax. Take it out." Gethers said, "But that's the big ending of Wallace's novel and of my script. Without it we have no third act." The network insisted that he invent another ending. He tried, finally gave up and told them it couldn't be done. So goodbye Gethers, and goodbye his script.

Then Rod Serling, a neighbor whom I know and who liked my book, was asked to take over. He told ABC that he thought they already had a good script. Apparently, he was told this wasn't the time to show an impeachment on television. So Serling did his best. Actually, he substituted a Congressional hearing for the impeachment. Then, loosely basing his new storyline on three or four story strands in my book, he combined them and created his own central fictional story. Serling confined himself to one story, instead of several, because he thought he was doing it for television. Had he known that he was writing a feature motion picture, I'm sure he would have approached the story on several levels, and with more depth.

Soon, ABC was casting. James Earl Jones, a magnificent actor and one not easy to find roles for, read the script and said he would do the part of the black President of the United

Irving Wallace and Paul Newman on the set of *The Prize*, 1963.

States.   There was tremendous excitement about getting someone of James Earl Jones' stature.   I met Jones at a dinner party at the Bistro given by ABC and Lee Rich Productions to celebrate the start of production.   I got off in a corner with Jones and asked him if he was satisfied with his role as Douglass Dilman.   "Do you feel too much was left out?"   I asked.   Jones' broad face took on the look of a wink.   "Don't worry, I'll put it all back in."   Meaning, he'd flesh out Dilman through his performance.   And in a sense, he did.

When the filming began, I did something I rarely do.   I went out to the set to watch James Earl Jones work.   He was a marvel.   I suppose his artistry oversold me, made me think that he could carry the film.   As it turned out, he couldn't.   As I said, I rarely watch the shooting of my films.   I skipped the making of *Chapman* altogether.   But when Mark Robson was directing *The Prize* at M-G-M, he invited me to drop by and watch Paul Newman and Elke Sommers do Craig's press conference scene in Stockholm.   I got to chatting with Paul Newman.   He said, half apologetically, that he had not read my novel, only Ernest Lehman's adapted screenplay.   Newman said he always preferred to read the novel after the picture was done.   If he read it first, he might be tempted to interfere with the screenwriter's version and get more of the book into the screenplay.

Anyway, here's my last private Journal entry on *The Man*: "Film of *The Man* shot in Los Angeles, at Goldwyn Studio, and in Washington, D. C., and turned out so well that the ABC executives decided to abandon idea of its debuting on TV and to release it as a full-blown theatrical motion picture in the United States and abroad.   Decision was made after two sneak previews in the Chicago area.   At once, a half dozen major distributors bid for the right to handle the film, and Paramount was selected.   *The Man* was released as a feature film nationally in June and July of 1972.   I saw it once in a projection room in Hollywood, and a portion of it again at a political press preview in Miami Beach.   Film received mixed reviews and did fair business.   It will have its

James Earl Jones in *The Man*.

television debut in near future."

SG: And along the way you made one of the most unusual contracts a novelist has ever made—sold three unwritten books to
a studio sight unseen. Has that ever happened before?

IW: No. This was a first, as far as I know. Although, after making that arrangement with me, 20th Century-Fox tried it
once more, in a limited way. They optioned or contracted
with Truman Capote for a novel he had not yet written.

But as to my unusual contract—no, it had never happened before, nor has it happened since. You want to know
how it developed step by step? Well, I'll let you in on how
the whole thing developed, chronologically. I shouldn't, because it is business, which is not my primary interest. It has
nothing to do with literary affairs or writing. It is one of
those Santa Claus gifts that can happen to a writer, but in
terms of creative writing it is a subsidiary event. However,
because it was small history, in a way, I have no objection
to letting the facts be known. Let me try to recall, as best I
can and with some help from my Journal notes, what happened and who was involved.

On Monday, February 8, 1965, in New York, at 2:30
in the afternoon, my literary agent and my attorney, Paul
Reynolds and Paul Gitlin, completed a contract promising a
$1,500,000 advance on my next three novels, *The Plot, The
Word, The Seven Minutes,* with Simon and Schuster and with
Pocket Books. I had the ideas for those future books, and
their titles, but had not written a word on any one of them,
except for notes. Also, I was informed that New American
Library-World had met the same terms, but my representatives chose to stay with my regular publisher. At 7:30
in the evening, old friends Helen Gurley Brown (on the eve
of taking over *Cosmopolitan* magazine) and David Brown,
executive story head of 20th Century-Fox, took me to The
Leopard Restaurant for dinner. Dave had heard of NAL's
offer, and I told him we had closed with Simon and

Schuster. David said he wanted to speak to Darryl Zanuck about a similar arrangement for the motion picture rights to these unwritten books for 20th Century-Fox. He said, "If book publishers believe enough in the consistency of your performance to contract for future novels sight unseen, then I don't see why motion picture studios can't do the same thing."

Negotiations were begun in mid-February with the Zanucks, and by early March Richard Zanuck was firmly interested in closing the three-book purchase. I remember Monday, March 8, a day Ziegler called three times. He told me the Zanucks were eager to see brief idea outlines and they would go ahead with the deal without a Board of Directors okay. They would buy the three book ideas outright. Ziegler and I decided we wanted around one million dollars for the package. Darryl Zanuck agreed that the price, and our terms, were "in the ball park."

I prepared three novel outlines for their perusal. Each ran about 2½ pages—just enough to give them a general idea of where the novels were in my mind, and might go as I wrote them. The outlines were specific enough for the Zanucks to get a feel of their direction, but general enough so I would not be pinched during their actual writing. The point is that I demanded, and got, my freedom to do what I wanted with my books, outline or no outline. I did not write my books to fit anyone's preconceptions.

About the second week of April, 1965, Ziegler arranged to meet with Richard Zanuck and Dave Brown to go over the outlines. Zanuck and Brown would read the outlines in Ziegler's presence, make notes, return the copies, and speak to Darryl Zanuck in Paris within 48 hours and give their final reply. I was at the dentist's when Ziegler called about their decision. He told me that Dick Zanuck said, "Wow! We don't like one or two—we like all three!!" I was delighted. Ziegler gave them until Thursday at six to make up their minds.

He called me that Thursday at about 4:30. He said the

Irving Wallace, Richard Zanuck and David Brown closing the contract for Zanuck Production's film rights to *The Plot, The Seven Minutes* and *The Word*.

Zanucks were willing to go for one and only one deal. They agreed to pay a high six-figure sum—guaranteed most of it for two of the novels, with a huge option on the third one. I discussed the matter with Sylvia, and called Ziegler back at 5:30 to tell him the deal was acceptable to me. The next evening Dave Brown telephoned me to congratulate me and say how delighted he and the Zanucks were.

The following Monday I went out to 20th Century-Fox and met with Richard Zanuck and Brown. They were happy, discussed the books, and Dick read me a two page cable from his father, Darryl Zanuck, listing the book ideas in order of his preference: *The Plot, The Word, The Seven Minutes.* He thought *The Plot* perfect in film terms, *The Word* excellent if more than a single central character could be added by their writers, and *Minutes* a good story, although it worried him because he does not like court room stories.

And that is the inside story of how it happened, as it happened.

SG: And this advance contract, with advance guarantees, this didn't affect your writing of the novels? I mean—did you, on any conscious level, think of movies when writing the novels?

IW: Not a bit. I gave the films not one iota of thought at any time after that. I wouldn't have, anyway, as I told you before. And in this case, why should I? I had the contract. I had the guarantee. There was no one to please but myself. If I pleased myself as I wrote—and hoped what pleased me might please the reading public—then I was sure the studio would be satisfied. They wanted a good book, written as a book, which the public would accept. If the novels proved to be bestsellers, no matter how difficult they might prove to convert into films, the movie studio would be totally satisfied. Well, each novel turned out to be a bestseller, and the studio was relieved and grateful for that. In all the years I was writing those books, the studio never once inquired about the books, about their progress, anything, and knew not a thing about each one until it was done and delivered to the publisher, and finally to them.

SG: Of the three, only one became a finished film, isn't that right?

IW: Yes, *The Seven Minutes*. During the time I wrote the novels, and in the years they were published, the old studio system was slowly disintegrating.

Although, I must say, *The Plot* was almost made. 20th Century-Fox had Lester Linsk preparing the production. John Michael Hayes, a fine screenwriter, who had done *Rear Window* for Hitchcock, did the first draft screenplay. But when he was done, the studio heads were uncertain. The studio was failing. *The Plot* would have to be a big budget picture. The executives were searching for a way to make the picture different, something that would guarantee boxoffice success. So Zanuck and Brown hired Erich Segal to do a rewrite. He hadn't done *Love Story* yet, but was supposed to have had something to do with a draft of the Beatles movie, *Yellow Submarine*. Erich Segal tried a new approach, but Linsk, Zanuck, and Brown were not happy with it. After that they brought in another writer, one I know well, John Sherlock, the novelist. He had just undertaken his rewrite, when the studio ran out of money. All their movies being prepared for production were shelved, including *The Plot*.

Too bad. Because *The Plot* could have been a significant and important film. In the book, I had created a story—projecting ahead a few years from publication in 1967—where the nuclear powers, at a crisis point, have a Summit conference in Paris. I included Red China as a recognized nation and a member of the Summit. Now, remember, I wrote this at a time when the United States pretended Mao's China did not exist. We recognized only Chiang's China on Taiwan. I thought that reality too ridiculous, and projected a more sane reality in fiction where mainland China was an accepted part of our world. I was told that when some newspapermen at the United Nations handed one of Taiwan's representatives my book, he glanced at it, became livid, and flung the book across the room.

In my novel I tried to show that the big diplomats at the Summit were not the ones affecting change. Rather, some little people, ordinary people, on the outside of the Summit, were the ones who unwittingly affected the outcome and changed the world by keeping the peace. I had a British girl who'd been involved in a Profumo-like affair, a former U. S. State Department official who had been disgraced and was in exile, an ex-President of the United States who had been ineffectual in office, a once renowned columnist who had fallen in favor—I had all of them attracted to the Summit in Paris for one personal reason or another. And then I dramatized how their lives crossed, and how together they unwittingly altered the result of the Summit and the future of mankind.

It would have been an excellent movie. It may still become one, of course. Part of the thrust of the book was to get Mao's China understood and into the psyche of the American people. I felt we were all on this earth together, and we had better learn to live in peace with one another. It's always amused me since, grimly amused me, that Nixon, the veteran hater and baiter of Communist China, was the one who used political opportunism to unofficially recognize Communist China. I remember when my wife and I met Dr. Henry Kissinger the first time, shortly after he and Nixon had conferred with the Chinese leaders in Peking. He told us that he had in his private possession forty hours of tapes of his own conversations with Chou En-lai. Much of it will be in Kissinger's memoirs one day. I wanted to tell him that I was one of many who had recognized mainland China long before Nixon had, but I didn't.

SG: What about *The Seven Minutes,* the film that was produced? The book seemed to say to me that this whole issue is so complex and so involved and so subjective that there is really no answer to it. But I felt that when Russ Meyer took the book and made a new screenplay, he was saying just the opposite. That there is a definite answer. He was using the book as a defense of his profession.

IW: Yes, that's true in a way. Russ Meyer felt my book was a perfect platform to attempt to justify on film his career as a skinflick producer and to inveigh against those who would censor skinflicks or anything else. To understand Russ Meyer's handling of the movie, you'll have to understand the climate in which the film adaptation was produced, so bear with me a minute.

You see, originally Russ wasn't supposed to have made the picture. Richard D. Zanuck and 20th Century-Fox had acquired the movie rights to my book sight unseen, before the book was ever written. The picture was to have been made by Richard Fleischer, who'd directed a whole string of pictures for the Zanucks from *Compulsion* to *Tora, Tora, Tora*. With *The Seven Minutes,* the Zanucks were not only giving Fleischer an opportunity to direct but also to produce. He hired Marvin Albert, a novelist who'd earlier adapted his own Tony Rome books for Frank Sinatra. In the summer of 1969, I met with Fleischer, who is an old friend, and Albert, and I saw the screenplay that was developing, and I thought it was a balanced, exciting job, and true to my book.

Then, suddenly—it was in November of 1969—the studio ran into terrible financial trouble. All productions or projects in the works were canceled or shelved. Apparently, the board of directors had determined the way not to lose money was not to make pictures. Most studio personnel were given notice, and one of the victims was Dick Fleischer. However, the Zanucks were still there, holding on, and were given the green light to make one or two more low-budget films. Casting around for a foolproof producer-director, their eyes lit on Russ Meyer—there'd been a big story on Russ in the *Wall Street Journal* which may have sparked Zanuck's interest.

Irving Wallace and Russ Meyer on the set of *The Seven Minutes*.

As I had it from David Brown, Dick Zanuck's righthand man, they said to each other—hey, look, there's this fellow Russ Meyer who made *Vixen* on a shoestring budget of $72,000 and it's grossed $4,000,000 to date—he must know something we don't know.   In fact, Russ had made *Vixen* in Canada, carrying a camera on his shoulder, creating his own story, and employing nonprofessionals for actors.

So, with the studio going under, Zanuck brought Russ Meyer in, told him—here are all our properties—take your pick and make that one for us.   Russ looked the properties over, and he selected *The Seven Minutes* as his first studio picture.   So, as I said, Fleischer was dropped—the greatest thing that ever happened to him, because as a free-lance he's done what he always wanted to do and has had any number of hits—and they brought Russ Meyer in from the bullpen to replace Fleischer.   Then the studio phoned me and asked if I'd like to meet Russ and see *Vixen*.   So I went over to the studio one evening and met Russ, a big bear of a guy, simple, sincere, artistically a primitive.   I was rather amused by *Vixen*. It was not hardcore pornography.   It was really like *Playboy* centerfolds—before they got into frontal nudity—converted into motion.   Russ, I could see, was not into obscenity but into titillation.   Big on breasts and buttocks and suggested sex, kinky, campy, with a little moral at the end.   Russ had a cult of followers around the country, was proud of the cult, and proud of a recent retrospective of his films at Yale.   He was also a man beset by lawsuits, constantly harassed by various local censorship boards, and angry about them, and determined to joust with each and everyone of them.

This offer from 20th Century-Fox was his first opportunity to work for a major and prestigious studio.   He said to me, "The story of *The Seven Minutes* is my story, what's been happening to me.   That's why I picked it as the property I want to do here."   This was also Russ's first chance to make a movie based on a book, on a published story—up to then he'd always just made them up—and to use professional actors. Above all, this was an opportunity for him to make a state-

On the set of *The Seven Minutes*. L-R: Olan Soule, Lyle Bettger, Irving Wallace, Stanley Adams, Philip Carey; seated, Jay C. Flippen.

ment about freedom of speech. So Russ set out to make his cinematic statement, but he committed one grave error: he tried to stick too closely to the book. Perhaps he was awed by working from a bestselling novel on which so much money had been spent. I don't know. But he tried to shovel the entire plot, all of the characters, into a tight ninety minutes, and by doing so he obscured whatever talent he had. Whatever the virtues in his previous kind of animated gatefolds, they were not apparent in his film adaptation of *The Seven Minutes*. The story got in his way. He didn't know how to move it. And yes, you're right, he overloaded the film with his own defense. He lectured too much, and he was on the nose, too obvious, all the way.

SG: I had a feeling that his style, which is very straightforward and obvious, didn't fit the subject matter of the story, which was complex and subtle.

IW: Correct.   The problem of censorship and pornography is exceedingly complex, has to be handled delicately, but Russ plowed into it like a bull in a china shop, to coin an expression. The picture opened nationwide in the summer of 1971, and was poorly received by the critics, and while it drew audiences, it didn't draw enough to break even—it cost $2,400,000, so the break-even point was double that sum. I suspect it let down Russ's fans, and I know it disappointed people who'd read or heard of my book. In fact, the distributors ran into such resistance to Russ Meyer's name on the marquees of certain Fox theaters, that they began to remove "Russ Meyer's *The Seven Minutes*" from the marquees and replace it with "Irving Wallace's *The Seven Minutes*"—feeling my image wasn't quite as bad as his. People around the country were sending me photographs of marquees featuring my name, and I'm not sure I was too happy about it, because it wasn't my picture.

Another reason for the picture's failure was that Russ tried to be serious and campy at the same time, and it just

Marquee advertising *The Seven Minutes* in West Los Angeles. Note it is Irving Wallace's not Russ Meyer's *The Seven Minutes*.

didn't work. At the outset, I thought that he might do something better. But when I began to see the scripts he was turning out with collaborators, I had a sinking feeling. Russ sent me the final shooting script when I was on the Riviera, asking for my comments for the revised final. Some of it was good, but I was troubled by much of the script. I remember going up to my suite at the Carlton Hotel—I lost a whole day on the beach writing him—God, how many pages of criticism did I write him?—ten or twenty or more. I wrote him point by point, telling him what was wrong with the script and how it might be repaired. I wrote him, in effect, Please, Russ, you've got to change this because it makes no sense at all the way you have it. In the end, he remained inflexible. He patched up a couple of minor things, but he couldn't see the major changes. Despite our good relationship, he had to do it his way. So he shot a Swiss cheese of a story—full of holes. The picture didn't do well domestically, but I'm told the studio won't lose on the picture—they should squeak through on foreign boxoffice.

It was quite an experience, since I had never before gotten even this minimally involved in a film based on one of my books. For me, the book is my statement, all I have to say. I want nothing to do with any film based on my work. Of course, I'm always curious to read the finished screenplay and see the previewed film. But the visual result is someone else's trip, not my own. And credit for a good film, blame for a bad one, should go to the filmmakers.

SG: Besides those you've already mentioned, what do you recall as some memorable moments, for better or for worse, or some memorable people you met, during your earlier time in Hollywood? I mean, before you became a well-known novelist and everything changed for you. Do any people come to mind?

IW: Well, it would take an entire book in itself to relate some of my earlier adventures in Hollywood. But a few encounters come immediately to mind.

During the course of my movie interviewing career, I met Adolf Hitler's great and good friend, Leni Riefenstahl, who made that powerful Olympic film. She was a real looker, and during the course of our talk, she lifted her dress up almost to her waist to show me a skiing scar on her upper thigh.

I remember interviewing Harry Cohn, head of Columbia Studios, a real tyrant who treated most of his hired hands like dirt. It was in speaking of Cohn's funeral, long after, and the large crowd in attendance, that someone said, "Just give people what they want, and they'll show up."

There was a lively afternoon with Orson Welles, when he was the boy wonder out here—we had in common the same grammar school, Weiskopf, that we'd both attended in Kenosha, Wisconsin. Then there was Judy Garland, a beautiful kid at M-G-M, and during a lunch and afternoon with Judy, I fell madly in love with her. Many years later, just months before her death, I met her again at a dinner party, and she looked like a sweet, sad ghost held together with pins. And there was a hilarious afternoon with Bob Benchley at the Old Garden of Allah apartment hotel—where Scott Fitzgerald stayed—since torn down, but God, Benchley was genuinely funny, and later when I was in the army and living off the post at the Royalton Hotel in New York, he was a permanent guest there. His suite had rooms separated by curtains of beads confiscated from some North African bordello.

One of the unforgettable persons I met out here, Polly Adler, got in touch with me because of a guest column I wrote for *The Hollywood Reporter* upon the death of one of the Everleigh sisters, America's greatest madames at the turn of the century. I had known and corresponded with the Everleighs in 1945 and 1946, and I would later write about them in my book *The Sunday Gentleman*. Well, Polly Adler, who had been America's most notorious madam in modern times, was living in retirement in Burbank. She had

Leni Riefenstahl gave Irving Wallace this picture of herself when he interviewed her.

read my guest column and telephoned me. She was writing her autobiography, and wanted permission to use my Everleigh material, and I gave her permission. We became quite close after that, and her autobiography turned out to be *A House Is Not A Home,* a tremendous bestseller.

I remember Polly phoning me one day and begging me to have lunch with her about something important. We had lunch and she said that Leonard Goldstein, head of 20th Century-Fox, wanted to buy the rights to her book, but she was afraid to meet the studio people alone. Would I accompany her to the studio? I was glad to do so. However, nothing came of the studio talks. Then I told Polly to get my agent, Ziegler, to represent her. She agreed. Ziegler was thrilled. He confided in me that, as a young man at Princeton, he used to visit Polly Adler's house of ill fame on weekends in New York. I repeated this intelligence to Polly when I introduced her to Ziegler, and she said to him, "Well, this is something—you used to be my client, and now here I am, your client."

Remembering my screenwriter period, one memorable evening comes to mind, an evening in 1952. My wife and I were at a dinner party for a visiting New York magazine editor. About a third of the way into the evening, the front door opened, and a ravishing, somewhat shyly nervous blonde entered. She was breathtaking. She was Marilyn Monroe. After a few introductions, she found a chair against a wall and never once moved from it the entire evening. Within minutes after Marilyn had sat down, the men at the party began to move in, surround her, and I confess I was one of them. I sat on the floor, literally at her feet, puffing my pipe and feasting my eyes upon her. All I can recollect of our own conversation was Dostoevski—we were discussing great novelists, and she was deep into Dostoevski, awed and shaken by him.

Which brings us full circle. It brings us to my latest novel, *The Fan Club.* While the idea for the novel was based on a casual conversation I overheard on a train about Eliza-

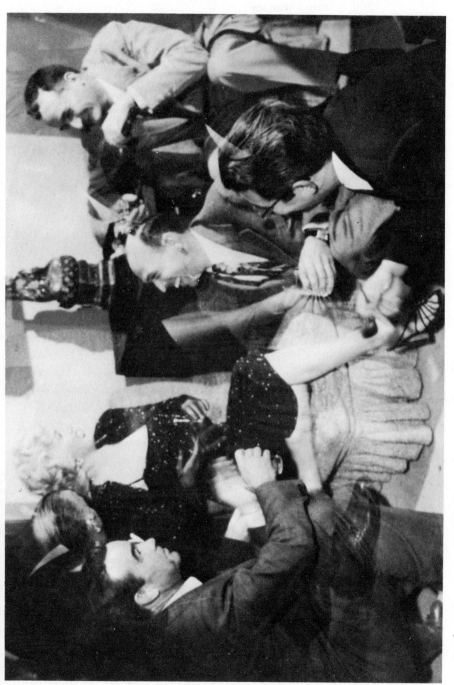

Marilyn Monroe at a 1952 Hollywood party. Irving Wallace in foreground.

beth Taylor, the fictional heroine in my book is actually much, much closer to Marilyn Monroe, the Monroe I've often thought about since that evening with her and the Monroe about whom I eventually came to know a good deal first-hand. Something about her haunted me as much as it did Norman Mailer. Recently, just shortly after reading Marilyn Monroe's last Will and Testament in which she left her personal effects to her onetime drama coach, Lee Strasberg, I attended a charity celebrity auction. At the auction, I found that Strasberg had contributed a silver cocktail shaker once owned by Marilyn on which she had etched her name. I bid for it, got it, and it now graces my bar.

Clearly, unconsciously, way back in 1952, I had filed Marilyn away in my mind—and I did not take her out again until writing The Fan Club in 1972 and 1973.

Apparently, for the novelist, the whole world—and everyone in it—exists only for his books. Crazy, egocentric, ruthless, yes, but true. I think William Faulkner put it best and put it right during an interview he gave in 1956. He said, "The writer's only responsibility is to his art. He will be completely ruthless if he is a good one. He has a dream. It anguishes him so much he must get rid of it. He has no peace until then. Everything goes by the board: honor, pride, decency, security, happiness, all, to get the book written. If a writer has to rob his mother, he will not hesitate; the 'Ode on a Grecian Urn' is worth any number of old ladies."

By Irving Wallace

Throughout his 40-year career as a writer Irving Wallace has kept notes of his stories, their development, and the circumstances under which they were rejected or published. What follows is a sampling of those notes and comments on magazine, film, book and other writings. They are taken from the author's handwritten notes, interviews, publicity releases, and other sources. Most of the material has never been published before, and should prove revealing as to what went into making the works, and what came out of them. [NOTE: Source references are dated as to when Wallace made the notes.]

"Racing Oddities" (1932)
    Magazine article
    My first published story. Non-fiction.
    Written July 2, 1932. Sold to *Horse & Jockey,* a Chicago turf magazine, July 21, 1932. It was published August, 1932, pages 15-16.

> —*From the author's bibliographic records. No date.*

My Adventure Trail (1935)
    Non-fiction book
    This was the beginning. *My Adventure Trail* is the first book I ever wrote—the experiences of an 18 year old romantic.
    I returned to Kenosha, Wisconsin in January, 1935 [after five month trip to Mexico, Guatemala, Salvador, Honduras, Panama, Colombia, Cuba]—began writing this—finished it in April, 1935,

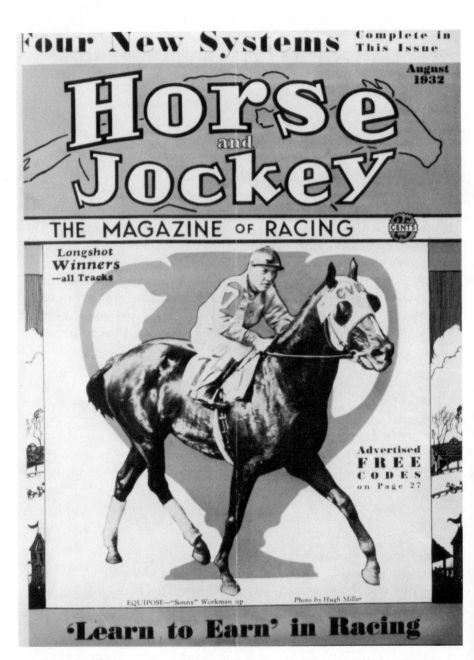

Cover of the 1932 *Horse and Jockey* in which Irving Wallace's first article appeared.

Principal + saw "Warrior's Husbands" with
Clare Lindi, who is beautiful.

December 13 — Thursday

I wrote a letter to Eddie, to Zin for
article type, to Scroll, to Harriet.
Wally was very sick with malaria
all day. We went to Coble + Wally
wired for $35 so we can leave on
time.
Paul out on evening date, Wally
asleep, I wrote — + to bed.

December 14 —— Friday

A red-letter day. Diario used our +
pictures on front page + we got 4 outs.
Minister Corrigan invited us to lunch.
Went + dressed, + got to his house at
12:30.
Chatted highball, Lucky Strike,
NY Times + rich house, chinese servants
novelist + reporter of Latino also present. ate
good meal. (learned editor gets 500 colons
a week, reporters 8 colons week.) Chatted in
smoking room, glanced thru Butenkey (must
get it!). At 4 we were informed we'd
interview President Menendez in 30 minutes.
Private car, generals, + then in
reception room to tune of construction
hammers, the President. Young Corrigan
interpreted. Chatted 30 minutes, took
snapshots, + President gave us

My Adventure Trail was written from notes taken daily during Irving Wallace's
Central and South American trip of 1934. The above is from that daily record
—these notes written in Salvador.

in my parents home.

Publishers were interested—but none finally bought and published it.

Three months after completing this I left to attend Williams College in Berkeley, California, on a scholarship.

> —*Handwritten note on title page of original manuscript of* My Adventure Trail. *1/11/73.*

The Sunday Gentleman: Biography of Daniel Defoe (1936)
Non-fiction book

I was 20 when I attempted my second book . . . a biography of Daniel Defoe, to whom I related as a youngster writing for periodicals [Defoe was one of the first magazine journalists before he turned to novels and wrote, among others, *Robinson Crusoe*]. The manuscript remains—a snapshot of my beginnings.

I was fascinated by Daniel Defoe—was unable to find any biographies on him—so I undertook to write this one. Apparently, I wrote this in 1936—when I had just turned 20—and the title and idea were favorites of my father. Two publishers almost bought it, but finally declined. Twenty-nine years later I borrowed this title for my tenth published book. [*The Sunday Gentleman*, a collection of essays published by Simon & Schuster in 1965.]

> —*Handwritten note on title page of original manuscript of* The Sunday Gentleman. *10/17/66.*

"He Played Jonah" (1938)
Magazine article.

My first major magazine sale. I wrote this in May, 1938, sold it to *Coronet* on July 11, 1938. Their $75 payment saved me from debtor's prison and was a great boost to my confidence. *Coronet* published the article in December, 1938; pages 139-141.

> —*From the author's bibliographic records. No date.*

Etcetera (1938)
Non-fiction book

Only one original draft of this unpublished book of mine exists. That draft is for my children. Early in 1938 I read that Harold Latham, the Macmillan editor who had discovered Margaret Mitchell's *Gone With The Wind*, was in Los Angeles to meet new writers. I made an appointment and saw Latham in his hotel. I told him I wanted to do this book. He liked the idea.

I went to work revising and organizing my twenty-eight favorite magazine stories—both published and unpublished. I then typed the material into this draft—the only one to survive the passage of thirty years.

I sent this manuscript to Macmillan. It was rejected. Other publishers considered it, but in the end never published it. I finally put it aside—a memento of my writers interests between 1934 and 1938. One day I may rewrite some of the stories for inclusion in another book.

> *—From handwritten notes on title page of original manuscript of Etcetera. 2/16/68.*

In the early 1960's—after my early bestsellers—I used to read that I got lucky and hit popular success overnight.

Going over my earlier unpublished book manuscripts—well that "overnight" business amused me—remembering how hard I worked, how many books or portions of books were rejected, remembering high hopes dashed.

Here is one I thought would be published in 1939 or 1940— but it was not.

> *—From handwritten notes on title page of original manuscript of Etcetera. 1/11/73.*

"Europe's Vest-Pocket Republic" (1938)
Magazine article

[First sale to *Ken*, a widely-read national political magazine.] Written June 9, 1938. Non-fiction. Sold to *Ken*, July 1,

- 168 -

CHAPTER 21

FATHER OF HIS COUNTRY

Never in his entire reign as emperor of Rome did Augustus Caesar make
an impromptu or memorized speech. Always he read from a script. Never·in
his entire career did he hold a spontaneous conversation. Always he wrote it
out beforehand.

This is amazing. Even with an x-ray machine you couldn't better look into the man's personality. Picture him, will you, that little Italian with the
ugly teeth, sitting at his dinner table, chatting with important guests — not
chatting easily, freely, but reading his ideas and small-talk from a prepared
manuscript on the table before him.

Suetonius, the lively Roman reporter and historian, is responsible for the
revelation. He writes clearly that Augustus scribbled out his conversations with
important persons ahead of time,· if only to prevent himself from saying too little or too much.

And when the last of the guests left, and Augustus was alone with his wife,
did he at last let down his hair? Did he relax? Did he banter, gossip and speak
with his beloved Livia as a tired husband speaks to an adoring wife? No. He did
not. Again the inevitable piece of paper. For Augustus was a busy man, and he

From *Etcetera.*

1938. Paid $75.00. Published September 22, 1938, pages 61-62.

"Peaceful San Marino, marooned in a turbulent sea of fascism, is the world's oldest-smallest republic; area, 38 sq. miles, population, 13,948 (Decatur, Alabama, is larger)."

—From the author's bibliographic records. No date.

"Hitler's Girl Friend" (1938)

An example of the typical course of submissions and rejections of an Irving Wallace magazine article.

Non-fiction.   2,000 words, 8 pages.   On Leni Riefenstahl [who made the Nazi propaganda film *Triumph of the Will*].
Submitted to:

Liberty, New York, Dec. 23, 1937; rejected Jan. 3, 1938.

Ken, Chicago, Jan. 4, 1938; rejected Jan. 23.

Mrs., New York, Jan. 23, 1938; rejected Feb. 4.

Picture Play, New York, Feb. 14, 1938; rejected Feb. 27.

Everyweek, Cleveland, March 17, 1938; rejected March 25.

National Jewish Monthly, Washington, D.C., April 1, 1938; rejected April 10.

Independent Woman, New York, April 10, 1938; rejected May 6.

—From the author's bibliographic records. No date.

"I Was The Real Kid McCoy" (1940)

Magazine article

This is the original draft of the article I wrote—my typing and revisions—which can now serve as definitive source material for prize fighting history. I met with and gathered this autobiographical matter from Kid McCoy himself in Hollywood early in 1940. I obtained his written release to ghost this for him. I finished this draft on January 26, 1940. I was unable to sell the story. Then, on April 18, 1940, at the age of 66, Kid McCoy committed suicide in a Detroit hotel room. I felt this should see print as a record of his life, and I persisted with it—and on October 4, 1940, *Fight Stories* magazine of New York bought it for $35 and published it

TRADE
MARK
REG.

FIGHT STORIES

…TION and FACT
…F THE RING

20c

N B C

LEATHER LIGHTN…
by MARK ADAM…

KID SOURPUSS…
by BILL COOK

THE TEN-COUNT TO…
by JOHN STARR

THE KILLER TAKES A TUM…
by TOM O'NEILL

I WAS THE REAL Mc…
AS TOLD TO IRVING WALLAC…
by KID McCOY

Fight Stories issue containing "I Was The Real McCoy."

I Was the Real McCoy!

By KID McCOY

as told to

IRVING WALLACE

YOU'VE heard the famous descriptive phrase—"the real McCoy."

There have been a lot of stories of how that originated. But I'm about the only person alive who knows the true one. Because that phrase was inspired by me.

I'll tell you the best-known story. At the turn of the century, when I was running a corner eatery in Manhattan, McCoy's Cafe it was called, there was at least one slam-bang free-for-all a week. Well, one evening a drunk came in and began messing up my joint. I kept my temper, until he threw a tray through my most expensive mirror. That was too much. I stepped out from behind the bar and grabbed him by the shirt.

"Get out!" I roared.

"Who in the devil are you?" the drunk wanted to know.

"I'm Kid McCoy, world's middleweight champion!"

"Yeah? The hell you are!" exclaimed the drunk, taking a wild swing at me.

I ducked, and let him have it with a sizzling right uppercut. He folded like an accordion, and fell on his side. Five minutes later, after one of my waiters brought him to with cold water, the drunk sat up, dazed. He touched his swollen jaw tenderly, then turned to the waiter with a sigh.

"Yeah," he murmured, "that was him, all right. That was the real McCoy!"

Two newspapermen were in the room. They published the story, and the phrase became popular throughout the United States.

> **I**N the spring of this year Norman Selby, "Kid McCoy," passed out of this game we call life, thus closing a career that was by all rights one of the strangest and most compelling the ring has ever seen. In this article, the last that was ever born in his drama-packed mind, he tells the origin of his famous fighting name—a name synonymous with lion courage and 'possum cunning—and touches on many a fresh, exciting little-known sidelight of the fight-game.

Well, sure, the entire incident was true. But that wasn't the origin of the phrase. Just to keep the records straight, I'll tell you how it actually began. It began years before, in San Francisco, and was invented by a reporter named Walter Naughton.

I arrived in San Francisco to tangle with a home-town favorite, tough Joe Choynski. Just a few months before, in the very same ring, a bum named Pete McCoy had fought and had been knocked out in seven rounds.

When I crawled through the ropes, someone shouted:

"Hey, what's this? Another McCoy?"

I won the fight, a thrilling battle. And the following morning Naughton's account of the fight in his paper began:

"Last night, the real McCoy beat Joe Choynski!"

That, citizens, was how the phrase originated, and don't let anybody tell you differently.

And speaking of Joe Choynski, I fought him four different times, and while he never became a champion, he was the most vicious fighter that ever lived. He gave me my hardest fight.

It took place at the Broadway Athletic Club, during February of 1900. We were scheduled to go 25 rounds.

DURING the first round, we looked each other over. Finally, I feinted Choynski open, and drove a terrific left to his stomach. He grabbed me, and as he did so, I whispered, "You want to watch your stomach, Joe. That's where I'm go-

24

in the Winter, 1940, issue.

It was a memorable experience for me—working with a man whose name was to become a public expression and part of the living language.

> —Handwritten note on title page
> of original manuscript of "I Was
> The Real Kid McCoy." 5/20/68.

Madame President (1941)

An original story for the screen.

Bette Davis read this—wanted to do it—she was a great star then—she called and discussed it with me but Hal Wallis, head of Warner Brothers, turned it down.   He didn't want her to do a costume picture.

> —Handwritten note on title page
> of the final manuscript version of
> Madame President, based on the
> life of suffragette Victoria Wood-
> hull.   No date.

This is a true story.   The backgrounds, the incidents, Victoria Woodhull's speeches, her nomination to the Presidency, her marriage to John Martin—all are based upon extensive research and are historically accurate.

Thus, excepting several sequences, romantic and action, which have been fictionized for the sake of plot continuity—the bizarre saga of America's Madame President is fact.

> —Author's note on page ii of the
> Madame President manuscript.

Japan's Mein Kampf (1942)

Non-fiction book

An incredible experience.

I'd researched this in Japan and occupied China in 1940.   I decided to write it as a book.   On Saturday, December 6, 1941, I sent an outline proposing this book to Bobbs-Merrill, Duell Sloan and Pearce, Reynal and Hitchcock, Lippincott, Greenburg [publishing houses].

MADAME PRESIDENT

by

Irving Wallace

It is a summer's evening in the year 1870, and
Delmonico's famous restaurant is crowded with the cream
of Manhatten society. There is gayety, noise, as couples
joke and laugh and converse -- when, suddenly, a hush
sweeps over the restaurant, then a silence. All eyes stare
in one direction.

For, during the excitement, two women have entered,
and taken a table near the doorway. Two women, unescorted,
in a public place after six o'clock in 1870! Unheard of!
Scandalous!

The two women -- Victoria Woodhull, and her sister,
Tennessee Woodhull, are once again shocking staid New York.
Everyone has heard of the Woodhull sisters -- those daring
Ohio suffragists battling for the equality of women.

Charlie Delmonico, genial restaurant owner, hurriedly
approaches them. He is tactful.

"There's only one way to save you," he whispers. "I
will pretend you just dropped in to speak to me, and then,
as we chat, I will escort you to the door."

Page one of *Madame President*.

The following day was December 7, 1941–Pearl Harbor.

The next day, Monday, December 8, 1941, all five publishers were at my door through wires, phone calls, their representatives.

I took the research, worked day and night, wrote this entire book between December 9, 1941, and January 29, 1942.

It should have been published–but the publishers were not yet oriented to Japanese history. By June 5, 1942, all had rejected it. A severe blow. It was never published. Here is the corpse.

> –Handwritten note on title page
> of the original manuscript of
> Japan's Mein Kampf. *1/13/73.*

Anything For A Laugh (1943)
An original story for the screen.

I wrote this improbable story on speculation for a film in October, 1943, when I was in the army and needed money. Sold it to producer Walter Colmes on March 10, 1944, for $2500.

Film starring Ellen Drew released September 1944. It was called *That's My Baby.*

The Hollywood Reporter said, "Blessed with a solid story line." They were wrong.

> –Handwritten note on title page
> of the final manuscript version
> of Anything For A Laugh. *No
> date.*

With Their Pants Down (1944)
Non-fiction book

This is an *unpublished* autobiographical book–concentrating on my first thirteen or fourteen years as an interviewer of big names, etc. Most of the material is personal and first-hand.

The book went out early in April of 1944. I had been in the army a year and a half–written this in Los Angeles at night and on leaves. It did not sell. Later I cannibalized sections and rewrote parts for my other books. This is immature, brash, sometimes vulgar–but I think it has gusto and good material–and is an excellent record of my work to that date.

> *—Handwritten note on title page
> of the only copy of the original
> manuscript of* With Their Pants
> Down. *11/2/61.*

Know Your Enemy Japan (1945)
Photographic Scenario

Carl Foreman and I were friends and enlisted men collaborating on this script in the Signal Corps. He went on to London to write the film version of *Bridge on the River Kwai* and produce *Young Winston*—and I turned to novels.

The war was nearly over, yet because of indecisiveness in Washington about what to tell our soldiers of the Japanese, we still wrote drafts of this orientation film.

> *—Handwritten notes on title page
> of "Restricted War Department
> Photographic Scenario of Project
> #11004,* Know Your Enemy Japan. *No date.*

From the Scenario:
Superimpose Title: "The Sword is our Steel Bible!"
           —General Sadao Araki.
Dissolve To: Montage of ancient and modern Jap scenes.
Narrator: "We shall never completely understand the Japanese mind. But then, they don't understand ours either. Otherwise, there would never have been a Pearl Harbor. But we must *try* to understand Japan because we have become locked in the closest of all relationships—war."

> *—From the 21 April 1945 draft
> of* Know Your Enemy Japan,
> *p. 1.*

A Young Wives' Tale (1950)
An original story for the screen.

This represents a memorable day in my life.

I got this marvelous idea—on January 3, 1950, I completed a 13-page version of it. It was a period when we were flat broke and I had a son not yet two years old.

I told the story at a half dozen studios and left the 13-page original. Everyone wanted to buy it.

On January 18, 1950, Dore Schary, head of M-G-M, bought it for $20,000—$12,500 for the original story, and $7,500 for me to spend 10 weeks developing it into a detailed treatment.

Starting at the studio on February 10, 1950, finishing on April 12, 1950, I wrote a 108-page version for producer Arthur Hornblow, Jr. It was well received. But with the coming of the Korean War this was shelved—though showing it got me many other studio jobs.

> *—Handwritten note on title page of 13-page version of* A Young Wives' Tale. *6/1/68.*

The West Point Story (1950)
Screenplay

The producer had the title—the idea—I was hired to go to West Point twice—research—then create a motion picture story or treatment.

[Final screenplay credit was given to John Monks, Jr., Charles Hoffman and Irving Wallace.] John Monks, Jr., did a rewrite of the screenplay Hoffman and I wrote—Monks was brought in to tailor the lead for James Cagney.

> *—Handwritten note on title page of the final screenplay version of* The West Point Story. *2/22/73.*

Split Second (1953)
Screenplay

On March 24, 1951, I completed an original story for the screen called *I'll See You in Hell*—the first story about what could happen to Americans under threat of a nuclear bomb.

When I learned that a famous director (*The Last Mile* on Broadway) and playwright (adapted *The Egg and I* for the screen),

James Cagney and Doris Day in *The West Point Story*.

IW

321 (CONTINUED)
                           DOLORES (983)
                    (snuggling her
                     arm under his,
                     drawing Alvie
                     to them)
          Love it!

322   TWO SHOT - Kathryn and Garven - bringing up the rear.
      Garven halts, turns, Kathryn joining him. He looks
      off at what they've left behind.

323   LONG SHOT - ruins of Last Chance City - with the
      atomic mushroom behind it - to include Kathryn and
      Garven in f.g. as they watch the awesome sight.

                           GARVEN (984)
                    The proving ground - old
                    Jellico was right about it
                    after all.

                           KATHRYN (985)
                    About what, darling?

                           GARVEN (986)
                    About the atom. About what it
                    can do _for_ people.

      They turn into the camera. She links her arm in his.
      He smiles down at her.

                           GARVEN (cont'd)
                    I'd say this was a highly
                    successful test - wouldn't you?

      She slowly, smilingly nods. They start off.

324   FULL SHOT - group. They are marching across the sand,
      together, heads high, confident of the future, their
      figures receding in the distance, as we

                                        FADE OUT

                           THE END

The happy ending of *Split Second*.

Chester Erskine, was interested in it—I agreed to collaborate with him on an expanded and improved version. He helped plot the treatment with me, I wrote it, and the version grew from 49 pages to 83, and we finished it on May 30, 1951.

On February 1, 1952, it was purchased by Howard Hughes as an RKO film for $27,500—$10,000 to Erskine for the story, $10,000 to me for the story, $7,500 to me to adapt it into a screenplay in 10 weeks.

On April 30, 1952, I delivered this first draft. On May 29, 1952, I delivered a revised version and left RKO to work at Columbia Studios. Then Harry Brown, the novelist, did a revision of it. Later, William Bowers did a final rewrite. The final credits said screenplay by Bowers and Wallace, original story by Erskine and Wallace—but it was my baby.

The RKO film, which I had renamed *Split Second*, was released to the public in 1953 starring Stephan McNally, Alexis Smith, Jan Sterling—directed by Dick Powell, his first directorial effort. The film had fine reviews, and was a great success in every way.

This story and screenplay is one of the few I wrote in Hollywood that I take pride in.

> —*Handwritten note on title page of the first draft screenplay of* Split Second. *2/24/68.*

Bad For Each Other (1954)
  Screenplay
  Scalpel was the last novel that my friend Horace McCoy wrote before his death. He also adapted it into a screenplay. I was asked by Columbia to rewrite Horace's screenplay. This is the draft I completed on my own in March, 1953. Later, Jerome Weidman joined me briefly to revise this draft. It was produced and directed by two more friends of mine—William Fadiman and Irving Rapper.

The picture, starring Charlton Heston, Lizabeth Scott, Dianne Foster, was greeted by dreadful reviews. It deserved them. It was released under the title *Bad For Each Other*. I shared screenplay credit with Horace McCoy.

—Handwritten note on a preliminary screenplay of Bad For Each Other. *5/18/68.*

The Second Bell (1955)
Preliminary story outline

Some years ago Jerome Weidman and I were collaborating on novelettes or original treatments—basically for the screen, but always with the possibility of a novel or magazine serial in mind.

Our last effort was a story called *The Second Bell.* We never wrote this story into its final form because suddenly, and simultaneously, we both signed contracts for sorely needed jobs—and we never got back to our collaboration—although we corresponded about it often and intended to do so.

—From handwritten notes on characterization and outline papers of The Second Bell. *3/5/65.*

The Fabulous Originals (Alfred A. Knopf, 1955)
Non-fiction book

I wrote the first three chapters between August and November of 1953. Based on these three chapters Alfred A. Knopf offered me a $1,000 advance for the collective biography.

I resumed writing it in what spare time I had—starting February 12—finishing this first draft October 13, 1954.

It was published October 17, 1955—my first published book— excellent reviews—it went into three printings and sold 12,000 copies.

Originals was later published by Longmans, Green for Great Britain, Kohler for Germany, Grijalbo for Spain—and as recently as October, 1967, as a paperback by New English Library of London.

—Handwritten note on title page of the partially complete first draft of the book. [The original draft of the first three chapters disappeared. But the original

To Jerome
From: Irving
Re: The Second Bell
June 6, 1955

Beloved Jerry,

I have had the weekend to think about your letter. I am full of what I
want to say so I had better get much of it down right now. I knew, about
three days after I wrote you the second batch of ideas that I was
wrong. My ideas on kidnapping a kid, etc., were too phoney, another
story really, and though it gave us a finish it lost us the entire
middle and all reality. I'm glad you saw that at once and I say forget
my last ideas - though not parts of my outline that preceded it.

In yours of June 1, now, I think you have gone off - in small
ways - all down the line. Your letter and ideas are persuasive - and i:
we both agreed we'd have a story quickly - but I'm afraid it wouldn't
be right. Anyway, that's how I feel - for I feel our original feeling.
were right, much righter. While I like the honesty of some of your
new thoughts, I generally feel several are somewhat special, too
underplayed and would invite construction problems in screenplay.
Let me elaborate, point for point --

1. I think you were using Westport, or its type of community, as
an example - but I think we would be mistaken to use so small a
community. It should be a big sprawling city like LA, Frisco, Kansas
City, St. L or Chicago - the city and suburbs - a fictional city. No
parents should be commutors. That's too unusual, too special. Where
do you find working folk commuting by train - or car - from a small
town to a big city except in New England, PA, etc., and NY. In several
places, yes - but not many. Or, at least, in the avg American city a
husband gets up in the morning and gets in his car, or on his bus or
streetcar, and goes to work within the confines of the community. This
is more familiar than the other. I think the city should be large in
area so we could move our bus around - get it lost among the millions
- have variety of incident and locale - etc.

2. I worry about making the day of our story a special day. I
think this defeats us in many ways. In Illinois and Wisconsin where I
went to school as a kid, in California where my kid goes, all big
public school systems, we never had and don't have Field Days. We have
a holiday PTA carnival, maybe; and always an open house for parents
at day in the East, in the evening out here. But still, my instincts
tell me an ordinary Wednesday or Thursday schoolday, like any day of
any week of any school month anywhere in America would be the best day
for us. This I feel is the commonplace we need. It could be any day -
tomorrow - and it could happen. Moreover, setting up a special, while
it helps get our parents to school naturally, seems such a coincidence
a convenience, for the melodrama we are setting up. Isn't it more
honest, really, to make it a regular day in the lives of all concerned
that is, as far as school is involved - and when the bus is missing,
and the parents finally informed, we at last bring them to the school?

3. You may be right about keeping it short, tight and fast - but
I think playing it within its own time, like Rope, has grave faults.
It doesn't give time for tension to generate. In 1½ hours you might
worry about a missing bus, wonder what happened, but it isn't time
enough for real emotional involvement and suspense. The time, however,

From Irving Wallace letter to Jerome Weidman concerning the writing of
"The Second Bell."

Dust jacket — *The Fabulous Originals*.

*first draft of the concluding five
chapters was retrieved from his
parents' garage in 1964. The
surviving first three manuscript
chapters are the revised final
draft, embodying the changes
and corrections made by the
author and Philip Vaudrin, the
Knopf editor responsible for this
book.] 3/13/68.*

Jump Into Hell (1955)
Screenplay

My God, where was my head when I wrote this?

Fifteen years later I became one of the most ardent opponents of French and then other USA power-play involvement in
Vietnam.

—*Handwritten note on title page
of final screenplay of* Jump Into
Hell. *8/24/54.*

[Jump Into Hell *concerns the last days of Dienbienphu.
Sample from the final screenplay:*]

Camera pulls back to reveal Major Riviere and Major Bonet,
with six Red prisoners, in padded jackets and torn trousers, stiffly
lined up against the far wall. Riviere is a lanky, angular, shrewd
intelligence officer. He is holding a pistol. Bonet is that dwindling
minority in France—a blue-blooded esthete out of Stendhal, snob-
bish, selfish, political, patriotic.

REVIERE:
That's right, sir. All are natives, except this one.
(he pulls the tidiest prisoner out of line)
He's Chinese.
(handing gun to de Castries)
And here is the pistol we found on him.

DE CASTRIES:
Well, at last we're getting some place. A Red Chinese

from Peiping. A gun from Moscow.
(putting gun down)
The complexion of our war is changing—now that Mao
and Malenkov are interested in our little valley.
(taking up paper from desk)
Lieutenant of the Chinese Red Army, attached to the
Viet Minh 17th Anti-aircraft. That's something new.
Until now the Viet Reds had only rifles and bamboo
spears.

CHINESE:
(matter-of-fact, but slightly arrogant)
They have more now—they have grenades, light machine
guns, heavy artillery, even rocket launchers—

. . . DECASTRIES:
(suddenly hard)
To free a neighbor from any hope of democracy—to
turn all Indochina into a Chinese and Russian slave mill—
producing for conquest.
(quietly)
But it will deceive no one. All Asia will soon learn the
truth—learn your real motives—

CHINESE:
(angrily)
They will learn no capitalist lies. Not from this Fort.
In a few days no one will be alive to tell them.

. . . DE CASTRIES:
. . . we will be ready, you may be sure. And we will
win. But should we lose—the world will still know that
our enemies were not nationalists—but conquerors for
Communism.

—From final screenplay of Jump
Into Hell, *pp. 4-5. 8/24/54.*

The Square Pegs (Alfred A. Knopf, 1957)
Non-fiction book
This is a complete copy of the original first draft of my

Larry Dobkin and Jack Sernas in *Jump Into Hell*.

second published book—as typed by me with my handwritten revisions. Later, I made more revisions that were incorporated in the final book published on July 22, 1957, by Alfred A. Knopf.

I started writing this first draft on January 23, 1956, and completed it on April 20, 1956. To write this book, I took a leave of absence from Warner Brothers Studio, where I was under contract as a scenarist, and worked on this in a spare room of my parents' home (Bessie and Alex Wallace, who had a place at 415 N. Edinburgh in Los Angeles).

This hard-bound edition sold 10,000 copies in the United States. The reviews were excellent. The book was a special choice of the New York Area Booksellers Association, Inc. and a recommendation of the Book-of-the-Month Club and the Book Society of London. *The Square Pegs* sold 100,000 copies as a paperback published by Berkley in 1962.

I spent many years researching the material in this collective biography—and the writing of this manuscript was truly a labor of love.

> —*Handwritten note on title page of the original manuscript of* The Square Pegs. *1/22/68.*

Paris Does Strange Things (1957)

Dialogue Transcript for a film by Jean Renoir.

Jack L. Warner financed this. When he saw the film he was appalled—it was not understandable.

As a contract writer at Warners I was asked to clarify this for the public by writing a prologue—which I directed—and by writing a narration over it which explains what is being said in dialogue.

I did it. Despite Jean Renoir's reputation this is a dreadful film that came and went—and happily is now forgotten.

> —*From a handwritten note on cover page of dialogue transcript done for* Paris Does Strange Things. *1/19/73.*

Dust jacket — *The Square Pegs*.

Magali Noel and Ingrid Bergman in *Paris Does Strange Things.*

Pantheon   (1958)
  Play
  Jerome Weidman, who won the Pulitzer Prize for his play *Fiorello,* and I wrote this three-act play in 1958. We plotted it when Weidman visited Los Angeles from Westport, Connecticut, then wrote it via correspondence, exchanging and rewriting each other's drafts. It was optioned for Broadway, but never produced. At last, on September 28, 1959, Anglia Television of BBC, London, bought it and later produced it as a live television play.

  Jerry and I based the hero on Albert Schweitzer, on a factual incident that occurred during the sinking of the *Titanic,* and his love of the construction of Conrad's *Lord Jim.* While the idea was good, neither one of us was ever quite satisfied with it.

> *—Handwritten note from title page of final manuscript draft of* Pantheon. *1/1/68.*

The Dog Who Would't Be (1958)
  Television Script
  A pilot television script instigated by Leland Hayward, written for producer Richard Whorf in 1958.

  The TV series was never made.

> *—Handwritten note on title page of final screenplay manuscript of* The Dog Who Wouldn't Be. *No date.*

The Big Circus (1959)
  Screenplay
  This was the last motion picture screenplay I wrote before I quit films. I accepted the job because I had to make a living. I did not relish producer Irwin Allen's story idea—which was trite. I took on this script in November, 1957—backed by Allen's researchers and art staff at Columbia Studio.

  I wrote the entire screenplay myself—Allen insisted on sharing credit because it was his idea.

  After I completed my chore, Allen hired another writer, Charles Bennett, to do more rewriting. All three of us shared

Dear Jerry,

I am working with carbon this morning - since I feel we must both have the final notes we now exchange. I can't remember when I've worked as hard on one of our projects as this one - I say this to assure you I believe in it that much and what it to be that good. At any rate, I worked all last night and until two in the morning, and I think I've come up with something. What was wrong, I now feel, with the last third was not that it was constructed or plotted wrong but that it was too thin - too many obligatory and truly theatrical scenes were left out at the very end. If these are inserted, we meat up the last third and have a fine balanced play. So much for prologue. I will not set down my notes in chronological order - mentioning your pages in the outline as I go along - and setting down all my suggested changes or adds. I am simply assuming you have retained a carbon of your long and magnificent basic outline of THE ARMS YOU BEAR. Incidentally, this title is fair. We might get a better single word one - if only Edna F had not used Giant. All the names of your characters are fine by me. At the end of my outline suggests I will set down some African names for us from research on Schweitzer, etc.

P. 2: a cure for sleeping sickness is too local; it does not effect Americans, Frenchmen, Britons, etc. The illness cure should be more universal - or, if not, at least less cliche. I will search Gunther On Africa for a better one.

P. 4: To give the whole thing bigness, more importance, I think Darlington should hold a press conference here - perhaps read a short statement, parry a few questions. Also, instead of Peppo, he should be the head of aluminum or steel or such, as was Kaiser. He established the Darlington Foundatio and this will be their biggest single grant yet.

P. 5: After press conference, perhaps they leave with Haight and Darlington to be shown about, one newsman remains behind. A cynical old hand at big stories and heroes with clay feet. Let's call him Slade for the moment (I entrust final names to you). Perhaps he questions Jack and Betty briefly, or examines the books and souvenirs in the room, with Helga hovering anxiously. Now Tweed appears. When Helga goes to fetch Marie, Slade has Tweed alone for a moment. With growing curiosity, Slade questions him. As it gets interesting, Marie appears, breaks it up. Slade sent packing. Marie tries to get rid of Tweed - but can't until she promises to deliver

a cryptic message to Fletcher:"Just tell him someone wants to see him about April 15, 1912." Tweed thinks he will hear from Fletcher soon enough; he'll be at the town's single wooden hotel, waiting. Marie shoos him out, and everyone else - as

From an Irving Wallace letter to Jerome Weidman concerning the development of "Pantheon."

THE DOG WHO WOULDN'T BE

by

Irving Wallace

FADE IN:

EXT. MOWAT HOUSE - FULL SHOT - ENTRANCE - DUSK

From the sidewalk, just outside the fence, shooting up the walk
to the front porch, we see a modest, somewhat elderly two-story
house. A ladder bearing a paint bucket is leaning against it.
The house is situated halfway up the block of a pleasant, middle-
class residential street in Midvale, South Dakota, a town of
thirty thousand situated between Pierre and Mount City. It is
a recent December day, chilly but snowless, and youngsters on
Christmas holiday are in the street.

UNCLE HECTOR, smallish, fiftyish, with a dry, often amused face
framed by old-fashioned spectacles, emerges from the house. As
he stands on the porch, pulling on a warm overcoat, his voice
as narration comes over.

                    UNCLE HECTOR'S VOICE
          I am Uncle Hector. Permanent realtive.
          Part-time handyman - when there's some-
          thing handy around. I have lived with
          the Mowat family for seven years.
          When they moved to South Dakota, I
          moved, too. What else was there to do?

Uncle Hector walks slowly to Camera.

                    UNCLE HECTOR'S VOICE
          I've seen Angus Mowat promoted to
          chief librarian. I've seen my niece,
          Bess Mowat, learn to cook. I've seen
          young Farley grow up. And, somehow,
          I've even lived through the latest
          addition to the family --

He has reached immediate f.g., as the door behind opens and
young FARLEY, aged nine, curious, extrovert, collector of
Things Animate, pops out.

                    FARLEY
               (shouting)
          Mutt! . . . Hey, Uncle Hector, have
          you seen Mutt?

credit when the film was made and released in 1959 starring Victor Mature, Rhonda Fleming, Red Buttons, Vincent Price, Peter Lorre. Incredibly—bad as it was—it was a big box office hit. For me it was a silly thing that helped get me out of motion pictures.

> —From handwritten notes on title page of a preliminary screenplay of The Big Circus. 5/28/68.

The Fabulous Showman (1959)
Screen story

After 10 years, off and on, writing in motion picture studios, this was the last film script I wrote—and I've never done another since.

During seven weeks in January and February of 1959, I adapted my biography, *The Fabulous Showman,* into this treatment for producers Martin Jurow and Richard Shepherd of Paramount Studios. I was paid $6,833. When this was done, I resumed work on my fifth book, *The Chapman Report.* Later, when I was offered the job of converting this into a screenplay, I refused it, saying I had quit movies and would devote myself to my one love— books.

Subsequently, Jurow and Shepherd split, and Jurow took this project to Columbia Studios. Two other writers developed screenplays—Robert Bassing and Herbert Baker—in 1963 and 1965, but the projected budget ran so high that the project has been temporarily shelved. [This film was never made.]

> —From handwritten note on title page of manuscript of the screen story of The Fabulous Showman. 5/20/68.

The Sins of Philip Fleming (Frederick Fell, 1959)
Fiction book

I began writing the manuscript on June 3, 1958, and finished it on August 30, 1958.

After many rejections, the book was published by Frederick Fell—who gave it its final title on September 30, 1959. [Originally

FIASCO

by

Irving Wallace

I.

SATURDAY NIGHT

It all began with a casual kiss in the hallway that led to the bedroom. What happened afterward lasted a week. It seemed a year. It was hell.

When they first bought the bungalow on Ridgewood Lane, six years before, Philip Fleming used to enjoy taking his breakfasts and lunches in the kitchen. From the dinette table, the view through the big picture window was incomparable. years ago, when he and Helen had driven from Paris to Rome on their honeymoon, hugging the mountains, above the clouds, between Rapallo and Spezia, he had seen what he then believed was the most breath-taking sight on earth. But when they had moved into Ridgewood Lane, he knew that only a name-conscious snob would deny that the mass of alabaster buildings, small in the sun, criss-crossed by broad boulevards stretching from West Hollywood across Los Angeles, was any less beautiful.

But that was six years before. Philip had lon

titled *Fiasco*.] Because Fell and I had a legal difference, he did not support the book. As a result, its hardcover sale was 2,659 copies. The published book differs from this version because Fell and his attorney deleted and altered passages to tone down explicit sex scenes.

The Signet paperback reprint edition sold well—242,000 copies to December, 1966. It was read widely in Great Britain and Italy, and also published in Spain, Germany, Israel, Norway.

In order to hold on to his share of paperback rights, Fell is reissuing a new edition of this book in April, 1968, almost nine years after it first appeared.

The book suffers from my inexperience as a novelist ten years ago—today I would do it much differently—but it is an honest, straightforward early effort—and its publication encouraged me to try another novel—*The Chapman Report*—which became an international best seller.

—*Handwritten note on title page of the first draft of* The Sins of Philip Fleming. *2/16/68.*

. . . early in 1958, my wife and I went to see a French movie based on Stendhal's *The Red and the Black,* one of my favorite novels. There was one scene where the hero was in bed, had finally almost seduced a woman, and he found himself temporarily impotent. It was played for comedy. After the movie, driving home, I said to my wife, "That was an interesting scene. It reminds me of something I read in Stendhal's *On Love,* you know, the collection of essays and notes." So when we reached home, I found that book, turned to the chapter on impotency. Stendhal had some amusing examples of Frenchmen in despair, and some serious ones, too. Then I began to remember case histories of men I knew—that was apparently in my mind all along —and suddenly I saw that this was the basis for a hell of a novel, a very exciting novel. The characters I knew. The storyline seemed simple. I felt it wouldn't be beyond my grasp. So the following day, since I wasn't working at a studio, I sat down and wrote the first ten pages, to see how it would go. It had been many years since I had done any fiction. I read the pages over, and I was not displeased. In fact, they were darned good. So I told myself, "I'm going to write this novel straight to the end," and I continued writing. I wrote steadily until I ran out of money. Then I did some television assignments instead of movies, because television jobs are short, and a movie job would take me from the novel too long. Then I resumed on the novel, entirely on my own, there was no contract, and I showed no one what I wrote, not even my wife. (This is a neurotic thing of mine. I feel too many writers show too much of their work, usually for approval, as they go along, and this inhibits the creative drive. No one sees a word I am writing until a book is finished. Then my wife is the first to read the manuscript and make the suggestions. She's a former editor, and she's astute and relentless.) When I'd completed that first novel, *The Sins of Philip Fleming*, my wife read it and said, "Gee, I think this is perfectly good, but I think it is just too frank. Why so candid? What got into you? You never wrote anything like this before. Tone it down a little." She was right in one sense. I had over-reacted to my new freedom as a novelist to the detriment of the work. I did tone it down a little, but very little, because I wanted to be honest, and I wanted to be liberated from research and fact. I had done some research on *Fleming,* but not much, and mostly in our neighborhood, where many psychoanalysts were my neighbors. Several of them were my friends. I went to one for advice on the psychological aspects of infidelity and impotency, and he gave me free advice in return for my promise that I'd give him a free copy of the novel if it was ever published. This analyst's replies, along with reading I did on the subject, and my own instinct, formed the basis of the hero's psychological problem —Philip Fleming was a married man who became involved in an extracurricular affair for the first time in his marriage, and at last, after a long flirtation, went to bed with the beautiful young widow. He brought her to bed, and that was all, nothing happened, no consummation. And then he became obsessed by his humiliation because he saw it as a symbol of all the failures in his life, his failures as father, husband, bread-winner. A valid idea. But it was not artfully done. I was too clumsy, inexperienced, unable to open up the novel.

—From Kirk Polking, "An Exclu-
sive   Tape-Recorded Interview
With Irving Wallace," Writer's
Yearbook, 37 (1966), p. 83.

The Fabulous Showman (Alfred A. Knopf, 1959)
   Non-fiction book
   Began it October 20, 1958, finished it Monday, December 1,
1958, at 4:50 in afternoon—320 Ms. pages.
   My fourth book—financed by Jurow and Shepherd [pro-
ducers] at Paramount Studios [$7,500], and New American
Library paperback [$4,000 advance]—my last book written before
I quit movie writing—it was published by Alfred A. Knopf in
hardcover and was a selection of the Literary Guild, my first book
club choice.
   This old and rare copy was made of my final revised version
and the corrections and styling are by Knopf editors before it
went to press.
   The most quickly written of my books—but "quickly" gives
the wrong impression—I was determined to free myself of screenwriting and wrote at least 12 hours a day, seven days a week to
complete this.

*—Handwritten note from title
page of the final revised manuscript of* The Fabulous Showman. *1/11/73.*

The Chapman Report (Simon & Schuster, 1960)
   Fiction book
   I'd long wanted to build a novel around fragmentary knowledge I had about several young married women in our circle. Then,
one afternoon, perhaps a day after reading a newspaper magazine
story about some woman who'd been conducting a sex survey,
the idea of a sex survey team superimposed itself upon the women
I'd long wanted to write about. The moment this happened, my

Literary Guild ad for *The Fabulous Showman*, December, 1957.

novel began to develop.

—From a questionnaire done for The Annenberg School of Communications, University of Pennsylvania. 3/31/70.

There was a good deal of nastiness here in Los Angeles. Many women I knew identified themselves with characters in *Chapman* and insisted that I had used them, undressed them in public. One married woman, an acquaintance, spoke out at a dinner party—I was not there, but this woman had always been friendly to me—and said the novel was vicious and she would not allow her husband to read it. That seemed odd to me. Then, a week later I ran into her in the street, and she came right up to me and said, just like this, "Am I in *The Chapman Report?*" I said, "How could you be? I don't know the least personal thing about you." She was mollified, but then I later learned that—by wildest coincidence—I had indeed related a portion of her private life in *Chapman.* Another young lady, whom I knew, came up to me at a party and said, "I wish you'd put me in a book—I wish I wasn't so damn dull." *She* had given me the idea (an episode in her life had) for the character of Naomi, the ailing nymphomaniac! Another young married dropped by our house for tea, and babbled on for an hour about her love life, and then after, she said to me, quite innocently, "How did you get all that true material about married women for *Chapman?*"

Eighty per cent of my letters are from married women, and at least a dozen women have written—so graciously—to thank me for the book and to tell me they had passed it on to their teenagers or married daughters, as something to go with Vanderbilt, Spock and Abraham Stone. The fan mail has been almost entirely favorable—completely understanding of what I had tried to do— and I can't tell you how wonderful it is to open a letter like this from a house-wife in Idaho or Iowa or New Jersey, knowing she has just cleaned the dishes, gotten the children off to school, and with the house and shopping and the heavy day ahead of her, and realizing that she has found a moment to sit down and dash off a

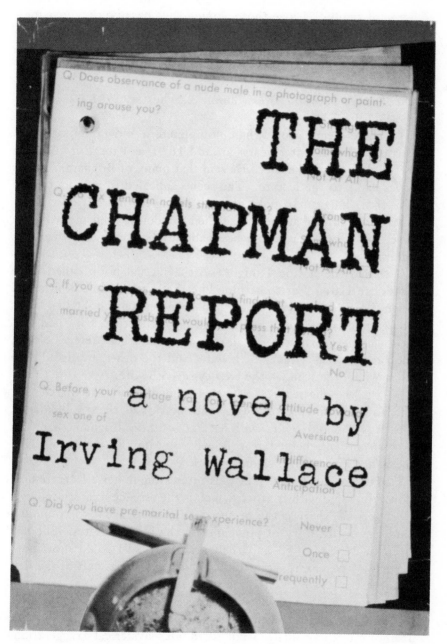

Dust jacket — *The Chapman Report*.

letter of thanks. I love those women—not because they love me—
but because they're so damn *sensible* about realities.

*—From a press release based on
publishers' question. 1961.*

The Twenty-Seventh Wife (Simon & Schuster, 1961)
   Non-fiction book
   Three years ago, I had completed a biography of P. T.
Barnum. In his latter years—around 1870, as I recall it—Barnum
lectured in Salt Lake City. He said that many of Brigham Young's
wives came to the lecture. The scene appealed to me—so, for the
fun of it, I began to poke around, trying to find out how many
wives Brigham had at the time. Then, suddenly, it hit me from the
blue—had there ever been a book about all of Brigham's wives, his
harem?
   I had the notion I might write a factual book called "The
American Harem" or something like that—if it hadn't been done.
Then I found that very little had been written about Brigham's
polygamous wives, and, as I looked into it further, I learned that
two wives, especially, were colorful. One was regal Amelia Folsom,
the favorite, the twenty-fifth wife—and the other, beautiful Ann
Eliza Webb, the scandal, the twenty-seventh wife.
   She was the story. I saw that immediately. She was the last
and youngest and prettiest wife—and, best of all, the troublemaker.
She was the only wife who walked out on Brigham, had him
thrown in jail, helped tear down polygamy in America. The
moment I knew that, I said: my girl.
   First of all, for me, she was interesting in herself. A tremendous life, filled with conflict, which is the essence of story-telling.
   Second, she was the perfect transmitting agent to communicate the entire story of polygamy in the United States. She had
been in it, part of it—and then against it—so I could show both
aspects of polygamy, good and bad. Also, she was part of the first
family of polygamy. That was good, too.
   It was a labor of love—but a terrible labor. She had written
her memoirs almost a century ago, so I started with that—but the
memoirs told too little, were filled with hysterical exaggerations

Irving Wallace

THE TWENTY-SEVENTH WIFE

Chapter	date started	date finished	No. pages	Total pages	DAYS IT TOOK
I.	July 27, 1959	AUG. 8, 1959	81	81	12
II.	AUG. 13-14 AUG-15-TO-SEPT-13 BUSY "THE CHAPMAN REPORT"	SEP. 14-Oct.3	59	140	21
III.	Oct. 5	Oct. 17	68	208	12
IV.	Oct. 19	Nov. 5	67	275	17
V.					
VI.	Dec. 3-15 Dec-16 To Jan 3 - CHAPMAN HOLIDAYS	JAN. 4-8	77	352	16
VII.					
VIII.	Dec. 11	JAN. 20	88	440	9
IX.					
X.	JAN. 23	FEB. 8	83	523	10
XI.					
XII.					
XIII.					
XIV.	FEB. 9	FEB. 11, 1960 Thursday, 4 o'clock afternoon	34	557	3

Work Sheet — *The Twenty-Seventh Wife.*

and contradictions—and unbalanced and incomplete—but that gave me my leads, anyway. After that I read everything, Mormon or anti-Mormon, concerning Brigham and his wives and Ann Eliza—all the books and pamphlets of the last century. I consulted experts in the field who gave me further leads.

In Salt Lake, I found a very close relative—Ann Eliza's first husband married a second time and there was this son by the second marriage still alive—he wouldn't let me in his house because Ann Eliza had maligned his father in her speeches—yes, that's how alive she still is to Mormons—and he didn't want to cooperate on a book that might revive Ann Eliza's antagonism. I pleaded with him, promised to show both sides of the first marriage—and so he let me in—and then we became very friendly—and I learned a good deal about Ann Eliza's first husband that she had suppressed.

> —From a press release based on
> publisher's questions. 1961.

The Prize (Simon & Schuster, 1962)
Fiction book

I began writing the original draft on October 19, 1960—and I completed it early Friday evening, February 24, 1961. Although I carried the idea with me since 1946, the actual creative writing was done in one great sustained yet disciplined burst of work. On the first day I wrote 5 pages, on the last 33 pages. In the final five days I did 124 pages. The longest period of no work was a four day period in November. Emotionally, throughout, I related closely to my hero, Andrew Craig.

Although published in 1962—the novel in continued reissued paperback is more popular than ever today—I get hundreds of letters from the young who find it happily anti-establishment.

> —Handwritten note on title page
> of the original draft of The
> Prize.   12/15/72.

It is not always possible to travel backward through the blur of years and remember the exact moment when a work of fiction was conceived. But in the case of my novel The Prize, I can even

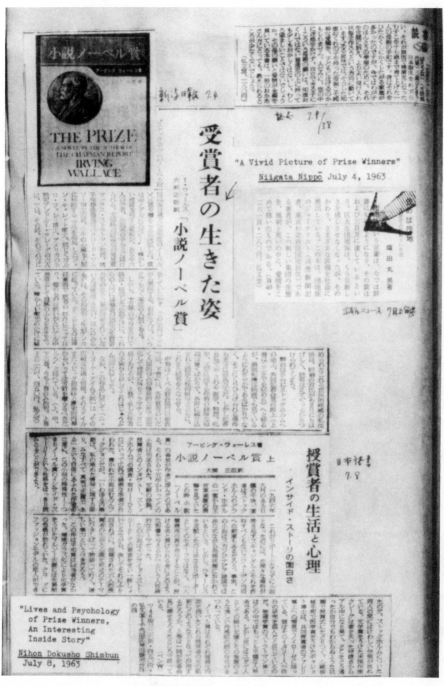

The Prize, as *The Chapman Report* before it, achieved international success.
Above are reviews from Japan.

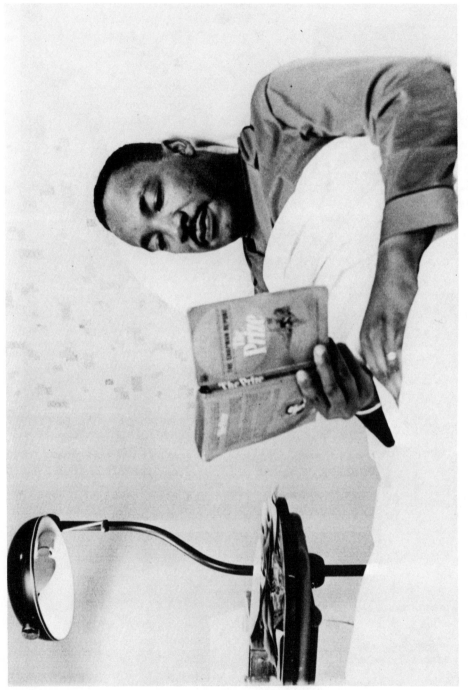

Martin Luther King, Jr., reading *The Prize*. *Jet* magazine took this picture the day King won the Nobel Prize.

now, although nearly twenty-two years have passed, remember vividly the moment, or several separate moments, of the book's beginning.

It began in 1946.

I had recently been discharged from the United States Army Signal Corps, demoted from sergeant to free-lance writer, and my wife Sylvia had resigned from her editorial job on a national magazine and was reduced once more from editor to helpmate. Together, we had taken a Swedish liner from New York to Goteborg, and then a train to Stockholm, to begin the research for the first of a series of articles I was to do for *Reader's Digest, The Saturday Evening Post,* and *Collier's* magazine.

It was the month of September in 1946, and I was constantly out in the chilly, wet northern city, trying to fulfill speculative magazine assignments and possibly find ideas for further assignments. I went everywhere in Stockholm, doing interviews and gathering information on stories that I had planned, yet always questioning, listening, observing in quest of subjects for additional stories I might write.

One name kept recurring in my numerous conversations. That was the name of Dr. Sven Hedin, who was listed in a government publication as one of Sweden's twenty great scientists of the preceding three hundred years.

I wrote Dr. Sven Hedin a note. He responded with an invitation to tea.

He wanted the publicity of my article, and he wanted it to be favorable. Suddenly, during some reply of his, he halted abruptly, and then he said to me, "you know I am a Nobel Prize judge, do you not?"

I had *not* known that, and I was quite astonished and, indeed, impressed.

Dr. Hedin was full of confidences.

Once, when I interrupted to ask Dr. Hedin why some prominent authors had never won the Nobel Prize, he asked me what authors I had in mind. Well, I said, Maxim Gorki for one. "Ah, he died too soon. His name came in several times; he would have got the prize eventually." What about H. G. Wells? "Too minor and journalistic." What about W. Somerset Maugham? "Too popular and undistinguished." And James Joyce. What about James Joyce? Dr. Hedin seemed puzzled. "Who is he?"

It was difficult to suspend disbelief, but these were the words and this was a Nobel Prize judge.

Two weeks later we met again. Some of my penciled jottings of the interview were explosive. The bitter personal prejudices of a single judge, Dr. Carl David af Wirsen, a poet and critic, prevented the Nobel Prize from going to Tolstoi, Ibsen, Strindberg. . . . The personal behavior of authors sometimes kept them from receiving deserved awards . . . homosexuality delayed Gide's receipt of the award for many years. . . . The anti-Semitism of one prominent Nobel Prize winner, the German scientist Philipp Lenard, may have been the major factor in keeping the award from Albert Einstein at a time when Einstein was expected to win it. . . . The selection of Gabriela Mistral for the literary award in 1945, over Hesse, Romain, Croce, Sandburg, and others, was made "because one of our judges, Hjalmar Gullberg, a poet, fell in love with her verse, and translated all of it into Swedish to convince us, and single-handed he swayed our entire vote."

Immediately, with the help of Dr. Hedin . . . I arranged to interview six more Nobel Prize judges. One of my key interviews proved to be the one with the formidable Dr. Österling, Secretary of the Swedish Academy. Dr. Österling was as candid as Dr. Hedin had been. Because of the historic Swedish fear and hatred of its big neighbor, the Nobel committees had ignored Russian genius, and the Swedish Academy had voted down Chekhov, Tolstoi, Andreyev, Gorki.

Only one Russian had ever been awarded the prize. In 1933, a minor writer, an expatriate who lived in Paris and had translated Longfellow's "The Song of Hiawatha" into Russian, Ivan Bunin by name, had been voted the Nobel Prize in literature. When I asked Dr. Österling why Bunin got the prize, he replied, "To pay off our bad consciences on passing over Chekhov and Tolstoi."

Dr. Österling frankly admitted that some of the Swedish literary judges, himself included, were prejudiced against certain American novelists. "I am against Americans getting it because they do not need our check and they receive more money from Hollywood than our Nobel Prize is worth." Unfair or not, such were the facts.

The moon was bright, but indeed, indeed, a dark side existed, and I had been there. Yes, I had a treasure, a true one, I knew at last. There remained only one problem. I had not the faintest idea what to do with it.

Another day or two passed, and I did other work, but always bothered and nagged by this new material, this revelation, and suddenly it was Sunday.

My wife and I slept most of the morning, and after we awakened, we had breakfast in our suite. Outside, the sun was shining. It was noon. I moved to the sitting-room window and looked down upon the Strömmen canal and idly watched and listened as the King's band played before his enormous Royal Palace across the way. The postcard grandeur of the scene, the outer unreality of it, struck me, and then I remembered my interviews and I was again reminded that all that lay before my eyes was a façade, and that plainer, cruder human events happened behind palace walls, behind academy walls, behind institute walls, behind any walls where mere mortals dwelt. And that was the moment of conception. At once I knew what must be done.

From that moment, I was possessed of a brainchild, faceless, almost shapeless, that I would not be delivered of for a decade and a half.

> —*From Irving Wallace,* The Writing of One Novel *(Simon & Schuster, 1968), pp. 13-26.*

The Three Sirens (Simon & Schuster, 1963)

Fiction book

I started page 1 on January 2, 1962, and I finished page 854 and the book itself on September 8, 1962.

Margaret Mead wrote me wondering why I took so negative view of characters—Ashley Montague read it and said he wanted to take me on a real field trip.

> —*Handwritten note on title page*

Oct 24, 1961

✓ Dr. Maud "Matty" Hayden (Dr. Adley R. Hayden) *anthropologist*

Marc Hayden

Claire (Emerson) Hayden

Thomas Courtney *lawyer*

✓ Rachel De Jong *psychoanalyst*

✓ Harriet Bleashka *nurse*

Sam Karpowicz *photographer*
✓   wife: Estelle
       daughter: Mary (Wollenstonecraft)
Louise or Lucy or Lisa
✓ ~~Rosalee~~ Hackfeld *dance*

Orville Pence

Alexander Easterday

Captain Ollie Rasmussen

Cyrus Hackfeld

Rex Garrity ... adventurer

                              Esq.
Godwin ... Daniel Wright,/John Wright, Joanna Wright, ~~Martha~~ *Prue*
               and Sheila.   *Daniel*
Chief ...   ~~Richard~~ Hapai or Tamaiti or Piahuru or Timaru
                                                       ^
Son ...   Johnathan or Hugh or Peter *or Richard*

Niece ... Katherine or Sibilla *or Kate*

Harriet's medical man ... ~~######~~ Edmund

Mary's teen ager ... Tino or Tobias

Early character and story notes for *The Three Sirens*.

of original manuscript.
12/15/72.

The Three Sirens was supposed to have been written before *The Prize*, but I was bruised by the terrible controversy over *The Chapman Report* and the sex scenes, and I was too shaken to write another novel about sexual problems right after it, so I did *The Prize* instead. With the success of *The Prize*, I said to hell with the critics, I'm going to continue to write what and as I please, and I did and have ever since. Not unexpectedly, I was belted by the critics for the theme of *The Three Sirens* (one wonders how some critics have children, or do they?), but I had done what I wanted to do, and this novel, too, was widely accepted by readers, and it is still doing very well.

> —*From Kirk Polking, "An Exclu-*
> *sive   Tape-Recorded Interview*
> *With Irving Wallace."* Writer's
> Yearbook, *37 (1966), p. 86.*

The Man (Simon & Schuster, 1964)
    Fiction book
    The original manuscript was begun October 31, 1963—completed March 8, 1964.
    The only entirely first draft pages of this manuscript typed by me and revised in my hand are Chapters I, II, IV, and VII. These original pages I have retained as a gift to pass on to my son and daughter. I have made this copy of those pages in my file for my collection. As for the other first draft pages, I have no idea what happened to them. The other pages of this manuscript—comprising Chapters III, V, VI, VIII and IX are copies of the revised final draft I submitted to my publisher upon which galleys and the first published book was based.
    This represents a copy of the earliest manuscript draft that exists—and differs from the printed novel.
    This draft was completed in the spring of 1964. *The Man* was published on September 18, 1964. It was the most widely read of my hardcover books—selling 103,000 copies in America—1,250,000 in paperback to date—2,200,000 in Reader's Digest

1963

THE MAN

DAY	PAGES WRITTEN			
October 31, 1963	7			
November 1	3			
2	0			
3	0.			
4	12			
5	8			
6	12			
7	3			
8	7			
9	3			
11	21			
12	10			
13	23			
14	17			
15	9			
16	0			
17	0			
18	21			
19	7			
20	16			
21	8			
22	4	President Kennedy assassinated		
23	2			
24	4			
25	0	JFK's funeral		
26	6			
27	8			
28	0	Thanksgiving		
29	21			
30	0			
December 1	0			
2	16			
3	18			
4	3			
5	8			
6	14			
7	0			

December 8	0		LIFE MAG interview	
9	0		"	
10	1			
11	18			
12	19			
13	9			
14	0			
15	0			
16	18			
17	22			
18	1			
19	4			
20	1			
21	0			
22	0			
23	11			
24	0			
25	0			
26	14			
27	9			
28	0			
29	0			
30	12			
31	0			
1964—January 1	0			
2	17			
3	15			
4	2			
5	0			
6	19			
7	9			
8	16			
9	17			
10	4			
11	0			
12	0			
13	18			

1964

THE MAN

DAY		PAGES WRITTEN
JANUARY	14	17
	15	15
	16	10
	17	9
	18	0
	19	0
	20	20
	21	13
	22	4
	23	17
	24	5
	25	0
	26	0
	27	10
	28	14
	29	12
	30	0
	31	0
FEBRUARY	1	0
	2	0
	3	20
	4	18
	5	16
	6	16
	7	7
	8	0
	9	1
	10	20
	11	4
	12	17
	13	18
	14	19
	15	0
	16	0
	17	16
	18	12
	19	17

VII

VIII

ill
ill

FEBRUARY	20	23
	21	14
	22	0	Rewriting
	23	0	"
	24	13
	25	11
	26	20
	27	14
	28	20
	29	14
MARCH	1	0
	2	24
	3	23
	4	17
	5	15
	6	21
	7	28	5:55 afternoon 5:16 afternoon
	8	12

Finished book on page 1166 at 5:16 in afternoon, Sunday, March 8, 1964.

Irving O'Halloran

Book Club—29,000 in the Book-of-the-Month Club edition—plus the sales of seventeen foreign editions.

—Handwritten note on title page of original manuscript of The Man. *3/20/68.*

. . . I've always been an active liberal, with a fierce belief in equality under the law and civil rights. I don't mean that I join anything, but I constantly feel that I want to write about a national or international human issue about which I feel deeply. I'm sure most of us have felt pain, alarm, even horror, about this whole Negro situation in America, the scandalous plight of the "second-class citizen," and at least twice I wanted to write novels about it. But you just don't write novels about a subject, you write them about people. Twice, in the last seven or eight years, I've had ideas for novels that dealt with American Negroes, with Negroes and whites in social and political contact, but each time I realized that though the ideas could convey my feelings, the ideas really weren't good novels. They were ordinary. Other writers, especially Negro ones, had said the same things before, and better than I could. And I didn't want to write a mammoth tract or pamphlet. (I'm ruthless with myself before I undertake a novel, commit myself to one. I know that once I become involved in writing a novel, I have to live with it for a long, long time, it has to become my entire life, it has to draw upon my feelings and imaginings and intellect, and it would be hell to be tied to a novel that you discovered, after a year, you didn't want to do, after all.)

Normally, a book gestates inside me for some time. . . . But *The Man* just came to me, and when it came I knew it was right. The characters were there. A fresh approach to the whole subject was there. Every major ingredient of the book came early. This was important, for when you have a strikingly unusual idea to superimpose upon your characters, there's always a danger that you'll get into trouble in the last part of the book, because the idea begins to dominate the characters, suffocate them, so that the characters can't evolve through the novel naturally, and you are left with an overwhelming idea that can't be resolved in the end.

Robert Kirsch, book critic of the *Los Angeles Times,* handing Irving Wallace the *Bestsellers Magazine* Award for paperback of the year, 1965. (Photo: L. A. *Times*)

I knew from the first day I began working on *The Man,* that I wanted it to end with an impeachment trial. The characters were heading that way. The trial seemed as vital as my opening idea. And also, an impeachment trial appealed to my sense of theatrics. And I had my Negro President, Douglass Dilman, whole, right away. I got him while I was sitting in the dining room one Saturday night, reading, and I can't explain how he got there. But suddenly there he was, a Negro President, and I jumped up and went into the kitchen to tell my wife and son about him.

> —*From Roy Newquist,* Conversations *(New York: Rand McNally, 1967), pp. 453-454.*

The Sunday Gentleman (Simon & Schuster, 1965)
Non-fiction book

In the years before I gave myself over completely to the writing of books, I had written and published at least 500 articles and short stories for magazines, and had perhaps written 200-300 more that had never been published. A handful of the published articles I had always wanted to preserve between book covers, but they did not add up to a book. Then, one day, coming across a few cartons of my old rejected articles, I found some that I realized had been too strong or unusual or offbeat to have been commercially acceptable in their time, but that today were worthy of book publication. Then it dawned on me that the handful of best published pieces, as well as the better unpublished pieces, were ones I had written on my own time, on my free Sundays, when I could write as I pleased, and they were not written on assignment for bread and butter. And so I gathered these stories together for a book. To bring some of the older pieces up-to-date, I instigated new research to learn what had happened to the young man who had undergone a prefrontal lobotomy operation that changed his personality, to the geisha union I had studied in Japan, to Alfried Krupp whom I'd interviewed in Essen, to the Orient Express since I first rode it and wrote about it. Then, I gave each chapter an up-to-date postscript. And, in 1965, my book, *The Sunday Gentleman,* was published by Simon & Schuster.

Wallace's World Full of Surprises

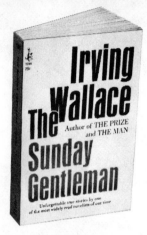

Pocket Books ad for

The Sunday Gentleman,

1967.

The $5.95 hardcover edition is now in paperback. only **75¢**

The personal adventures, the extraordinary people, places and ideas that have fascinated one of the most widely-read novelists of our time: Irving Wallace, author of **THE MAN, THE PRIZE** and the forthcoming **THE PLOT.**

THE SUNDAY GENTLEMAN is an international carnival of surprises, with Irving Wallace as your companion and guide. Join him. Rub elbows with spies on the glamorous Orient Express. Visit the most luxurious bordello in the world. Meet the head of the Japanese Geisha Guild. Tour John F. Kennedy's Oval Office, nine weeks before Dallas. Let Irving Wallace show you a world only a few have ever witnessed.

"... *Wallace writing at his best.*" LIBRARY JOURNAL

"... *a feeling for mood and character; a responsive eye; a recording ear; an individuality* ..."
LOS ANGELES TIMES

"... *Amusing and expert* ..." London TIMES

"... *well-written, altogether human and absorbing* ..."
NEW YORK POST

"... *consistently interesting* ..." CHICAGO TRIBUNE

"... *his fifth consecutive smash.*" WALTER WINCHELL

Published by **POCKET BOOKS** First in Paperbacks

—From copy provided for Professor Al. P. Nelson for Writing The Nonfiction Book (text for English A64, University of Wisconsin, 1970).

The Plot (Simon & Schuster, 1967)

Fiction book

I remember precisely when and where I thought of the central idea of *The Plot*. The idea came to me at 4 o'clock in the afternoon, on August 26, 1964, while I was having a sandwich at an outdoor table of Fouquet's on the Champs Elysees in Paris. I suppose, like everyone else, I was preoccupied with the possible emergence of Red China as a world power (this was less than two months before China exploded its first atomic bomb). And all at once—I can't tell you how or why, because I do not know—the entire central idea of *The Plot*—a life-and-death Summit Conference on disarmament and arms control—came to me. This idea was the catalytic agent for the entire book. Within a few minutes after having been struck by the idea, all of the characters I had thought about in the years before came crowding back into my head. And the characters and the idea merged, belonged together.

Anyway, with the book crystalizing in my mind, I left Fouquet's, hastened to my suite in the California Hotel, a few blocks away, stuck a page in my portable typewriter and typed— *The Summit* (which I changed to *The Plot* five months later)—and then I began writing down all that I knew of this book. As I wrote, the central idea of it was altered by the five characters who had been so long in search of a plot, and the five characters, themselves, began to take on different shapes and personalities in the light of the idea of the book.

After that, I started to impose a writer's discipline on the raw material. I developed the characters, their backgrounds, their personal stories, their relationships with one another, and simultaneously I developed the thread of the main story. All of this seemed an unending process. I wrote pages and pages of biographical material about the fictional characters. Then I wrote three

THE PLOT

Second Outline -- Step Sheet

by

Irving Wallace

CHAPTER I:

Jay Thomas Doyle, in Vienna, fails to get a deal on his book, The Conspirators Who Killed Kennedy.
He learns Hazel Smith, of CNA (Cosmos News Agency), is arriving in Paris with Russian delegation. She is the key to his book. He flies to Paris.

Ex-President Emmet A. Earnshaw, in London, learns a former business friend, recently released from Spandau, Krupp's foremost rival, Dr. Dietrich von Goerlitz, is in Paris for Summit to meet with Red Chinese -- and make contracts with international publishers #### for his memoirs, My Life Among The Big and The Little -- containing a chapter on Earnshaw that can destroy his fading reputation.
Earnshaw, and his niece Carol, take the Golden Arrow to Paris.

Medora Hart, in Juan-les-Pins, has been banned from England, so as not to stand witness in the Sydney Ormsby scandal - and Sir Austen Ormsby is responsible.
Medora learns Sir Austen and his bride, Fleur, will be in Paris for the Summit. Medora obtains an early nude painting of Fleur from Nardeau, her great artist friend. She takes her car and drives to Paris.

Matthew Brennan, former diplomat disgraced in a security in which he and his Russian counterpart, Nikolai Rostov allowed a Professor Varney to defect with H-Bomb secrets to Red China during a conference in Zurich four years before, lives as a leper in Venice. Only good thing in his life is Lisa Collins, a young fashion designer, with whom he is having an affair.
After Lisa goes to Paris for the shows, Brennan learns the missing Rostov, who alone can clear him, has been reinstated into power and is coming to the Summit as an adviser to Premier Zabbin. Brennan hastens to the Orient Express, joins his Lisa, and heads for the showdown in Paris.

———

CHAPTER II:

Having dropped Lisa at the California hotel where in better days he stayed with his wife and daughter, Brennan phones an old faithful friend, at the US Embassy, Herb Neely - who, despite Brennan's reluctance, has him to Embassy to discuss Rostov's whereabouts

Second outline of *The Plot*. Irving Wallace calls it a "step sheet" — a term used for film script outlines, 1966.

chronological outlines of the story, and the third and last of these outlines, prepared for my own eyes and own guidance in undertaking a novel so broad in scope and intricate in detail, ran to about 25,000 words. Meanwhile, there were many factual things I did not know about my characters, about the backdrops of the book, so I began to read, interview, and travel for purposes of research.

Then, back at my home in Los Angeles, I began the formal writing of the book—often departing from my outline—often going off on unexpected tangents. For example, one female character I had thought would be minor became major as the novel was being written, and another female character I had expected to be major became a lesser character. And one secondary character, locked in my mind, who begged to be put into the book, I ignored completely until the entire book was done, and only then did I realize I missed this character on paper and only then did I go back and carefully weave this new character into the book.

I worked compulsively on the novel, night and day, seven days a week. It was as if the only life that was real to me was that which I was creating on paper. The actual world outside my typewriter seemed utterly unreal in that period. But in truth, thinking back, the outside world was very real, indeed. In those two years, while I was writing, a thousand extraneous events, yet events close to my life—all involving family and friends, some painful, some pleasurable, all time-consuming—swirled around me. Yet, despite distractions, despite slings and arrows and skyrockets, a writer must write, and so I wrote on, constantly building and rebuilding my make-believe paper world.

And when the first draft was finally finished, I took a brief rest and then began to rewrite. In all, I did five revised versions of *The Plot* before it went to the printer.

This process absorbed almost every waking hour of two solid years—two years and two months—although the entire growth span of the book from conception to pre-publication took ten years.

In physical size, as well as in the story's scope, *The Plot* was the biggest book I had ever written. The first draft came to 1,369 manuscript pages—about 350,000 words—or the length of

Dust jacket — *The Writing of One Novel.*

three normal-length novels.   It would have been better for me
emotionally, even better for my health, to have contrived to write
a shorter book in that time, but I could not cheat myself. This
book had to be written the way it demanded to be written, and so
I wrote it and did not worry about the time that it took or the
energy that it required or its ultimate length. I suppose that it
came out at this length because it was so heavily populated with
so many different characters, and several of the characters might
have deserved complete books by themselves. But, to my mind,
they all belonged in this one book, and there they are, in *The
Plot,* today.

> —*Unpublished notes on the writing of* The Plot *(done for Roy
> Newquist's collection of interviews,* Conversations*).
> 1/15-16/67.*

The Writing of One Novel (Simon & Schuster, 1968)
> Non-fiction book
This is the original draft of this autobiographical book—as
typed and corrected by me.

I began writing it on October 2, 1967, and finished writing
it on November 17, 1967.

Off and on until January 2, 1968, I made revisions and rewrites in this draft—and after that I released it to be retyped.

For many years I had in mind a book such as this for students,
writers, and curious readers. When a publisher asked me to do a
40-page piece on how I'd written one of my books, I agreed to
try it. But when the project grew into a 251-page book of my
own, I decided to publish it as a book of its own—since it was too
long for the anthology on writing.

Although I sometimes had to improve the writing of my
original letters and journals, I never altered the facts—and so this
is an honest and candid account of my life with one novel. This is
the draft that will soon be submitted to my publisher.

> —*Handwritten note on title page
> of original manuscript of* The
> Writing of One Novel. *1/14/68.*

First edition, second state.

In the first printing of 7,500 copies on November 8th, a printer's error appeared on page 18, when the third line from the top of the third paragraph was repeated in the seventh line. This was replated before 5,000 more copies of the first edition were shipped last week—and the correct omitted line seven of paragraph three of page 18 was restored here in this second state of the first edition.

—Handwritten note on flyleaf of
The Writing of One Novel.
12/5/68.

The Seven Minutes (Simon & Schuster, 1969)
  Fiction book

Published September 28, 1969—in three printings sold 115,000 in this edition—with an additional hardcover sale of 353,000 copies sold via Literary Guild and Doubleday Book Club.

I found the reception gratifying because this book meant a good deal to me.

*—Handwritten note on flyleaf of
first edition of* The Seven Minutes. *1/19/73.*

I got the idea for the book in 1964. That was the time when I was supplying an affidavit for my Italian publisher in Milan for use in the Italian censorship trial—a criminal trial—against my novel, *The Chapman Report.* At the same time, in August, 1964, I received word from Dublin that my novel, *The Prize*, and Edna O'Brien's novel, *Girl With the Green Eyes,* had been banned by the Censorship Board in Ireland. And those two occurences may have been the spark of inspiration. I may have said to myself — You are being censored so why not draw upon this experience to write about a fictional author and his book which are being censored—and once and for all tackle the whole vast subject of pornography and censorship? My answer must have been — Why not indeed? And so I conceived *The Seven Minutes.*

—From an interview conducted

THE SEVEN MINUTES

by

Irving Wallace

By early morning, heat had begun to lay its dank,
moist hand on the Main Street of Midvale, California, a small
community just outside Los Angeles.
Local police officers Corrigan and Otto, walking in lock
step up the street, are uncomfortable not only because they
are in civilian clothes at this hour, but because they must make
~~at up whookst~~ ~~~~ an arrest . . . a minor,
unimportant arrest which, they cannot know at this moment,
will create an international earthquake of controversy, and
will become a cause celebre in every civilized corner of the
world . . .

The most famous, the most notorious pornographic novel
in English, long banned from the United States, is a book
entitled The Seven Minutes by Jonathan Jadway, a brilliant
expatriate American author of the Henry Miller- D. H. Lawrence
school who died in his youth, shortly after privately
publishing the novel in Paris back in 1935. (The contents
of this novel, so long banned, will be revealed during the
course of a sensational trial which dominates my story. The
frontispiece quotation reads: "While there is great variety in
individual response, our survey of 250 females who ~~had~~ have had
orgasms reached the climactic state ~~###~~ after seven minutes
of intercourse." This banned novel ~~at~~ ~~the dead Jadway's is~~ by
stream of consciousness narrative ~~is~~ one woman's mind during inside
seven minutes of sexual intercourse, in which she reviews her
life, the men in her life, her acts of love, until in the ~~###~~
~~###########################~~ climactic moments the reader learns . . .
what choice she made and who ~~###~~ is making love to her and
how the seven minutes have resolved her future,).

In my novel, the bright, decent but weak son of a
tyrannical father who has built up a huge publishing house seriously
has just taken over the firm, because his father is ill.
determined to keep the firm from others, to save it and in
the process prove himself, he chooses as his first project a
daring venture. Supported by his best friend, a young and
rising attorney, he determines to defy the old banning and
censorship and, in this new time of enlightenment and freedom
of speech, bring The Seven Minutes ~~out~~ in the United States.
He invests all his resources in it, knowing if anything goes
wrong he will lose control of the firm, and it appears he
will win. From advance reports, The Seven Minutes will be
allowed to be ~~published~~ unmolested, and it will be a sensation solo
and a smash hit.
                    on publication day,
And then, in a tiny, sleepy California city, two policemen

by Censorship Today *(October/November, 1969)*.

The Nympho and Other Maniacs (Simon & Schuster, 1971)
    Non-fiction book

Most books devoted to the lives of liberated ladies focus on those who were pioneer suffragettes, strong politically-minded ladies out to get women the vote, job equality, emancipation. With three exceptions—Caroline Norton, Margaret Fuller, Victoria Woodhull, who were dedicated to the cause of female emancipation, I have avoided the familiar approach. Most of the women in *The Nympho and Other Maniacs* were not reformers, not crusaders for equal rights. Most of them weren't breaking the rules for any lofty principle or to achieve anything for their sex. They broke the rules simply because they were individuals, determined to live as they wished in a man's world. Whatever my women accomplished for their sex was accomplished accidentally.

The earliest inspiration for the book came to me when I came across a reference to Lady Jane Ellenborough, how she had married four husbands in four different capitals of the world, started out as the young bride of a British Lord and wound up as the wife of an Arabian Bedouin sheik—and I decided to look into her past, investigate it, with the idea of writing a biography of her or making her part of a biographical collection of similar scandalous women.

Of course there were many criteria to go by. I wrote about some women whose names might be familiar to readers when I felt that, familiar as they might seem, the truth about them was really not known and the readers would be as surprised as I to find out what they were really like. Then, too, I selected women who I felt were actually little known to most readers, ones inexplicably overlooked by other biographers and who deserved to be more than mere postscripts and who I felt should not be forgotten. I judged each woman by the dramatic impact she had on her time, by her fearlessness in the face of scandal.

Among the little-known names, how could I not write about Anne Royall, America's first female journalist? When President John Quincy Adams refused to give her an interview, Anne deter-

NEWS

from THE INNER SANCTUM *of*
SIMON AND SCHUSTER
publishers · 630 FIFTH AVENUE
ROCKEFELLER CENTER, NEW YORK 20
TELEPHONE: 212-245-6400

For Immediate Release
Contact: Dan Green
February 26, 1971

The NYMPHO *And Other* MANIACS

"This consistently popular novelist once again hits the bulls-eye, this time in non-fiction. . . .This is hard-to-put-down stuff, written with Wallace's own brand of verve, ironic detachment and keen observation."
—*Publishers' Weekly*

"In *The Nympho And Other Maniacs,* I am writing about individual women of the recent past who, whether by plan or by accident, wittingly or unwittingly, refused to accept any simplistic biological definition of the female as a mere childbearer and the second best of the sexes. The wild women I've written about, by their various expressions of revolt, by doing their thing and implying that society's rules be damned, challenged and modified the role of the female in the age in which each lived. Because of these individual ladies, the organization of modern-day Women's Liberation Movement was made possible." writes Irving Wallace. *The Nympho And Other Maniacs* (Simon and Schuster, March 22, $8.95) brings together thirty of these women, each of whom, in her own way, contributed something to the cause of individual freedom.

They include: Ninon de Lenclos, who founded a School of Lovemaking in France; Emma Hamilton, who became pregnant by England's greatest naval hero without her husband's noticing it; Napoleon's sister, Pauline Bonaparte, whose intense sexual activity was the despair of her gynecologist; Napoleon's mistress, Maria Walewska, who was asked to sacrifice her virtue to the Emperor to save Poland from his wrath; Lord Byron's reckless females (among them the sensuous Teresa Guiccioli, the unhappy Caroline Lamb, and the unfortunate Claire Clairmont); and Victoria Woodhull, who ran for President of the United States in 1872 on a platform advocating free love, short skirts, birth control and world government.

The Nympho And Other Maniacs is a magnificent *tour de force,* a book that goes far beyond the amusing and incredible adventures of the uninhibited ladies themselves to make some wise and unexpected points about life, love, marriage and women.

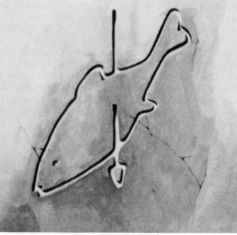

Dust jacket – *The Word*.

mined to trap him into speaking to her. She learned that the President often took a swim in the Potomac River near The White House at daybreak. One morning, she crept up on him during his lone swim, and caught him paddling about in the nude. She sat on his clothes, refused to let him have them, until he gave her the interview—which he was forced to do while naked in the water.

It took a long time, from having the idea for the book to completing it—nearly thirty years—but I finally completed it, and here it is.

—From a description of The Nympho and Other Maniacs *done for Cassell and Company, the British publishers who brought out the English edition of the book on June 24, 1971. No date.*

The Word (Simon & Schuster, 1972)

Fiction book

The regular Simon & Schuster edition of this No. 1 bestseller was 576 pages. This Literary Guild edition is 568 pages, cheaper paper, and the list of my previous titles has been removed from the back jacket.

The trade edition sold 130,000 in hardcover—this edition via the Guild and Doubleday Book Club will sell 350,000 minimum.

—Handwritten note on flyleaf of Literary Guild edition of The Word. *1/12/73.*

The inspiration for *The Word* came to me in 1961. It grew out of two things: an inner spiritual crisis, when I thought I had everything and found I had very little and sought for something to believe in (and decided to create a protagonist in my own image to undertake the search for an answer); and a persistent curiosity about historic Messiahs like Christ, who offered reason and purpose, and my private speculations on whether such men had actually once existed on earth. The ideas merged, gestated for nearly ten years, took form in a story, which was finally published

Irving Wallace

IK, JACOBUS

roman

DE BOEKERIJ
BAARN

Title page of Dutch edition of *The Word,* published in The Netherlands in the fall of 1973.

in 1972.

—From unpublished notes done for Contemporary Authors. *1/8/73.*

The Fan Club (Simon & Schuster, 1974)
  Fiction book

"Did you really mean it—what you were saying—about doing anything in the world, even risking your lives, just to make love to Sharon Fields for one night?" Malone asked the three other men in the bar.

Thus begins Irving Wallace's sensational and breathtaking new novel about man's ultimate erotic fantasy—and perhaps woman's, too—the longing and desire for the perfect sexual partner. Four men who live unsatisfying, ordinary lives in a society where only the wealthy, powerful, and famous enjoy blatant sexual license with the most beautiful women on earth, conspire to act out the most primal of all man's carnal dreams—the physical possession of the world's most coveted and worshipped Love Goddess. Obsessed by the sensual image of Sharon Fields, the magnificent young movie star who has become the sex symbol for a new and liberated age, and whom they see as glamorous, provocative, available, these four very different men join forces to convert fantasy into reality by planning a crime which seems to them not so much criminal as the legitimate enactment of their fantasies—and possibly hers . . .

It is Adam Malone, a gentle idealist whose private life is devoted to being a one-man, obsessional fan club of Sharon Fields, who first thinks of kidnapping her in order to share with her his dreams of erotic perfection, of supreme lovemaking. With the fervor of a true believer, he persuades Howard Yost, an unsuccessful insurance agent whose life seems pointless when compared to his past football glories and his constant reveries of sexual conquests, and Leo Brunner, a mild-mannered accountant, haunted by the hopeless gray dullness of his life and marriage in a society which flaunts its pleasures in his face. The fourth convert is Kyle Shively, a coarse, bitter, redneck garage mechanic, with a chilling potential for violence. Together, lightly, then seriously, they

1.

IT WAS NOT LONG after daybreak this early june morning—ten minutes after seven o'clock, according to his wristwatch—and the sun was continuing to rise, slowly warming the vast sprawl of buildings and the long stretch of Southern California country.

He and his friend were there again, the two of them,flattened on their stomachs in the scrubby growth at the edge of the cliff, concealed by a high hedge of bushes from anyone living in the nearby houses or entering this dead-end street called Stone Canyon Road on a hilltop in exclusive Bel Air.

Both of them held binoculars to their eyes, still waiting.

Tilting the glasses higher, peering beyond the object of his surveillance, he could clearly see Stone Canyon Reservoir, with the miniature figures of several early-rising sightseers promenading along the artificial lake. Lowering the glasses slightly, he could follow the ribbon of Stone Canyon Road where it wound up toward this high elevation in Bel Air. Then his glasses moved to catch a glimpse of a narrow, steep side street—that would be Levico Way—which he knew led to a cul-de-sac where stood the security gate that guarded entry to her well-photographed estate.

Now, once more, his binoculars were probing inside her estate, focusing down on the secluded asphalt road far below, the driveway that led from the locked gate between clusters of heavy trees and an orchard to the palatial mansion standing on a gradual rise beyond. For him, it was as impressive as ever. In other times and other places, only kings and queens lived in such splendor. In this time and this place, the great houses and modern palaces were reserved for the very rich and the very famous. He did not know about riches, but he did know for certain that none other in Bel Air was more famous, more world-renowned, than the mistress of this estate.

The magnified section of the asphalt road between the gate and the cluster of elms and poplars remained in focus, as he breathlessly watched and waited.

Suddenly, someone moved into his field of vision. He reached out with his free hand, tapping his partner's shoulder. "Kyle," he said urgently, "there she is. Can you see her coming around the trees?"

He could hear his partner shift slightly, and after a brief interval his partner spoke. "Yeah, that's her. Right on the dot."

They lapsed into silence, their binoculars trained on her, steadily, relentlessly holding the small, distant figure in view as she reached the end of her familiar quarter-of-a-mile stroll to the locked gate. They continued to hold on her as she turned away from the gate, halted, knelt, stroked and then spoke to the tiny excited Yorkshire terrier that had been prancing at her heels. At last, she stood up, and briskly began to retrace her steps in the direction of the huge mansion at the head of the driveway. In moments, she disappeared from view, obscured by the thick cluster of trees.

Adam Malone lowered his binoculars, rolled over on his side, and carefully packed them away in the leather case attached to his wide belt. He would not need them again for this purpose, he knew. It was exactly a month to the day that this vigil had begun. He had found this observation site, and first used it, on the morning of May 16. This was the morning of June 17. He had been up here, mostly alone but occasionally with

August 29, 1972

All American Bowling Emporium Fourteen Bar

CHARACTERS FOR THE ~~WISH~~: FAN CLUB:

Actress	... Sharon Fields
Writer-clerk	... Adam Malone
Mechanic	... Kyle Shively
Salesman	... ~~████~~ *Howard*, Yost *his children ... Harry & Timothy*
His wife	... Elinor Yost
Accountant	... Leo Brunner
His wife	... Thelma Brunner
Actress's personal manager	... Felix Zigman
Her lover	... Rodney Clay
Her secretary	... Nellie Wright
Her housekeepers	... Pearl and Patrick O'Donnell
Her producer	... Justin Rhodes
Her public relations man	... Hank Lenhardt
Her hair stylist	... *Terence Simms*
Detective	... Sgt. Chester Culpepper *Officer Lopez in...*
His assistant	... Sgt. ~~████████████~~ *Willie* Trigg *Detective Neuman*
Shopkeeper	...Mr. Middleton
Newscaster	...Sky Hubbard Show
His young assistant	...~~████~~/Owen *Charley*
Teletypist with L.E.T.S.	...Marion Owen
FBI / *FBI*	... *Agent ~~Sierceson~~ / Agent Wescott*
Shively's woman	...Mrs. Gilbert (Kitty) Bishop
Shively's boss	...~~████~~ *Jack* NAVE *'n Crony gasoline station*
Yost's insurance ~~family~~	...Mr. and Mrs. Livingston and Gale
Brunner's account	...~~████~~ RUFFALO
Sharon's father, mother	...Thomas and Hazel Klatt
Boy~~s/#~~s and men in her li~~fe~~	...John, then Duane, ~~then Clark,~~ Geiger, ~~Jurgeson, Parmelee,~~ Olson,
Bartender	... ~~████ Einstein~~ *Reese,* Wescott

create The Fan Club, the innocent cover name for their monstrous conspiracy. It is Malone who convinces the others that The Fan Club not only can seize Sharon Fields, but can persuade her to cooperate willingly in their dreams of sex; but it is Shively whose tough-fisted approach carries through their daring plan—and who transforms what has been merely a collective orgiastic fantasy into a horrifying and sadistic reality of bondage, savagery, and murder.

With mounting tension, Irving Wallace describes their brilliantly conceived plan and its success, and the playing out of each man's repressed sexual wish in the hidden mountain cabin they have chosen as the hideaway for The Fan Club. Here, alone with their Love Goddess ("Picture Elizabeth Taylor or Marilyn Monroe or Brigitte Bardot lying in the next room naked," one of them says with incredulity), each of the four men confronts the embodiment of his dream with unexpected and shocking results. And here, in the confinement of her barred room, at the mercy of her captors, Sharon Fields, a different, smarter, and more vulnerable person than their image of her, recklessly uses all the histrionic talents and wiles that have made her the world's most renowned screen sex symbol, to play one man against another in a desperate and deadly sex game that may win her freedom—or cost her her life.

—From copy written for the Spring, 1974 Simon & Schuster book catalog. 10/73.

The Square Peg

an Afterword by **Ray B. Browne**

Irving Wallace is a man of many lines and angles, and the profile of this writer must contain a firm outline. But within it there need to be considerable shadings.

Wallace the man and writer is and always has been, to play on the title of one of his books, a square peg in a round society. He is a staunch individualist who though highly respecting society and holding out great hope for it has been intrigued by the quaint, the curious, the unusual. He is the type to appreciate the story told during World War II of Mrs. Franklin Roosevelt one night observing Winston Churchill, on one of his many visits, stalking up and down the hall of the White House dressed only in his smoking cigar. The story shows Churchill's unflinching individualism, his marching, in words of Henry David Thoreau, one of Wallace's favorite writers, to a "different drummer." And Wallace steadfastly has marched in his own way and to his own rhythm. This trait in his personality accounts partially for his great appeal to the average reader.

The titles of many of Wallace's books reveal this bent: *The Fabulous Originals, The Scandalous Ladies, The Square Pegs, The Nympho and Other Maniacs*. And to a certain extent this interest is exemplified in all his other books, for they search out and develop the peculiar, unexplored, unexploited aspects of the human being or of society. At his best he has been remarkably far-sighted. In *The Prize* (1962), for example, he pictured two doctors developing a serum that neutralized the body's rejection of a foreign organ being introduced into it. Six years later it was revealed that such experiments were underway, and the next year Dr. Christian Bernard succeeded in his first heart transplant.

Wallace early displayed and began to develop this interest in the unusual. As a high school student and writer for his Kenosha, Wisconsin, high school paper, the *Kenews,* he concentrated on the extraordinary. His first venture into commercial writing had to do with informing the public about the real location where Buffalo Bill was buried. Wallace's first original story for the screen was about John Hix, a collector of odd facts. To a large extent the John Hixes in life have dominated Wallace's interest.

Another obvious characteristic of Wallace's writing is his great interest in accumulating and telling facts whether they are always relevant or not. This trait undoubtedly accounts for much of his appeal to the general public. To read one of Wallace's books is to peruse the shelves of a major library, to handle and glean facts from hundreds of books, and to talk to dozens of experts in the field being discussed. Wallace likes to repeat the facts and to give the anecdotes, even if he feels that he might be telling some of his readers more than they want to know.

Wallace's love of facts for their own sake, his desire to accumulate them, has been strengthened by his careful cataloguing and filing of them. Malvin Wald, a writer who knew and worked with Wallace when he first came to Hollywood, recalls that even then Wallace had his detailed filing system, and he, Wald, knew that eventually Wallace was going to succeed. He was simply too meticulous to fail. This method of working allows Wallace to document and make viable his philosophy. He is a humanist, a political liberal, who has always fought for the right to prove that "life is worth living, worth fighting for, worth defending against the forces of death."

This philosophy also undoubtedly accounts at least in part for Wallace's style of writing. Coming from a poor background, a fact that he has never forgotten, and never having graduated from college, through the years he has been determined to prove that he knows a great deal and can write his knowledge very well. This urge to transmit facts—to improve society—has always dominated his style. In his eyes the writer has a responsibility beyond his art. "It was because I believed in the responsibility of the writer to his art as much as I believed that he had other responsibilities beyond writing, it was because of this ambivalent feeling toward my work, that I determined that six days a week were enough to give of myself to avoid a debtor's prison. The seventh day of the week, I felt, belonged to me." He was especially pleased with his novel *The Man* because he felt it "affects the reader for the better, improves him, gives him more love and understanding of his fellows."

In his writing Wallace has never been a follower no matter how great the royalties he has received, or merely out to make money. On the contrary, he has generally insisted on following his own Dream and writing in his own style. Even when he was penniless and skirting disaster he still determined to write his own way. As he said, he would whore around and write six days a week to live, but never on Sunday. That day he reserved for satisfying himself.

Part of his Dream has always been to learn and to teach. Wallace's reading and scholarship are staggering and shame many of his academic critics. He always has a paid researcher working for him, and often she will have many aids helping her. He will not write on any subject until he has learned everything he can about it, until he has lived with the experts in the field, and knows precisely that his resulting book cannot be faulted for its facts by any expert in the field.

Ignorance of material, if it appealed to him, has never been a deterrent to his accepting the challenge of a subject that he liked. He has set about informing himself, making himself into an expert. When he began writing *The Prize,* for example, his knowledge of the fields in which the Nobel prizes were awarded was better than average, but not precise enough for him to write about them with any expertise. He therefore set about informing himself. The result was that even experts praised him for his knowledge of fields that he should know little about.

As he recounts in another section of this book, Wallace once talked with Clifford Irving, long before he became notorious for his faked autobiography of Howard Hughes, who was complaining that he wanted to write a novel about lawyers but knew nothing about them or their profession. Characteristically, Wallace told him that all he had to do was to meet and talk with lawyers—live with them for a while—until he learned their business. Research, to Wallace, provides the answer to all questions—reading the printed word, talking with people, learning about new ways of life.

Naturally, then, when he was researching *The Prize* over a fourteen year period, he sought out the recipients of the Nobel Prize—Albert Einstein, Pearl Buck and others—and asked them questions that would allow him to write on the subject knowledgeably. Wallace's files are always active and his memory retentive and responsive. If he ever learns anything it is subject to conscious or unconscious recall. His fiction, he says, demands "every resource of my imagination, my passions, my feelings," his nonfiction requires his "mind and intellect to do it well."

It is common knowledge that there is no single type of "popular writer." There are dozens of types that appeal to the vast body of persons known as the "popular reader." As a "popular writer" Wallace's intentions, like many other's in his business, have been misunderstood. Because he does not write formulaic fiction (such as detective fiction, science fiction, the Western, or the like) he is not easily classified, and not being classifiable he is not easily pigeonholed. Wallace refuses to produce the same kind of story over and over, to write by formula. He gave up this kind of writing because he found that it wearied and restricted him even though he knew there is safety in formula fiction. As long as a popular writer sticks to his type he may be judged good. But once he tries to branch out or break through into something else he is severely criticized and is urged to get back into the groove he has worn for himself. The criticism leveled against Ross Macdonald for his latest book, *Sleeping Beauty,* is an excellent case in point. Macdonald has been told that he is a superb writer of detective fiction but should not try to write anything beyond that.

Like Mark Twain before him, Wallace has written for the masses, for the millions. He knows, or thinks he knows, what appeals to them, and tries to reach that quality, because he feels, like W. Somerset Maugham whom he likes to quote, that a book is incomplete until it has a reader and the more readers the better. But Wallace determines to be the cutting rather than the dragging edge of change, and will not—can not—sacrifice his independence of mind and action to coddle and cater to public demands that he does not agree with. Fortunately he does not have to.

A good example of Wallace's independence is found in the way he insists on structuring his novels. His plots are extraordinarily complicated and complex. Beginning with a problem, as Wallace sees it, they develop through conflict and drama, which he loves, in the characters. "Every human face has two profiles," Wallace says. "As a novelist, it is my duty to show not one but both." Wallace's interest is "in people and the hidden things in their lives," he once said in an interview for the New York *Herald-Tribune*. "My instinct is to take what's never been shown on the surface and to bring it to the surface. That's what makes a novel. . . ."

In development, Wallace's novels start from a large and ranging base. Then they grow pyramidally, gradually concentrating the plot and shedding sub-plots and details as they rise until eventually the top is reached and the problem is solved. These plots are rich and complex, or they are overly complicated and confusing, depending on the reader's point of view. But Wallace, like John Barth, Truman Capote, Gore Vidal, Norman Mailer, Irving Stone, and dozens of other contemporary writers, must have room and time to develop his novels in considerable detail to get across his message.

Once this message has been developed, however, after the puzzle has been solved, Wallace seems to lose most of his interest in the book. He begins with a situation which seems to say, "What if. . . ?" and goes on from there. "What if a black man, through the force of events, suddenly became President of the United States?" "What would happen if suddenly a new portion of the Bible were discovered—how would the world, including religious leaders, be affected?" Wallace is fascinated by such possibilities, and although he is interested in the people who would be involved in such events, and although he realizes that characters bring novels alive and memorable, he is actually mostly gripped by the themes themselves. Little wonder then that after the questions and answers have been demonstrated and worked out, the author rushes to close the book, apparently content to erase the characters once they have illustrated his point.

In *The Sins of Philip Fleming,* for example, Fleming, the

protagonist, has been playing around with other women and has very nearly destroyed his writing ability and chance for a big job with a Hollywood producer. But he comes to his senses and returns to his wife, who understands and is waiting for him. In the final scene, at home with his wife to stay, he pulls back from her. " 'I'm hungry,' he said. 'Whip me up a couple of eggs. I've got a lot to tell you.' She started into the kitchen, and after a moment, he followed her." End of book. At the conclusion of *The Man*, Douglass Dilman has just become the first Black President of the United States and is assuming his Presidential duties. Wallace concludes the book: ". . . Dilman lingered outside briefly . . . and then, feeling assured and purposeful, feeling good, he entered his Oval Office to begin the day's work."

Such endings have often been called fairy-tale, "They-lived-happily-ever-after," terminations. But Wallace has been explicit in answering the criticism leveled against them. An interview he gave on *The Prize* to the editor of *Information & Documents,* a French Cultural magazine, on endings and certain other aspects of his works is revealing and should be given at some length (as quoted in *The Writing of One Novel,* pp. 185-186): "I've always been told I have a dangerous tendency toward happy endings, such as in *The Prize*. But I am at heart an extremely optimistic person. I am not childishly so. For it is also true that I have a balancing tendency to be cynical. I've seen so much that goes on behind people, their greed and hypocrisy. I am also dismayed by and curious about man's condition on earth—why he was put here, so uniquely, to have so much learning and passion poured into him, and then to be snuffed out of existence so quickly. Yet the very miracle of man's existence at all in the scheme of things excites me, and makes me believe that for every person's problem there must be a possible solution. I believe man is too complex and gifted a marvel not to be able to resolve his own or another's difficulties. . . .

"As for coincidences, I believe life is filled with them. I feel it is nonsense to say 'we mustn't contrive a meeting, a situation which produces such and such because this is a convenience for the writer to make the story go ahead.'

"A story creates its own truth. A novel does not have to

represent real life, but one often has to go way beyond life to make it seem real."

Wallace assumes that after the problem raised in the novel has been settled, the world, which he does not see as having been really endangered, will rock on at about the same keel. Wallace's world is not as dark as those of many other writers—Mailer's or Capote's, for example. Agreeing with the British politician who said that one should never allow the threat of national calamity to interfere with a good night's sleep, Wallace can rest and awake to a world that he insists has some promise. Like William Faulkner in the speech he gave upon receiving the Nobel Prize in Literature, or Andrew Craig in his acceptance speech for the same award in *The Prize,* Wallace thinks the world will be safe because the individual, when developed into his full potential, is strong. Wallace believes that perhaps his best statement on the subject is Craig's speech, and readers of the novel will remember that it does have a fine ring:

" 'This is the foremost of earthly honors that you have offered me,' he found himself saying aloud. 'I am moved and grateful beyond inadequate words. But I believe Alfred Nobel would have understood what I will say next. It is this—that all man's honors to man are small beside the greatest prize to which he may and must aspire—the finding of his soul, his spirit, his divine strength and worth—the knowledge that he can and must live in freedom and dignity—the final realization that life is not a daily dying, not a pointless end, not an ashes-to-ashes and dust-to-dust, but a soaring and blinding gift snatched from eternity. The ultimate prize is to know that each new day's challenge is meaningful and offered for use, that it must be taken to the bosom, and it must be used— and to know this, to understand this, is the one prize worthy as man's goal and all mankind's summit.' "

Perhaps, to many readers, it may seem absurd to say that Wallace can be embarrassed by sex and uses restraint in portraying it. But the statement holds. Wallace is the first to admit that sex sells books and that he wants to sell his works. But he also insists that sex is life and that he, if he would be true to life, must demonstrate that sex is a dominant force. Freud, whom Wallace admires,

The Kinsey Report and other scientific studies have demonstrated, as have far more sensational writers of the past and present, that sex is a vital part of our daily lives. Further, as everybody knows and the U. S. Supreme Court has recently ruled, there are the truthful though frank writings about sex and there are, on the other side, the prurient exploitations of it.

Wallace correctly feels that he falls into the former category. He is as explicit as he needs to be to demonstrate his point. But he is not salacious, not obscene, although he has been criticized for being so. Searchers for the pornographic need not look into his books. If his own restraints were not sufficient, there is always his wife, Sylvia, whom Wallace characterizes as "sharp, sensitive, perceptive, unsparing," who somewhat in the manner allegedly played years ago by Olivia Clemens, Mark Twain's wife, redirects Irving's prose if it tends to become too racy.

Wallace grew up in a family that revered the old masters—Tolstoi, Dostoevski, Balzac. Throughout life he has carefully read everything he could get his hands on. He dedicated *The Seven Minutes* to the characters of John Cleland, D. H. Lawrence and James Joyce, the last two among literature's most respected stylists. Believing in the importance of style, he has worked as hard as any other dedicated writer to improve his own. As he says in the interview in this book, he early discovered that "the only way to become a writer is to write!" On *The Prize*, as he catalogued in his work *The Writing of One Novel,* he wrote 3,101 hours in a total of 582 days, or an average of more than five hours out of every twenty-four.

As a result of his dedication to the art of the novel, through the years Wallace has developed an effective style. It is direct, carefully chosen and clear. It is never tortured and egoistic, as is the case with other contemporary writers. If at times it appears wordy, this is because of Wallace's insistence that clarity of message is more important than brevity.

Both message and style have combined through the years to create works of considerable impact. *The Prize* set a kind of high-water mark in subject and accomplishment. Since that novel Wallace has continued to explore new areas of investigation and to provide rich entertainment. *The Three Sirens,* his next book, was generally felt to be more readable than *The Prize*, as it surely is. *The Man,* Wallace's next book, the one he feels is his best, contained both readibility and importance of topic; it is one of my favorites of his works. In *The Plot*, his next book but one, Wallace expanded from a national to an international theme, which though a book of real strength, is not more powerful than *The Man*. In his next novel, *The Seven Minutes*, Wallace turned to a thoughtful examination of the problem of pornography and censorship. Here as elsewhere his research was exhaustive; the result is a stirring work with great impact. *The Nympho and Other Maniacs,* Wallace's next book, was in many ways a return to the author's interest in quaint and unusual persons, this time women. Although it is extremely well written and interesting, it fails to have the impact of his more conventional, larger novels.

After these formidable achievements, Wallace produced his finest accomplishment to date—*The Word*. Here he is probing the very foundation of human nature—pondering the question what would happen if a new Gospel were discovered, and what would be its reception. Into the answer Wallace poured all his research, his talks with noted Biblical scholars, and his observations on mankind in general. The result is a powerful book which forces upon the reader the suspension of disbelief. The writing, though the book concerns itself with three continents and scores of people, is compelling. Although the reader knows that no such Gospel has ever been discovered, he reads on, gripped by the power of the subject and the author's presentation. This, indeed, as they say in show biz, will be a hard act to follow. What *The Fan Club*, his next book, will achieve remains to be seen. To discover the power of the many books he is now planning and working on, we simply must wait and see.

Taken on balance, in the last few years Wallace obviously has not suffered from his critics. People from all walks of life read and enjoy his works. The audience of *The Prize*, for example, included among its millions of readers the typical housewife from Wauseon, Ohio, the secretary of the campus of the University of Michigan, the Nobel Prize-winning chemist J. C. Urey, who loved it, and

Martin Luther King. With each book Wallace's reading public, in this country and abroad, continues to grow.

But Wallace is sensitive to his critics. Unlike many other writers, he reads his reviewers with interest. Perhaps he is too thin-skinned; maybe he reads out of curiosity. Anyway, he is quite aware of and resents the obvious contradiction in this domocratic America, where critics reviewing for the mass media usually impose elite standards that are essentially alien. All too frequently the American critic is so ashamed of the culture he lives in and so intent on improving it that he refuses to evaluate a work on its own grounds on the basis of its medium and its audience. When Wallace commented on the subject to the reporter of *Politika*, the Belgrade magazine, as quoted elsewhere in this volume, he sounded almost as bitter as Mark Twain might have been:

"In America, it seems to me, there is a wide schism between what is wanted and loved by the professional reviewers and critics, and what is wanted and loved by the broad reading public. The critics, not all but the great majority, have shown a tendency to prefer precious writing, concave writing. The broad reading public, which for the most part ignores the critics, seems to prefer direct writing, plain writing, exciting writing, topical writing (that is, characters who bear some relationship to the lives of the readers)."

Wallace, like many others in this country and abroad, is a writer working in a genre and in a medium that need to be recognized for what they are, what they try to do. That is, Wallace is a "popular" writer, is proud to be one, and does not want to be among the "elite." Actually the differences between the two are more apparent than real—shadings on a long continuum. But these differences have long generated much hard feeling.

The controversy goes back at least to the Classics. To Plato the non-elite people were "oxen," and their arts were dung. Aristotle, however, recognized that, "There is nothing in the intellect that is not first in the senses"; therefore all levels of life—and art—are important. Terence, the second century B. C. writer of comedies, appreciated all of life: "I am man; nothing pertaining to man repels me."

The real break between "elite" and "popular" art came, how-

ever, in the eighteenth century, with the rise of the Industrial
Revolution, when wealth and poverty more sharply divided people,
and when rapid printing presses developed a medium for mass
communication. The controversy raged through the nineteenth
and the first half of the twentieth century.

But now under the irresistible impact of the mass media and
a liberalized new thinking, the whole concept of what constitutes
"elite" and "popular"–"highbrow" and "lowbrow"–arts has been
challenged. Despite the holding action of some influential critics
the walls are tumbling down.

Abraham Kaplan, a distinguished professor of philosophy at
the University of Michigan, used to argue that the popular arts
should be considered as newly born artifacts that were growing
toward maturity in a "higher" form. But such arguments are fast
losing any influence. Susan Sontag, one of America's most perceptive critics, insists that there is an altogether new attitude creep-
ing into our consideration of the so-called "popular" arts. These
arts are a new dimension, having nothing to do with the presumed
"higher" arts, and must be judged on their own merits and standards. "One cheats himself, as a human being," she says in *Against
Interpretation,* "if one has respect only for the style of high
culture."

Perhaps the most revealing, the most honest, statement of
this kind was made by Ross Macdonald, the creator of the Lew
Archer series of detective fiction. Macdonald, proud to be a popular writer, insists: "We learn to see reality through the popular
arts we create and patronize. That's what they're for. That's why
we love them."

Critics more and more are recognizing their proper function
and are devoting their time and effort to the proper study of their
proper subject. Robert Kirsch, book review editor for the Los
Angeles *Times* and one of the more perceptive of the newspaper
reviewers, was particularly acute in commenting on *The Prize* (as
quoted in *The Writing of One Novel,* p. 58): "Irving Wallace is, in
my opinion, a better writer than, say Sinclair Lewis, and in time
may emerge as a writer of real importance on the American
scene. . . . In order to understand why these writers have found

and kept a large audience, one has to examine what people want from a novel and what they have always wanted. It is, basically, entertainment." Entertaining—that is, telling a good story—was originally and always has been the primary purpose of the novelist, though many critics and academics tend to forget, to play down, or to condemn this perfectly honorable object. In so doing they try to frustrate human nature and often do succeed in falsifying it.

But critics come and go, they learn, and they change their standards and their minds. Popular novelists survive—or disappear— by producing what the paying public—not the critics—want. Wallace has always wanted to be a good storyteller. In the art of generating a story that people will want to read and in the telling of it, he has few peers among popular writers today. He is quite correct in feeling that the standards critics set are arbitrary, capricious, cultist and changeable, and that he, and other artists, working in their own ways to their own purposes will ultimately prevail. There is no doubt that popular fiction in general—and Wallace's in particular—deserves and will receive in the future more recognition for its role in society and for its intrinsic merit.

It is in the context of "popular" writer—writer for the multi-tudes—that Wallace must be considered if he is to be judged fairly. Any writer who has sold 92 million copies of his books, who can expect to sell 2-3 million of any book he writes, must be doing something right. He is. Wallace is producing the kind of book that teaches and entertains—an unbeatable combination. To cavil and condemn him for doing this is foolish and beside the point. To criticize him for not writing other kinds of books is absurd.

While crafting his many works through the years, Wallace has marched to his own drummer as Thoreau did a hundred years ago. Wallace, in Thoreau's words, "steps to the music he hears, how-ever measured or far away" or, perhaps better, Wallace creates his own music, a music that many people like. He is still the square peg in a round society. His four corners of independence have never been ground off: he has remained true to himself, to his way of life and philosophy, and beholden to no one. Those who lead lives of quiet desperation—as most of us do—have reason to thank him.

Index